# The Therapy of Education

# The Therapy of Education

## Philosophy, Happiness and Personal Growth

Paul Smeyers, Richard Smith and Paul Standish

First published 2007 by
PALGRAVE MACMILLAN
Houndmills, Basingstoke, Hampshire RG21 6XS and
175 Fifth Avenue, New York, N.Y. 10010
Companies and representatives throughout the world

PALGRAVE MACMILLAN is the global academic imprint of the Palgrave
Macmillan division of St. Martin's Press, LLC and of Palgrave Macmillan Ltd.
Macmillan® is a registered trademark in the United States, United Kingdom and
other countries. Palgrave is a registered trademark in the European Union and
other countries.

ISBN 13: 978–1–4039–9250–5    hardback
ISBN 10: 1–4039–9250–9          hardback

This book is printed on paper suitable for recycling and made from fully
managed and sustained forest sources.

A catalogue record for this book is available from the British Library.

Library of Congress Cataloging-in-Publication Data

Smeyers, Paul
    The therapy of education : philosophy, happiness and personal growth /
    Paul Smeyers, Richard Smith & Paul Standish.
        p. cm.
    Includes bibliographical references and index.
    ISBN 1–4039–9250–9 (cloth)
        1. Education–Philosophy. 2. Psychotherapy. I. Smith, Richard. II. Standish,
    Paul, 1949– III. Title.

    LB14.7.S64 2007
    370.1–dc22                                          2006049480

10   9   8   7   6   5   4   3   2   1
16   15   14   13   12   11   10   09   08   07

Printed and bound in Great Britain by
Antony Rowe Ltd, Chippenham and Eastbourne

*For Nigel Blake*

# Contents

# Acknowledgements

This book is the latest in a series of collaborations, the most salient of which are *Thinking Again: Education After Postmodernism* (1998), *Education in an Age of Nihilism* (2000) and *The Blackwell Guide to the Philosophy of Education* (2003). Nigel Blake contributed to all of these, as he did to our early discussions of the present project, and we record here the extent to which we have benefited from working with him. *The Therapy of Education* might not have taken shape without him, and it is to him that we dedicate the book.

We thank the following: the many colleagues and conference participants – in particular at Leuven, Madrid, Oxford, Oslo and Sheffield – who have responded to earlier presentations of our work; Jenny Laws, of Durham University, for many helpful discussions; Naoko Saito, of Kyoto University, for the research work in which she has shared; Cassie Higgins, who provided invaluable support in the preparation of the final manuscript.

Some of the chapters rework or substantially reprint material that has appeared before, in whole or part, and we thank the various editors and publishers for giving permission for their appearance here.

Ch. 1 appeared as Self-esteem: the kindly apocalypse, *Journal of Philosophy of Education* 36.1, 2002, 87–100.

Ch. 2 appeared as On diffidence: the moral psychology of self-belief, *Journal of Philosophy of Education* 40.1, 2006, 51–62.

Ch. 9 is a revised version of Abstraction and finitude: education, chance and democracy, *Studies in Philosophy and Education* 25.1-2, 2006, 19–35.

Ch.10 is a revised version of Unfinished business: education without necessity, *Teaching in Higher Education* 8.4, 2003, 477–91.

Finally, Daniel Bunyard, our Commissioning Editor at Palgrave Macmillan, has been patient and encouraging beyond anything we had a right to expect.

# Introduction

Any consideration of therapy, and its relationship with education today, takes place against a background of three prevailing climates of thought. First, there is the conception of therapy as an obvious good, a practice that helps people lead more fulfilled and less unhappy lives. The prevalence of this assumption, and the fact of the proliferation of therapy in its various forms, hardly needs illustration. Second, and partly in reaction to the first, there is increasing scepticism, even hostility, towards therapy and its influence (see, for example, from the last few years, Frank Furedi's *Therapy Culture: Cultivating Vulnerability in an Uncertain Age*, and Christina Hoff Sommers' and Sally Satel's *One Nation under Therapy*). Therapy is charged with encouraging a debilitating climate of dependence to which it then presents itself as the solution, and eroding our natural capacity for coping with the various obstacles we find in our path in the course of life. Third, it may seem to some that the only essential and important questions concerning therapy are whether or not it can be proved to be effective and if so how to do it. Here as in many areas of life our pragmatic age is principally interested in 'what works'. We return below to the limits of such instrumental thinking.

In this book we attempt a more balanced and nuanced treatment of therapy and its connections with education, one that eschews caricature and is sensitive to what therapeutic practice involves. In doing so we reject the idea that a sharp conceptual division can be made between education and therapy. That division has often been drawn along the following lines. Education has intrinsic aims, while therapy seeks to restore mental health and so its aims are extrinsic. Therapy involves 'doing things to people' while education respects and tries to enhance their autonomy: it treats them as responsible agents and not

1

as the patients or clients on whom the psychotherapist or counsellor will exercise her kindly manipulative techniques. To assimilate education to therapy, or to exaggerate the degree to which they overlap, is to fail to recognize the extent to which people may reasonably hold different ideals and preferences. It is to neglect the fact of legitimate value diversity. These points are made by, for example, David Carr (2000); they have their recent ancestry in familiar distinctions drawn by earlier analytical philosophers of education such as Richard Peters.

Two responses suggest themselves. The first is to observe that an over-sharp distinction here tends to rest on a misunderstanding, or perhaps a parody (maybe even a fantasy) of therapy. It is far from true that all therapy consists in doing things to people, as if every therapist is essentially engaged in behaviour modification from a position of complacent superior assumed understanding. (MacIntyre's well-known anathematizing of therapy in *After Virtue* has done much damage.) Many therapists in fact are concerned precisely to distinguish therapy as a relationship between autonomous human beings from therapy as a set of techniques. James Hillman, for example, connects therapy with the ideas of attending and serving found in the Greek word *therapeia*: 'a *therapeutes* was one who attended, was a servant of, and thereby could heal' (Hillman, 1995, p. 80). David Smail writes:

> Psychological help, then, is gained by those who seek it first and foremost in the context of a *relationship* in which they are *undeceived* about the nature and significance of a real, often complex and possibly insolubly difficult, painful predicament or set of circumstances, and *encouraged* to confront *bodily* those aspects of the predicament which admit of any possibility of change. In essence this procedure is a moral, not a technical understanding, since at every point it necessitates judgements being made by both therapist and patient about what is *right* and what is *good* for either or both to do... . (original emphases) (Smail, 1984, pp. 139–140)

Unsurprisingly, our technicist age – obsessed, as we noted above, with the question of 'what works' – tends to reconceive the qualities of a *relationship* as skills to be acquired and exercised (the chapter from which the quotation above is taken is entitled, with proper irony, 'The Experts'). It is not difficult to find counsellors and therapists who have, as Smail puts it (*ibid.*) 'scurried behind the ramparts of objectivity', from which position they like to talk of the 'simple but effective techniques' which can put the distressed and the neurotic to rights. Smail however shows how they represent the debasement of a very different ideal. And that ideal, Smail's remarks above show, is remarkably close to a traditional notion of education as leading the learner to make autonomous and morally informed judgements about the right, the good and the true. Elsewhere, indeed, Smail complains that both in therapy and in education we have 'substituted a mythology of training for a philosophy of learning' (1987, p. 137).

A second line of response is to consider how much of education does *not* consist in the straightforward acquisition of knowledge or skills (or even of attitudes, to complete the popular trio) which can then conveniently be distinguished from the affective or therapeutic. Any teacher of children with 'special educational needs', for example, is confronted not only with the pupil's particular difficulty (for instance dyslexia or mobility problems) but also with the damage that the difficulty has inflicted over many years on the child's confidence and sense of his or her worth. Or consider students, young adults, embarking on their first Shakespeare play, *Antony and Cleopatra*. Teaching Shakespeare presents peculiar difficulties. The Bard is a cultural icon, the Greatest Playwright in the English Language. To some students that means that he cannot be approached without armour, the protection of Notes and Guides. In this example, taken from life, the teacher recalled how the previous year he tried to show that Shakespeare tells us all we need to know in the opening lines:

> Nay, but this dotage of our general's
> O'erflows the measure...

– the groundlings at the Globe neither having nor needing the latest Key to the English Classics. But the students, alarmed by some remarks in the Introduction to their edition of the play, demanded a full account of the Seleucid dynasty before they could be expected to approach the text. The teacher wondered if the subject-matter of the play – erotic love and its conflict with duty, rebellion against authority and suicide – was experienced by these teenagers as something that needed to be made safe, defused. Knights (1992, p. 8) writes:

> A group of people trying to think about the text is attempting to integrate knowledge (about the text, the author, historical context, language) with fantasy and emotion. Many of the strategies evident in this process may well be defensive: literary texts are invested with considerable affect, and much of a discussion may represent an

attempt to keep threatening emotions at bay. This negotiation (which is never finished) on the subject of a text reproduces tensions and conflicts inherent in the text.

The English teacher of our example has found that 'a secure group where mutual trust is fostered is one capable of contemplating and joining in the play of meaning' (*ibid.*, p. 22), and sometimes feels less like a Shakespearean scholar than a therapist who facilitates group relations, as the jargon has it.

The idea that education involves a kind of therapy goes back to ancient times: Socrates was, at least in part, concerned with a kind of care of the self, and Plato in his early dialogues presents education – the education that consists of rigorous philosophical discussion – as a cure for bad intellectual and moral habits. As Martha Nussbaum (1994) has shown, the post-Socratic philosophers saw the question of how to learn to live well in terms of a 'therapy of desire'. In our own time therapeutic approaches tend to be connected with progressive conceptions of education. But education as traditionally conceived has often been tied to a more or less pessimistic assessment of human nature and hence associated with releasing us therapeutically from certain inherent weaknesses. In short the connections are more traditional and widespread than they appear to those hostile to therapy, and more complex than they seem at first sight.

We are, then, concerned with the ways in which education can serve as, or indeed simply is, a kind of therapy; but we are also interested in ways in which education may itself stand in need of therapy – perhaps through the incorporation of therapeutic approaches but especially, and more importantly, in terms of the need to retrieve education from its current state of debilitation. The condition that has come to be called 'performativity' – the fixation with assessment and league-tables and the reconstitution of the pupil or student as a collection of programmable skills – has joined forces with managerialism to threaten older and more vibrant notions of education as a liberal ideal. Here is the dominance of instrumental thinking that we referred to at the beginning of this Introduction. There is a compulsive quality to such thinking: a purely intellectual critique of its limitations and dangers seems to leave it unscathed, perhaps because some of our most stubborn fantasies about control and order are at stake here, as well as our profoundest fears about contingency, personal responsibility and the finitude of human life.

The second part of our title – 'philosophy, happiness and personal growth' – points to areas where the connections between education and therapy can be most readily examined in detail. We attempt this examination in two ways. In the first place, we consider a number of developments in educational practice in recent years that show the influence of ideas drawn from various kinds of therapy. From Circle Time in the primary school to assertiveness training and stress management for executives in industry, from counselling and guidance to self-esteem and well-being, from spiritual education to citizenship, there is growing evidence of extensive crossover. Ideas inspired in particular by Carl Rogers to the effect that one should regard others with unconditional positive regard have become dominant in thinking on pastoral care in education, while Paulo Freire's work has left its legacy in notions of empowerment and ownership. In countries where the pressure to improve standards in schools has brought new levels of stress and anxiety to children, there is growing concern with children's happiness and well-being, and a rejection of the idea that these learners will require merely academic and vocational knowledge. Within the counselling world, there is a current boom of interest in the expanded role that is planned in many countries for professional counsellors in the school context. There are, moreover, various practices outside formal education that are characterized, in one way or another, by working on the self. The self-help shelves in bookshops are heavy with guides to improving one's sense of self-worth, developing assertiveness, enhancing leadership skills, managing stress and finding 'the real you'. In critically examining such tendencies, we note that the kinds of empowerment that they promise are generally individualistic. We seek to understand ways in which therapy's benefits may be achieved without undermining community and solidarity, and without diminishing possibilities of political engagement.

In the second place, we are also interested in this book in the ways that philosophy has been understood as a working on oneself, an idea given new currency by Michel Foucault. The ways in which philosophy is supremely and uniquely conducive to personal growth have been emphasized by thinkers throughout history. A part of such personal growth comes through unravelling tangles in the understanding that are often caused by popular theories (as well as tangles caused by aspects of philosophy itself). Our view is that thinking about education and therapy is also subject to confusion and mystification. Such thinking itself stands in need of the kind of philosophical attention that

Wittgenstein described as therapy: in his memorable image, the fly needs a way out of the fly-bottle.

It is in this spirit that the picture on the cover of this book, reproducing *The Extraction of the Stone of Madness* (also known as *The Cure of Folly*) by Hieronymus Bosch, should be viewed. The charlatan doctor offers – for a fee – to relieve the patient's headache by cutting out an imaginary stone, here transmuted into a tulip perhaps because 'tulip head' is a slang term for 'mad' in Dutch. The inscription around the picture reads *'Meester snyt die Keye ras – myne name is lubbert das'* ('Master, cut out the stone – my name is Lubbert Das': the 'patient' identifies himself as a proverbially stupid character from Dutch folktale). The book on the head of the nun and the funnel on the head of the 'doctor' indicate that those performing the operation are themselves not free of the grip of folly. No doubt there are charlatans enough in the world of therapy. However they are less our targets in this book than the stone of muddled thinking and confusion that we here attempt – not without some diffidence and occasional irony – to excise.

Part I, *The Kindly Apocalypse*, which takes its title from Philip Rieff, focuses on the self. It deals in critical but not unsympathetic ways with the various manifestations of our therapeutic culture as they have found their way into education. Therapy promises much but cannot always live up to the expectations it raises. Our discussion attempts to distinguish the ways in which this culture is helpful to us from ways in which it is not.

In Part II, *Coming to Terms*, we explore a variety of aspects of our ordinary world that are not usually understood in terms of the therapeutic. In these we find something that was not evident in the therapeutic practices in education that we considered in Part I. In speaking of 'coming to terms' we have in mind the ways in which the finitude of our lives, spatial and temporal, governs our condition: that we are subject to contingency, and live in a fragile and uncertain world. We are interested in the ways in which we can learn to live well within these limits.

In Part III, *Redeeming Philosophy, Redeeming Therapy* we argue that the alienation that characterizes much human distress consists partly in a disenchantment with the world and a kind of scepticism. There is a rich tradition that sees philosophy and literature as *the* disciplines that transfigure the ordinary, restoring it to us as our proper home. Education, rightly understood, is thus one of the richest kinds of therapy.

# Part I
# The Kindly Apocalypse

# 1
## Self-Esteem: The Inward Turn

> What apocalypse has ever been so kindly? What culture has
> ever attempted to see to it that no ego is hurt?
> (Philip Rieff, *The Triumph of the Therapeutic*, p. 27)

## I

Ruth teaches in a primary school in a poor part of London. Many of the
children are recent arrivals in the UK; there are few whose first language
is English. Many parents are unemployed, and many are refugees. Ruth
and the other teachers devote much time and energy to raising, as they
put it, the children's self-esteem. For example, in Ruth's class every day
is some child's Special Day. He is fêted, sung to, permitted to fill in the
register. Great care is taken to emphasize what children have achieved
rather than where they fall short. Exercise books display a wealth of
stars and smiley faces. An outsider might wonder whether some particular, rather indifferent piece of work deserves such raptures but, as
Ruth says, if you knew what an achievement it represented for that little
girl ... ; and besides, how much more important that she develops
confidence, acquires positive attitudes to the world, than (say) masters
the spelling of English – an achievement now in any case overshadowed
by the existence of the computer's spelling checker.

Thus it is that Ruth's school declares its mission as 'Aiming to raise the
self-esteem of each and every child'. School policies on assessment, bullying, home-school relationships and others all make reference to this
concept, which is clearly seen as an essential building-block – perhaps *the*
essential block – in a good education. Who could be against the development of self-esteem, when even in a developed and in many ways civilized country so many children grow up with a view of themselves as

useless, 'not worth bothering with', doomed to failure? And if our ambitions are focused on examination results and league-tables, won't children with high self-esteem be likely to succeed better in these academic terms anyway?

Jane too is now a primary teacher. In the middle of the summer vacation she appeared in the University Education Department where she was about to start her last year of training, in a search for someone to tell she was leaving the course. It emerged that she had just taken her small child and walked out on her emotionally abusive partner, taking refuge in the home of parents who are themselves emotionally cold and deeply unsupportive. Jane was persuaded to finish her training. She now has a good degree, a permanent job in which she is successful, and her own home. However she finds it almost impossible to believe that anyone can like her or see her as anything other than 'dull and useless', a phrase she frequently applies to herself. Any new challenge, even the beginning of a new school term (and sometimes even a new week), drains her of any vestiges of self-confidence and often brings panic attacks.

It is familiar enough that those who have not been loved as children grow up to see themselves as unlovable, and that those who by contrast have enjoyed the unconditional love of supportive parents tend to turn into what we think of as well-adjusted and successful adults. The examples above seem to show that there is something worthwhile we want, when we seek to build self-esteem, or something important that talk of self-esteem calls attention to. In *The Drama of Being a Child* (p. 21) Alice Miller writes:

> The child has a primary need to be regarded and respected as the person he really is at any given time, and as the centre – the central actor – in his own activity. In contradistinction to drive wishes, we are speaking of a need that is narcissistic, but nevertheless legitimate, and whose fulfillment is essential for the development of a healthy self-esteem.

Thus it is tempting to say of Jane that *she has low self-esteem*. Reference to self-esteem here brings with it those ideas about the connection between childhood experiences and adult self-perception alluded to by Alice Miller. It acts as a kind of shorthand, indicating that reference is being made to a common theory about why some people are the way they are. We find this theory helpful; it suggests for instance that Jane needs to resolve issues in her relationship with her parents, and this in turn points to ways in which she can be helped.

Nevertheless we shall argue that there is a shadow side here that needs attention. Consider Hannah, who was six years old when her parents were inspecting possible schools for her in their suburb of Boston, Massachusetts. They were initially impressed with one which foregrounded the building of self-esteem among its aims. As she showed Hannah and her parents around the school the Principal drew attention to the various arrangements that were meant to embody this philosophy: no competitive sport, plenty of Circle Time for children to listen respectfully as their peers talk about their feelings, an emphasis on praise for good behaviour rather than blame for bad. Hearing the phrase used so often, Hannah asked, 'What's self-esteem?' 'It means we *love* you, Hannah', the Principal replied. 'No you don't', Hannah burst out. 'Mummy and Daddy love me, and grandma and granddad, *but you don't even know me*'. This too is a real example; many others from North America can be found in Maureen Stout's *The Feel-Good Curriculum: The Dumbing Down of America's Kids in the Name of Self-Esteem*, and in Christina Hoff Sommers' and Sally Satel's *One Nation under Therapy*.

Meanwhile, back on this side of the Atlantic, there are periodic attempts to eradicate racism and bullying, and prepare young people to live peaceably together in the community, through exercises designed to enhance their self-esteem. An example which received media coverage and the Minister for Education's disapproval involved adolescents standing in a ring and saying to their neighbour, 'Hi, Peter, I'm really glad you're here at school today'. Circle Time has arrived: Jenny Mosley's *Quality Circle Time in the Primary Classroom* is subtitled *your essential guide to enhancing self-esteem, self-discipline and positive relationships*. Not only are we to prioritize improving children's self-esteem, we are to start with our own. Part 1 is entitled 'Working on Yourself', on the reasonable grounds – it would seem – that we shall not be able to do much for children's self-esteem if our own is low. Sixteen questions are included to help us assess our self-esteem. Do you worry about asking colleagues for help? Do you worry about work when you're at home? Are you often absent through illness? (pp. 18–19). 'If you find you're saying "yes" to too many, then maybe you really need to spend time working on yourself' (p. 18).

Self-esteem is entering higher education too. A poster on the corridors of a northern UK university campus is headed 'Managing Self Esteem'. It asks: 'How much do you value yourself? Do you criticize yourself for the way you are? Are you successful and yet feel something is missing? Do you worry about what other people think of you? *If these experiences are familiar you could benefit from the Managing Self Esteem course'* (our emphasis). It seems odd to think of 'managing' your self-esteem. Presumably this would require an element of self-deception, since you could hardly have high self-esteem if you were aware that you had deliberately brought it into being, for instance by associating only with people who reflected back to you a positive image of yourself. The conscious pursuit of self-esteem, and the general idea of 'working on yourself' in this kind of way, thus seem to involve a paradox.

There are absurdities, then, in some versions of self-esteem talk, which risk bringing the whole notion into disrepute. For this reason, if for no other, it is healthy to offer criticism. It is emphatically not our intention simply to dismiss Circle Time, for instance, or any of the other techniques or movements that foreground self-esteem. We have no doubt that much valuable learning often happens in these ways, though it is not entirely obvious that self-esteem is what is at stake: it might be that children are benefiting from *attention*, perhaps, or from explicit attention to the dynamics of working together. Balanced critique is important here too because of the dangers of over-reaction against the idea of self-esteem. A recent study (Emler, 2001) is highly critical of the idea that 'a limited sense of self-worth lies behind just about every social and personal ill from drug abuse and delinquency to poverty and business failures' (from the Rowntree Foundation *Findings* website). The study notes that there is 'imperfect agreement' about the nature of self-esteem, yet confidently declares that 'levels of self-esteem can be reliably and easily measured' (*ibid.*). How can we reliably measure what we cannot agree on? The need for more careful thinking about self-esteem could not be better illustrated.

## II

In what follows we move among but try to keep some sense of the distinctions between three levels of self-esteem talk. There is, first, the level of the 'self-esteem movement', where the development of self-esteem is taken to be one of the chief, or even the overall, purpose of education. Secondly there is the level of the therapeutic approach to education, where certain underlying philosophies of psychotherapy or counselling come to be transferred to education. Here education is seen in affective terms as much as in cognitive ones, and in particular formal education is conceived as a site where the individual's (or the group's) emotional problems can be addressed and repaired, or self-fulfilment or self-mastery achieved.[1] Thirdly there is the level on which we simply make significant room for the idea of self-esteem in our scheme of things as one of the ends of education among many. Although we shall cautiously argue in favour of this third level, we remain tempted by the thought that there are flaws in the very idea of self-esteem itself. It is after all a concept we use for various purposes, and one which is at home in the life of persons *who choose to live in a particular sort of way*, a point to which we return below. It is open to us to give up these purposes, or achieve them differently, and we may decide that we do not want to live in this sort of way.

There is of course considerable overlap between these levels, but there are some significant distinctions to be noted. Not all therapies would see increase in self-esteem as their goal, particularly if self-esteem is seen as a matter of 'feeling good about yourself'. Therapies derived from Freudian psychoanalysis, whose founder famously hoped for no more than that it would help patients replace neurotic misery with ordinary human unhappiness, entertain no utopian fantasies of personal beatitude. Some versions of psychotherapy are particularly sceptical of happiness as an overarching end of human life and, *a fortiori*, as the aim of therapy. David Smail, in a book significantly entitled *Taking Care: an alternative to therapy*, writes (p. 141):

> Our most reliable guide in the formulation of our conduct...is not the longing for an unattainable bliss but rather the private knowledge of pain. For although the knowledge is private, the pain is not merely personal, but arises from an embodiment in the world which is our common fate. It is not only you who are the victim of the other's indifference, contempt or spite, but the other is the victim of yours...This is a fact which is necessarily overlooked in the struggle for resources which the pursuit of happiness entails; the inevitable individualism of the latter reduces universality to, at most, a grudging reciprocity, and transforms the public world into a projection of private dreams in which others become sacrificed to the needs of an insatiable 'self'...

Nor does the engendering of self-esteem necessarily have to be particularly therapeutic, if the essence of therapy is to repair some damage in the individual's psyche. Simply to feel better about yourself without such repair, even if it could be securely achieved, is not a matter of being 'cured' (perhaps it is more like being drugged). Conversely, repair might well lead to *lower* self-esteem: consider Pip, in *Great Expectations*, whose release from his delusions about Miss Havisham and Estelle is achieved at the cost of greater humility (not that it is clear that humility and self-esteem are necessarily at odds; the issues here are discussed in Chapter 2).

On the first level, which we have loosely characterized as that of the 'self-esteem movement', a distinction can be made between instrumental and non-instrumental attitudes to self-esteem. For instrumentalists, we should develop children's self-esteem because children with high esteem make better learners. Lee and Marlene Canter declare in their influential book *Assertive Discipline* that 'It is your response style that sets the tone of your classroom. It is your response style that impacts students' self-esteem and their success in school' (p. 25), suggesting that self-esteem is necessary for academic success. For non-instrumentalists, self-esteem is a distinct and legitimate aim, perhaps *the* aim, of education, to be pursued without reference to the traditional goals of acquiring knowledge and passing examinations. The Canters themselves often blur the distinction:

> A teacher who responds in a hostile manner is one who may be able to get her needs to teach met in the classroom, but who does so at the expense of the feelings and self-esteem of her students. (p. 26)

as if the 'need to teach' were a function of the odd psychological make-up of the particular teacher, here unable to see what the real business of the school (attending to students' feelings and self-esteem) should be. This seems to be the Canters' general view of the matter:

> It is our belief that by enabling children to be successful in school we are empowering them with the skills that will become the foundation for their self-esteem and future success. (p. xix)

Here, it seems, academic success itself is only a means to the end of becoming an adult with high self-esteem. So students are to acquire self-esteem for the sake of academic success, *and* vice-versa; and at the same time self-esteem appears to be the real goal of education, independent of any reference to knowledge or learning. This latter comes close to what we have called the 'therapeutic' approach to education. It is unsurprising that Marlene Canter writes that in her early days, when she intended to become a social worker, 'I wanted to help children feel the best about themselves'; later she 'decided that teaching would allow me to be close to the children that I wanted to help' (p. xvii).

The very fact that the different levels and distinctions are so easily blurred in thinking about self-esteem shows us that there is work to do here. A good example of the blurring occurs in an American publication called *Brain Gym*, which is about the 'relationship between movement and whole-brain learning'. Under the heading 'Self-awareness skills' (p. 37) we find the sub-heading 'Self-Concept: Inner Sunshine'. This is glossed as 'self-esteem is both the goal and the means of self-directed learning', and followed by talk of having confidence within the boundaries of personal space. Is self-esteem the goal or the means to another goal, that of learning? The connections here are not at all clear. It seems that straightforward talk of personal space as where we feel safe, 'the immediate working area around the body', is used to lend respectability to the less straightforward notion of *inner* personal space which may be irradiated by the inner sunshine of self-esteem. Self-esteem can only be both the goal and the means of learning since learning has been assimilated to, or identified with, the acquisition of self-esteem. We should note, too, that whatever is going on here, it is 'self-directed'. we return to the solipsistic tendencies of the self-esteem movement below.

Examples of the third kind, where we make room for the idea of self-esteem in our educational scheme of things, can be found wherever teachers pause in the pursuit of their more traditional goals to wonder if there are costs and drawbacks here which could be avoided: when it is good to display the best work in the class, but also good to ensure that every child's work is represented somehow, or when the teacher makes feedback on poor work a discrete matter rather than asking each child to announce his or her mark for the register. In many such small but important ways like this we have learned to ameliorate, often in the name of self-esteem, the inhumanities of mass education.

## III

Given the reality of this amelioration – of the kindliness of the apocalypse, as Rieff puts it in the quotation that prefixes this chapter – why should we have reservations about self-esteem and therapeutic tendencies in education? At the first level, and especially for instrumentalists, there is the obvious problem of devaluation of the currency. The teacher who lavishes praise on what to the outsider may seem an indifferent piece of work that a child has done will find it more difficult to respond with commensurable currency to truly outstanding work. It is possible that children will simply be confused by such stratagems. Adults may similarly be confused. We recently listened to a conference paper where the speaker responded to the first question at the end by saying 'That's a very fine question, a really interesting and important question'. This seemed a fairly straightforward question, and we puzzled over why he thought it so significant. But this was intellectual energy wasted: every question, it turned out, was interesting, important, truly insightful or a question the speaker was enormously grateful had been asked.

There is a kind of dishonesty here, and if it is practised for benign reasons it is dishonesty nevertheless. It seems characteristic of self-esteem instrumentalists. The Canters write of sanctions that they call 'consequences' (Canter and Canter, 1992, p. 82). Carl is told that poking someone means that 'you will choose to sit by yourself at the table. It's your choice'. Soon Carl is poking another child. 'Carl, you poked Fred. You have chosen to sit by yourself at the table'. Carl might reasonably respond that while he was told this was to be the punishment he hardly wants to sit by himself, and hasn't *chosen* to. But there is to be no talk of punishment, because of course punishment would damage pupils' self-esteem.

> Remember, consequences are not punishment. Punishment is something that teachers *do* to students. Punishment takes the form of criticism, humiliation or even physical pain. Teachers who try to curb disruptive behaviour with punishment do so at the expense of student self-esteem and growth... Consequences, on the other hand, are actions students know will occur should they choose to break the rules of the classroom. Consequences must be seen as natural outcomes of inappropriate behaviour. (*ibid.*)

The moral quality of the dishonesty and manipulation here is nicely captured by E.M. Forster in his novel *The Longest Journey* (ch. 17). The young schoolmaster Rickie, newly down from Cambridge and largely unreflective about his vocation, 'grasped the school regulations, and insisted on prompt obedience to them. He adopted the doctrine of collective responsibility. When one boy was late, he punished the whole form. "I can't help it", he would say, as if he was a power of nature. As a teacher he was rather dull...'.

It is not enough to complain about manipulation: perhaps all teaching has an element of it. What is objectionable in the cases both of the Canters' teacher dealing with the incident of poking and Forster's schoolmaster is that they disavow personal responsibility. Whether Carl pokes Fred is itself not a natural fact but a matter of interpretation (is it a nudge, a touch, an accident?), here the teacher's, who is quite reasonably invoking a sanction in order to make the classroom run smoothly. If our class rules say 'no yelling' we have to decide when an utterance constitutes a yell. (The visitor to the infant classroom tends to hear a lot of yelling where the experienced teacher hears a hum of activity.) And there is an irony in the teacher disavowing responsibility while supposedly fostering the children's sense of responsibility: has she not been told she will not build their self-esteem unless she works on her own self-esteem? How will she teach them to take responsibility if she equivocates about her own?

More broadly, to see in a disaffected or bored pupil someone suffering from low self-esteem is to make a large assumption. If a teacher's lessons are disorganized, her subject-matter ill-chosen; if (say) there might be something thoroughly alienating for adolescents to shuffle round a decaying school from lesson to lesson, their developing understanding of the world arbitrarily cut into forty-minute segments of unconnected facts ... if any of these reasons for their disaffection have any force, then explanations in terms of their self-esteem begin to look remarkably like an attempt to shift the blame. And there is something extraordinarily arrogant in the idea that the teacher knows all these children sufficiently well to *diagnose* low self-esteem in individual cases. It is more likely that she is *assuming* an absence of self-esteem either in general (that is she is in the grip of a theory, whether it is a good or bad one), or in the case of certain sorts of pupils – pupils for whom low self-esteem springs readily to mind as an explanation of their attitude to school. Here we have a danger particularly highlighted by Maureen Stout (2000), that we may entertain generalizations about the self-esteem of children from particular *backgrounds* (black, working-class, single parents) that would be clearly unacceptable if expressed in terms of their likely *intelligence*.

Much turns here on whether we think it is easy to know people, or rather difficult; whether we are inclined to be impressed by our own perspicacity in the matter, or by contrast regard the inner lives of others as a welcome mystery, their very *otherness* as something to be respected. (Rieff, 1966, p. 22, writes: 'We are, I fear, getting to know one another. Reticence, secrecy, concealment of self have been transformed into social problems; once they were aspects of civility...'.) Of course people begin to look much more transparent in the light of a simple theory, whether about self-esteem or anything else. Thus too because of the insistence that these techniques are successful (both Jenny Mosley and the Canters begin their books with pages of plaudits from fellow-professionals) the theory and the transparency come to seem confirmed. We say more below (p. 21) about the claim that *it works*. Since we cannot adjudicate here on the question of whether people tend to be opaque or easily read, perhaps it is enough to note that if we make facile assumptions about what it is like to be them then we are being profoundly *disrespectful* of their personhood and their privacy; which, if we thought we were raising their self-esteem, would be paradoxical. Those who are treated with disrespect, even if only the implied disrespect of condescension, are unlikely to feel more self-respect as a result. Most of us have at one time or another experienced the well-meaning attention of those who thought they knew us better than they did, and can confirm that it has peculiarly chilling and alienating effects.

The foregrounding of self-esteem, although we have distinguished it above from therapy, is recognizably part of the 'triumph of the therapeutic', to use Rieff's well-known phrase (Rieff, 1966). There is a familiar line of criticism here (though Rieff's own critique is subtle and ambivalent), followed in different ways by (for example) Alasdair MacIntyre (*After Virtue*), Charles Taylor (*Sources of the Self, The Ethics of Authenticity*) and Christopher Lasch (*The Culture of Narcissism, The Minimal Self*) and Robert Bellah and his co-writers (*Habits of the Heart*). One element of the criticism is that 'truth has been displaced as a value and replaced by psychological effectiveness' (MacIntyre, p. 29); while we agree with this, it is far too easy to draw a clear dividing line, as some want to, between on the one hand education (seen as the realm of truth) and on the other therapy (seen as the realm of manipulation, exclusively means-end reasoning and techniques to make people more 'psychologically effective'). In fact one very useful thing the self-esteem movement has done is cause us to blur that dividing line. Is it in no sense the business of education to help us lead more fulfilling lives, cope with our emotions, understand ourselves a little better, empathize with very different people and cultures? Our sense of what education can be stands to be enriched, not diminished, by a sufficiently nuanced appreciation of its connections with therapy.

This is something that the early dialogues of Plato should have taught us. Dialogues such as the *Theaetetus* or the *Phaedrus* present us with fleshed-out persons who fall in love, drink too much, suffer the vicissitudes of war and disease. The dialogues show them having their prejudices challenged and their ideas changed, being thoroughly confused, and being offered inspiring and thought-provoking visions. 'Phaedrus' is not just a name for a character in a philosophical treatise which Plato put into dialogue form to make its timeless truths more palatable to the reader or to display his virtuosity. But Plato's dialogues have not been altogether well treated by later philosophers, especially in academia. Even when they were not largely neglected in favour of the apparently more substantial works, such as the *Republic* and *Laws*, they became subject to an academic philosophical reading which marked out distinctively philosophical *topoi* as the province of the philosophical curriculum and so ignored the powerful element in those dialogues of engagement between the Socratic teacher and the taught as someone with an embodied and contextualized *life*. Narrow conceptions of philosophy, particularly ones that insist on the radical separation of philosophy and literature, have perhaps done at least as much harm here as clumsy conceptions of therapy.

## IV

A crucial criticism of the idea of self-esteem (in its non-instrumental dimension in particular) is that it encourages the 'inward turn' often (but wrongly) associated with therapy in general. The distressed individual, suffering a catastrophic loss of self-esteem, so to put it, turns away from the world which fails to praise or affirm her, and tries to find the solution in her *self*: in analyzing it (or having it analysed), in constantly going over the smallest remark made by a colleague (what must I be like for her to have said that?), perhaps in joining a therapeutic group where the dogged, mutual unconditional positive regard practised by members as they listen to each others' stories promises no threat to the fragile self. In his classic treatment of the topic Nozick (1974; cp. Cigman, 2001, who takes what is in many ways a similar line) concludes that self-esteem is essentially competitive: we cannot evaluate our own standing separately from that of others. Writers (such as Keshen, 1996) who argue by contrast that self-evaluation can be conducted without comparing the self to others drive a further wedge between the individual and her peers, and strengthen the idea that the development of self-esteem is connected with turning away from the outside world.

To criticize the inward turn is not to deny that psychoanalysis or psychodynamic approaches in general may offer real insights. It is simply to suggest that certain *versions* of the inward turn may prove worse than the original disease. That is because the process does not, perhaps paradoxically, always lead to the discovery of a rich and multi-faceted self 'within' – a self which could be esteemed for its depth and complexity. As Lasch (1985) explains, the troubled individual responds to feeling threatened by shrinking his core being: by the psychological equivalent of curling up into a tight ball in order to make the target as small as possible. Thus he (we, for these are, Lasch says, troubled times for all of us) reconceptualizes the qualities of his personhood, the virtues that might be held to constitute his identity, as skills which are not so much *him* as things which he *has*. To be an inadequate parent, for instance, is to be found wanting in something fundamental to your identity; to lack parenting skills, by contrast, is more a matter of happening not to have various things which you can go off to acquire relatively simply, probably by attending parenting classes. Not for nothing is there so much talk of *ownership* in education and management.

Furthermore, this reconceptualization is all the easier and more tempting because liberalism, the prevailing flavour of modern western societies, requires the self to be understood in 'thin' terms. No one version of the good life is either bequeathed or dictated to us in such a society. It would be intolerable for a person's selfhood to be established once and for all by the accidents of his or her birth, and a liberal society allows us the lifestyles that we prefer, within the constraints imposed by the requirement that we permit others to live their lives their own way as well. Thus we come to think of ourselves as essentially *choosers*, a tendency which becomes stronger as liberalism shades into neo-liberalism and the ideology of the market prevails. Michael Sandel (*Liberalism and the Limits of Justice*, 1982) has shown us how liberalism and its associated ideas of freedom and justice bring us to a picture of the self in which more becomes *mine*, and less becomes *me*. The self must possess, rather than *be*, its ends. For if I *am* my attributes then any change in them changes me. This is the psychological threat that tempts us to reconceive attributes, qualities and virtues as skills and competences. If a family doctor, for example, prides himself on being a sensitive and caring person, it may be intolerable for him to discover that he is 'really' short-tempered and tetchy when the numbers of his patients increase and bureaucracy multiplies. (If he is in the grip of the wrong kind of theory perhaps he will turn to stress management skills.)

The theory of the moral subject implied by liberalism requires that the self is antecedently individuated, prior to its choice of ends: otherwise any change in those contingently chosen ends or attributes changes the self. So it is that we arrive at a picture in which our personhood is constituted less by the ends we choose than by our capacity to choose them: by our capacity for deliberative reflection. And if the self is felt to be fragile, impaired or otherwise inadequate, what more natural than to undertake yet more deliberative reflection? Thus the inward turn is driven from many sources, and the sense of emptiness it brings inspires yet further spirals. As Lasch writes (1985, p. 168): 'Only a complete disavowal of experience…can protect such fantasies against the reality of helplessness and dependence, and a schizophrenic withdrawal from reality not only incapacitates a person for ordinary life but brings a new set of terrors all its own'.

David Smail (1993) writes with great insight of the deleterious consequences of the mistake – of which, as he notes, philosophy ought by now to have disabused us – of thinking that our beliefs and attitudes are somehow 'inside us', things we can change at will (by 'working on our self'). People, Smail notes, cannot readily control their beliefs and attitudes, not simply as a matter of empirical fact, but because 'people *are* their beliefs and attitudes' (p. 82). The notion of 'inner' self and 'inner' resources is seriously misleading.

> My propensity to meet threat without anxiety ('confidence' or 'courage') [and we might add 'self-esteem'], no differently from my ability to speak French, is something I have learned or been enabled or empowered to do at some previous point of my existence. I can no more summon confidence up from some kind of inner space than I can a knowledge of French if I have not acquired them from the outer world at some time in the past; and just as one might find it rather strange to think of 'my French' as existing in 'inner space', it is precisely as strange to think of confidence or courage in this way. (p. 83)

It is in this context that we might be particularly cautious of claims to the effect that programmes for enhancing self-esteem 'work'. May it not be that focusing on the minimal, bare self of modern society exacerbates the very condition for which increase of self-esteem is proposed as the answer? Rieff (1966, p. 36) writes: 'The process of receiving help in finding out what is inwardly wrong presupposes establishment of that inner attitude whereby the patient, or the worshipper, may become more receptive to the sources of help'. 'It works' does not even claim more than that someone has been made to feel good; there is 'nothing at stake beyond a manipulatable state of well-being' (p. 13), comparable to the effects of a drug with no particularly damaging side-effects except the craving for ever larger doses. The claim that 'it works', here as in many other contexts, serves to limit our conception of what counts as success, or as doing or living well, and of course to limit it according to those criteria which the alleged solution can be shown to meet.

# V

The importance of self-esteem, estimated in the way that the self-esteem movement does, falls into that category of 'propositions over which everybody is in fundamental agreement' which so enraged Nietzsche (*Ecce Homo* 3.5). His examples include 'man strives after happiness' and 'pleasure and displeasure are opposites'. Nietzsche complains that 'the Circe of mankind, morality, has falsified all *psychologica* to its very foundations – has *moralized* it...' (*ibid.*). Circe turned Odysseus's men into pigs. So too moralizing psychology represents us not as the complex, even perverse beings that we often are (beings who sometimes put duty before happiness, for whom 'pleasure and displeasure' may be oddly mixed) but as creatures whose lives are governed by relentless platitudes. 'Everything we do we do to make ourselves feel good, and to have self-esteem is to feel good, therefore...', 'You can't change the world but you can change yourself': these are the kinds of propositions, commanding fundamental agreement in certain quarters, that should provoke *us* to Nietzschean exasperation.

Perhaps it sounds odd to hear this described as 'moralizing psychology'. The description would certainly be resisted, for those responsible for it pride themselves on advancing the understanding of the human condition beyond moral or any other kind of philosophy (sometimes dismissed as mere 'head-stuff'). Yet it is morality, in large part, that supplies the system of demands and remissions (thou shalt not...under certain circumstances you may be forgiven for...) which gives our lives a structure of meaning. By replacing this with its own precepts, implicit and explicit (You're only working so hard to please your internalized parent...you should chill out and do some work on *yourself*) much counselling psychology precisely takes over the role of morality.[2]

Nietzsche helps us to see that many of the 'agreed propositions', of his day as well as of ours, are the results neither of empirical research nor of alertness to the human condition. They are the outcome of *a priori* theorizing about the human soul and how it *must be*: must be since (as it is alleged) human beings pursue happiness and therefore want to feel good about themselves. Hence such cruel absurdities as the depressed student who came back, now confused and distraught as well as depressed, from her first meeting with a counsellor to tell me: 'He says that if I'm depressed it's because I really want to be'. This is truly moral psychology, of a horribly over-simplifying sort. (It might be a different matter if the insight that the girl in some sense *wants* to be depressed is the outcome of long and patient exploration of how things are for this particular person.) The *a priori* quality of these ideas accounts, we suspect, for the intensity with which they are often held and the pain and anger with which criticism is often met. To challenge such claims as that enhancing self-esteem should be the basic aim of education is sometimes to be made to feel that one has violated some sacred precept, or that one must have hidden motives, dark and unpleasant, to have made the challenge at all. Or both at once: debased morality and crude psychology are comfortable bedfellows.

What kind of people, then, choose to live like this, at the level of the 'self-esteem movement', where self-esteem has been raised to the status of chief organizing principle of education? First, perhaps, it is people who have given up on the world, despaired of having political effect or influence, and chosen to 'work on the self' instead.[3] And that should no doubt be connected in turn to the great difficulty of achieving any influence in an education system such as we have experienced in recent years in the UK, where curricula, schemes of work, teaching methods and so on have been laid down in great and mandatory detail by central government. But what a difference there is here from the aspirations of those educationalists of previous generations for whom it was axiomatic that education existed in order to achieve greater social justice: who wanted through education to change the public world, not only the 'world within'.

Secondly, although this might be a kindlier culture of unbruised egos it is a tranquil and tranquilized, muted sort of culture. Ideas of risk, associated with openness and vulnerability, of the necessity of the pain without which there is no possibility of sympathy and solidarity, seem alien to it. We do not here find Nietzschean self-affirmers boldly creating value and 'becoming what they are'. Self-esteem of the kind discussed in this chapter is too much like the 'slave morality' of those who, in their oppression, make virtues of the powerlessness – here that of those who 'work on themselves' rather than making a difference to the world – to which they are in any case condemned.

The difficulty here is to do justice both to the distortions which the wrong kind of emphasis on self-esteem can introduce, and to the fact that there is something here that we want: a culture 'purchased at lower cost to our nerves, and at larger magnitudes of self-fulfilment', as Rieff puts it (1966, p. 12). We suggest that self-esteem can usefully be admitted into our educational scheme of things as a significant good, but not one pursued directly, still less exclusively. The attendant risks and costs, particularly those involved in the 'inward turn', need to be appreciated far more than they are. Furthermore the good teacher has often raised her pupils' or students' self-esteem (so, once again, to put it) without having that goal in mind. Ordinary perceptive attentiveness to the detail of their work ('I thought the essay rather lost its way in the middle of p. 3, but then got back on track on p. 5 where you turned to the issue of...') seems more properly *respectful*. And experience certainly suggests that pupils and students respond better than if such occasions are seen as self-esteem opportunities ('That was a very interesting essay. Well done, you really should be delighted with your progress this year').

To say that we might make room for self-esteem without allowing it to take over the entire house of education or of therapy is to say that we need to see learning, personal identity, motivation and related matters through a wider lens. It is a poor conception of therapy, still more so of education, that allows emphasis on a single good to conceal the complexity of human existence and the great range of goods, sometimes incompatible, that human beings pursue. It is an impoverished conception of both that focuses on the inward turn, a working on the self, at the expense of efforts to achieve change in the world outside. The kindly apocalypse of self-esteem can be revealing, but it also obscures.

# 2
## Diffidence, Confidence and Self-belief

### Introduction

The concepts with which we describe aspects of self-belief, or the lack of it, are both interesting and puzzling. The qualities of diffidence and shyness, for example, are more complex than they often appear. Self-esteem has become a notorious case, particularly because it is often held to be a symptom of the 'therapy culture'. Frank Furedi, in *Therapy Culture* (2004), shows how 'self-esteem', a term with no particular therapeutic associations until the 1990s, has now colonized our picture of the good, or at least the well-adjusted, life to the point where sport, museums and art galleries are commonly justified in its name (pp. 2 and 167). It is claimed as a 'core skill' in the teaching of citizenship and democracy in schools, and as a goal of sex and relationship education (p. 167).

We pay particular, though not exclusive, attention to self-esteem below, for three reasons. First, it has received fresh energy from the growing interest in individual or 'personalized' learning (see for instance the UK government-sponsored website 'Personalized Learning' and other internet material linked from this). Here the idea is that the pupil flourishes when learning tasks are pitched at just the right level for her – not too simple as to fail to stimulate, nor so challenging that they daunt her. Behind what may seem a perfectly commonsensical approach lies of course the assumption that the individual's fragile self-esteem may not survive a homework assignment that is too demanding or a particularly difficult set of exercises from the text-book. The notion of, in W.B. Yeats's phrase, 'the fascination of what's difficult' has given way to the reassuring fantasy of perfect 'matching' – as if the pupil's current level of attainment could be known with any degree of certainty (as if there *were* any such thing to know beyond such truisms that there is no point in setting her exercises in simultaneous equations if she has not been taught them), and as if there were no problems of condescension or self-justifying expectations.

Secondly, in a recent partial defence of the concept Ruth Cigman has made out an interesting case for saying that many of the problems with the idea of self-esteem disappear so long as self-esteem is 'situated', that is so long as it is based on and reflects genuine achievement rather than being a function of the kind of grandiosity she calls 'psychological fraudulence' or a result of indiscriminate attempts to praise and boost the ego. Given such caveats, she concludes, in repudiation of an earlier critique (Smith, 2002; here substantially reprinted as Chapter 1), that 'self-esteem matters in education' (p. 105) and that it is the proper job of teachers to help children with low self-esteem.

Thirdly, we want to go beyond the earlier critique and develop and expand on the previous chapter here. Although we shall in turn criticize some elements of Cigman's defence this chapter is only incidentally a response to Cigman, who in our view has taken the discussion forward very helpfully. It now seems to us that, at the very least, we need a much subtler and more nuanced picture of the moral psychology of self-belief, which is how we shall refer to the tangle of concepts such as diffidence, confidence, shyness, self-esteem and so on. We shall argue that we need more than this, however. It seems to us that there is a lability, an instability, indeed a violent contrariness, to these concepts, to which justice needs to be done. And we shall further suggest that it is literature and the kind of philosophy that goes by the name of *deconstruction* – a particular way of reading texts – that can best effect this justice.

## I   A thicker moral psychology

'If only', J.L. Austin (1957) wrote, 'we could forget for a while about the beautiful and get down instead to the dainty and the dumpy'. His point was that more philosophical progress is made by investigating 'a field where ordinary language is rich and subtle', yet where philosophers have not (so far) trodden the ground into 'bogs or tracks' to the point where ordinary language is corrupted by the jargon of their efforts, as has perhaps occurred with 'the beautiful' and 'the sublime'. So too with self-belief: it is not just that the therapists have made the ground difficult to navigate: after all, navigating difficult conceptual terrain is precisely what philosophers are sup-

posed to attempt. It is rather that the therapy literature has suc-
ceeded in shifting the discussion of psychological phenomena onto
a very general level – especially that of talk of self-esteem – with
much the same results as occurs if we concentrate discussion of aesthetics on the beautiful and the sublime or ethical debate on the
right and the good.

At the equivalent level to where we find the dainty and the
dumpy in aesthetics, the moral psychology of self-belief offers a
rich and nuanced vocabulary. People may be mild, quiet, meek,
self-effacing, lacking in self-confidence, shy, humble. By contrast
they may be smug, conceited, proud, pompous, grandiose (cp.
Cigman, p. 94). It is not obvious that any of these equates to 'low
self-esteem', or that they are helpfully to be understood as positioned anywhere on the self-esteem scale at all. These qualities are,
rather, just what they are, and not some other kind of thing; and
each repays further investigation. Humility, for instance, can be of
the bad kind or the good kind. Charles Dickens constantly explores
the distinction, with Uriah Heep at one extreme and Little Dorrit
and Esther Summerson (*Bleak House*) at the other (and Little Nell in
*The Old Curiosity Shop* disastrously off the scale). Shyness seems to
work both ways: we can be concerned that one of our children is
shy, yet be relieved that she is not like one of her friends for whom
we uneasily – because we have absorbed the lesson that shyness is
not good – search for the right adjectives: bold, 'forward', precocious, too 'in your face'? Of course shyness can be crippling, but a
degree of reticence, even reserve, can seem part of good manners of
a rather old-fashioned kind. The word 'demure' once did useful
service here.

Somewhere close by here is the idea of 'diffidence'. Dictionary
definitions largely depict it as an undesirable disposition, emphasizing
its connections with timidity and lack of confidence in our own capacities, but they tend also to indicate that it has connotations of
modesty and reserve. It is attributed to the Socrates who was sure only
that he knew nothing. It is valued in part of the Christian tradition,
where diffidence in ourselves is seen as a necessary condition for
having confidence in God; in this tradition it is sometimes found in
the company of wonder and worship.[1] In something like this spirit
Abigail Adams writes to her son, John Quincy Adams, that diffidence is
'the most amiable and most useful disposition in a young mind',
because it leads a young person to seek 'advise [*sic*] and instruction'. It
is an attractive disposition in that a diffident person appeals to our

instinct to protect, reassure and nurture. Hume puts the matter admirably (1903, Part III, Essay IV):

> *Diffidence*, in the mean time, not daring to approach the great house, accepted of an invitation from POVERTY, one of the tenants; and entering the cottage, found *Wisdom* and *Virtue*, who being repulsed by the landlord, had retired thither. *Virtue* took compassion of her, and *Wisdom* found, from her temper, that she would easily improve: So they admitted her into their society. Accordingly, by their means, she altered in a little time somewhat of her manner, and becoming much more amiable and engaging, was now known by the name of *Modesty*.
>
> *Confidence*, though more refractory to counsel and example, degenerated so far by the society of *Vice* and *Folly*, as to pass by the name of IMPUDENCE. Mankind, who saw these societies as JUPITER first joined them, and know nothing of these mutual desertions, are thereby led into strange mistakes; and wherever they see *Impudence*, make account of finding *Virtue* and *Wisdom*; and wherever they observe *Modesty*, call her attendants *Vice* and *Folly*.

Yet at the same time this is rather misleading. We love the diffident person for her very diffidence and not because, by being 'improved', she will become otherwise. Her diffidence, insofar as it is a fault, is a behovely fault, a *felix culpa*, which opens the possibility of a kind of redemption; even if it is the endless promise rather than the achievement of redemption that is most *felix*, most happy, here.

Where then does the diffident person, or the shy or self-effacing one, stand in regard to self-esteem? If we explore these qualities in sufficient depth and with sensitivity to their nuances – which we do not pretend to have made more than a start in doing above – the question no longer seems worth asking. In much the same way a 'thick description' (in the *locus classicus*, of the Balinese cock-fight: cp Geertz, 1993) dissolves the need for explanation, the desire to translate phenomena into a different and more generalizing language. Cigman's story of the black South African township boy, Bulelani, makes this point well, although she does not use it for this purpose (Cigman, 2002). Does the diffident person lack self-esteem? As well ask whether a William Blake etching is 'beautiful'. It is more complex, and difficult, and more interesting, than that.

## II  Three case studies

It was T.'s first day at school, and he went off excitedly. Things went well until C., one of his new classmates, sneered at him for the clothes he was wearing – on the second day too, after T. insisted his mother dress him in something different. Watching C.'s work being awarded a gold star by teacher was especially galling. On the third day T. was delighted to find C. wearing the same shirt as him, and drew attention to it: 'No', said C., 'you are wearing the same shirt that *I* am'. And C. seemed to be the most popular member of the class, while T. found himself alone in the playground and the dining-hall. When he got home T. told his mother he was never going back to school. *A phone-call from mother alerted the school to the problem. Clearly T.'s self-esteem was being damaged. The class teacher arranged some sensitive Circle Time sessions where the pupils were encouraged variously to talk about how it felt to start at school or how you could feel threatened by new arrivals. In the third session C. declared he was very glad T. had come to join them, and after that there were no further symptoms of school refusal.*

F., a bright and perceptive girl whose schooling has nevertheless been intermittent, comes from a poor home in a large town on the south coast. There are many siblings, of which she is the eldest. F. has little privacy. Father is often unemployed, drinks more than is good for him and tends to get out of bed late. Mother works hard to manage on what money is available, and to hold the family together. She appears constantly harassed. Her sister, who has made a good marriage and is in comfortable circumstances, offers to have F. live with her and her own family both in order to relieve some of the pressure in F.'s household and to give F. the opportunity to realize her potential. The offer is accepted, not without mixed feelings. The new home includes four cousins who seem to F. to be full of self-confidence, as well as a maiden aunt whose insensitivity and sharp tongue often remind F. that she is not a full member of her new family. When the head of the household goes abroad on business F.'s cousins and their friends take advantage of his absence to behave in characteristically adolescent ways. F. does not join in, but does not have the temerity to tell the others to stop. She is teased for being a kill-joy. *Her eldest cousin, seeing the effects of all this on F., arranges for counselling. The counsellor diagnoses low self-esteem and recommends an assertiveness skills course.*

D. is a successful and physically attractive, but somewhat tense man in his early thirties. He and a friend move to adjacent properties in the midlands, where they meet several sisters from a family a little lower than them on the social scale. D. is strongly attracted to one of them but is awkward and brittle in her company. Her intelligence seems to intimidate him and what started as a promising relationship seems to be drifting into the sands. She complains he is standoffish and rather too fond of himself, he complains that she is too clever by half. *She cares enough for him, however, to put him in touch with a 'life coach' she has found on the web. This person suggests that D. is suffering from the narcissism that conceals lack of real self-esteem.*

It all works out in the end, of course. The events in italics never took place. There was no Circle Time in Timothy's class. Things picked up for this anthropomorphized small furry animal (Rosemary Wells, *Timothy Goes to School*) when he met Violet, who was having the same problem with a rabbit called Grace ('She sings. She dances. She counts up to a thousand, and she sits next to me!') Eventually Timothy plucked up courage to ask Violet, 'Will you come and have cake with me after school?' On the last page we see the pair carefree, hand in hand. The text reads: 'On the way home Timothy and Violet laughed so much about Claude and Grace that they both got the hiccups'. As for F., Fanny (Jane Austen: *Mansfield Park*) when Sir Thomas Bertram returns from his estates in the West Indies it becomes clear that she is the only member of the family who has kept her head and displayed good judgement. Her cousin Edmund now perceives that she is 'more wise and discrete' than other people (chapter 21). She may be 'timid, anxious, doubting', in the words of the author (chapter 48), but he appears to see these qualities as innocence, reticence and unassuming-ness. They marry. Darcy, or D. (Jane Austen: *Pride and Prejudice*), revises his judgement of Elizabeth Bennet a little: enough for her to draw him out of his proud ways, which may or may not conceal fundamental insecurity, and they too marry. Perhaps she found that awkward and aloof manner of his challenging to her own high spirits, and believed that life with him would be more lively than with a more convention-ally well-adjusted man ('She remembered that he had yet to learn to be laughed at, and it was rather too early to begin', chapter 54). There are no counsellors, therapists, life-coaches or analysts here, and there is no talk of self-esteem.

We have used (and distorted a little) these examples from fiction to point up what seems to go wrong when the idea of self-esteem moves to the centre of our picture of the self. As Cigman (2004) notes, it becomes a kind of gold-standard, a scale on which, supposedly, people can be ranked as having more or less of the precious metal. The trouble with standards (cp. Blake *et al.*, 1998) is that they both assume and demand commensurability, consigning to oblivion all values that cannot be expressed in their terms. Like any other standard, that of self-esteem thus represents a totalizing tendency, demanding that all other kinds of qualities of persons be translated into its coinage. And so all kinds of subtleties of character, of the sort that Jane Austen writes about with insight and perception, are lost. Consider again Fanny Price. There is the finest of lines between being quiet and unassuming, on the one hand, and insipid and uninteresting on the other. The distinction may take a lifetime to explore, as we come to see that, as Iris Murdoch (1992) puts it, the bad person is always surrounded by his own ego-racket, and so can appear interesting and different from moment to moment, while the good person is quiet and always the same. The shyness Fanny can be said to display is an ambivalent quality: we worry about our children being too shy but would not want them to be brash, precocious, forward. A shy person can seem exasperatingly self-effacing in one light, while in another light exactly the same quality is a balm and a delight (the companion who is great fun for a night out might not be our choice for forty years of marriage, as Edmund perceives in his dealings with the effervescent Mary Crawford). Sometimes shyness is entirely proper: when Sir Thomas returns to Mansfield Park and the family circle loses its animation, Fanny comments that this is a natural consequence of the head of the household returning after absence: 'There must be a sort of shyness', she says (chapter 21).[2]

Certainly Darcy might be cured of his narcissistic self-esteem, or pride, by a life-coach, or even the right self-help manual, and the Circle Time sessions might well help Timothy to settle at school and Claude to become reconciled to his new class-mate. Perhaps assertiveness training would indeed equip Fanny with the skills to deal more firmly with tradesmen and hotel waiters. What the therapeutic approach here seems to miss, however, is that these characters are not unambiguously flawed, possessing defects which they would be improved by being cured of in just the same way as they would be better off without haemorrhoids or arthritis. These sins are behovely. Without Timothy's diffidence there is no laughter for him and Violet. Without Fanny's shyness Edmund will respect her for her integrity, but his love for her rests partly, we may speculate, on the feelings of care and protectiveness she inspires in him. Unless Darcy preserves at least the remains of his pride there will be few occasions for Elizabeth to use her wit to tease him. There are dangers here, as in all human relationships: of Edmund's chivalry shading into condescension and chauvinism, of Darcy never learning to be laughed at and of Elizabeth's mischievous wit developing too sharp an edge. But a world without these possibilities of laughter, care and wit would seem a poorer place, and the lives that are built on them, with all their ambiguities, seem fuller and richer than lives solemnly dedicated to the acquisition of self-esteem.

## III   Unsettling self-esteem

One attraction of the idea of self-esteem is that it can seem to bring order to this complex and immensely variegated picture. It promises to make the 'inner life' *manageable*, whether it is one's own (as when we are enjoined to 'Manage Your Self-esteem') or that of pupils in school.[3] In Chapter 1 the question was posed just what kind of people would choose to live with such an idea at the centre of their map of moral psychology: it now seems to us that a significant part of the answer is that they are people who are instinctive managers – systematizers, lovers of diagnosis, prescription, reliable solutions and no doubt of lists. Even Ruth Cigman, though the general tenor of her approach is to observe a proper reticence in this respect, writes of the need 'to identify the psychological fraudsters' (2004, p. 98), that is those whose bravado, arrogance and so on (see previous section) conceals low self-esteem, as a preliminary to offering them appropriate help. She regrets that the discussion of self-esteem to which she responds (Smith, 2002) is 'hard to interpret in terms of classroom technique' (*ibid.*). And though she is clearly right to favour situated self-esteem, ie self-esteem that is based on real achievement rather than the shadow of it created by the empty praise and blandishments of therapism, there is something chilling about the prospect of teachers carefully setting up just the right activities for children to succeed at and so improve their self-esteem. Of course good parents and teachers have always acted on their instinct that last year's Duke of Edinburgh's Award expeditioners came back with a new confidence in themselves, or that it did something for George when after years of academic struggle he discovered a talent for web design. It is the thought that such attunedness to young people could be turned into something like the techniques of 'personalized learning' that disturbs: and, just as much as this, the assumption that the dispositions in this area of moral psychology are readily manageable.

In order to unsettle this assumption we offer a reading of one of the most famous and popular[4] of all English poems, Rudyard Kipling's *If –*. It is not, we believe, to prejudice the reader unfairly if we remark that it is generally taken as an inspiration for fortitude (one of our mothers used to recite it in times of trial, but we digress). Wikipedia notes that it is 'a memorable evocation of Victorian stoicism and the "stiff upper lip"' that are among the traditional British virtues. We reproduce it here in the same format in which it originally appears at the end of Kipling's short story, 'Brother Square-Toes', in the *Rewards and Fairies* collection (1910). The format is not insignificant, despite the many versions, particularly on the internet, that appear to suppose otherwise, thus treating the poem as a mere vehicle for transferable content – the inspiring thoughts that it is imagined to immortalize.

The context, positioned at the end of 'Brother Square-Toes', is also interesting, and gives no comfort to those who see Kipling as the Laureate of British imperialism. The children Dan and Una are nearly at the end of their visit to the seaside, and are strolling 'over the Downs towards the dull evening sea'. The coastguard comes out of his cottage, and walks away into the distance. With this symbol of adult authority removed, Puck and 'a dark, thin-faced man in very neat brown clothes and broad-toed shoes' appear. This man is Mr Lee, also known as Pharaoh. He is a smuggler, and tells the children the story of how he sailed to Philadelphia – not entirely of his own free will – on a French warship shortly after the revolution in France, and at the time when France was encouraging the United States to begin its own revolutionary war against Britain. (Since the children appear to live in the England of Kipling's time, this makes Pharaoh well over a hundred years old, or perhaps he is simply timeless.) He tells them of his adventures in America, where he was particularly impressed by the members of the Moravian Church, who 'used to wash each other's feet up in the attic to keep 'emselves humble: which Lord knows they didn't need...' ('"How very queer!" said Una')... 'I haven't yet found any better or quieter or forbearinger people'.

The climax of his story concerns the attempts of the French to persuade Washington to join them in their war against the British. At a meeting in a clearing in the woods Washington faces down those who are pressurizing him to make war, and declares he will make a peace treaty with Britain. His adversaries slink off; two native Indian chiefs or sachems who have observed all this from the other side of the clearing come up to him and make a gesture that signifies their respect for him. He simply responds 'My brothers know it is not easy to be a chief', and declares that the message to go out to all the native people is that there will be no war. The keynote is quiet dignity. Pharaoh's story, and Kipling's, finishes a few lines later.

Thus attuned, we are now ready to read the poem that is printed, without explanation, at the end of 'Brother Square-Toes'.

*If –*

If you can keep your head when all about you
    Are losing theirs and blaming it on you,
If you can trust yourself when all men doubt you,
    But make allowance for their doubting too;
If you can wait and not be tired by waiting,
    Or being lied about, don't deal in lies,
Or being hated, don't give way to hating,
    And yet don't look too good, nor talk too wise:

If you can dream – and not make dreams your master;
    If you can think – and not make thoughts your aim;
If you can meet with Triumph and Disaster
    And treat those two impostors just the same;
If you can bear to hear the truth you've spoken
    Twisted by knaves to make a trap for fools,
Or watch the things you gave your life to, broken,
    And stoop and build 'em up with worn-out tools:

If you can make one heap of all your winnings
    And risk it on one turn of pitch-and-toss,
And lose, and start again at your beginnings
    And never breathe a word about your loss;
If you can force your heart and nerve and sinew
    To serve your turn long after they are gone,
And so hold on when there is nothing in you
    Except the Will which says to them: 'Hold on!'

If you can talk with crowds and keep your virtue,
    Or walk with Kings – nor lose the common touch,
If neither foes nor loving friends can hurt you,
    If all men count with you, but none too much;
If you can fill the unforgiving minute
    With sixty seconds' worth of distance run,
Yours is the Earth and everything that's in it,
    And – which is more – you'll be a Man, my son!

The crucial thing to notice is that we are here recommended two kinds of virtues. There is the manly, vigorous kind – keeping one's head under pressure, forcing 'heart and nerve and sinew', and the willingness to take significant risks. But there is another kind, which consists of quieter qualities, which are themselves touched in quietly in the poem (too quietly, indeed, for many people to hear them). Making allowance for people's doubts when it is you they are doubting is no particular part of stoicism or the stiff upper-lip: it is the mark of an almost saintly patience. In the last four lines of the first stanza there is a suggestion that the *really* difficult thing is not so much to practise the virtues described as to do so without looking too good, or talking too wise. The same is true of the first four lines of the third stanza. To risk everything you have achieved – how many of us could do that? And then, when it all goes disastrously wrong, to start over? An extraordinary feat. But the repeated 'And' at the beginning of three consecutive lines seems to require the reader to give third one particular emphasis: which is when it seems that the *really* difficult thing is not to become the kind of person who bores the pub with talk of how he lost everything but built it all up again from scratch. It is modesty and forebearance that the poem talks of, as much as the more vigorous virtues. And this is confirmed by the promise that the one who has achieved what is there to be achieved will be granted the Earth. Here we surely hear a Biblical echo: Blessed are the meek, for they shall inherit the Earth. Not the strong and the hardy, nor the entrepreneurs, nor even the tough, who famously get going when the going gets tough. *Blessed are the meek.*

There is further interest in the question of just who we are to understand as the voice of the poem, if they have the power to bequeath the Earth, and whom they are to be understood as addressing, if He is both Son and Man. It cannot then escape us that Jesus is celebrated, in the words of Charles Wesley's hymn, as gentle, meek and mild. Now perhaps we can see the point of the poem's title: not *If*, as in so many bastardized versions, nor even *If...*, as though the title either simply abbreviated the poem, or anticipated a resounding *Then...* Kipling's *If –* is an aposiopesis, a breaking off, a falling silent, a reticence (another name for this rhetorical device is *reticentia*), as of one overcome with emotion, or modesty. One who hesitates, falters; perhaps through diffidence. As, introducing such a speaker and such a listener, one well might.[5]

## IV  Any text to head as rest in chapter

Our language presents us with binaries: present/absent, true/false, man/woman. These binaries generally imply that one of the pair of terms is superior while the other is lacking, deficient and inferior. On the one side proud, robust, vigorous, forceful, with high self-esteem: on the other, meek, humble, shy and suffering from low self-esteem. *If* – disturbs this binary. It is not just that we are reminded that there are gentle virtues as well as red-blooded ones: we are drawn into the comfortable, familiar assumption that the latter are the virtues of the major key, only for this assumption to be overturned.

The binary is inverted. But it is worse than this, because after a moment's discomfort we discover a nagging voice insisting that we won't get very far without vigour, a measure of stoicism and at least the occasional capacity to display a stiff upper-lip. Who is going to protect all these meek and mild characters, anyway? This voice would no doubt have nagged Kipling's contemporaries, citizens of Empire at its zenith, more loudly still. Then it is time to revisit the poem and experience Kipling's inversion: and so the binary turns, endlessly and vertiginously.

However it is worse even that this, because the occupants of each part of the binary will not stay still. Pride – but not King Lear's kind. Forcefulness – but it is not hard to think of contexts where we prefer people not to be forceful. (Contrast a virtue such as courage, which is always a good thing or it becomes foolhardiness or recklessness.) We have seen how there is a good kind of humbleness and a bad kind; shyness seems thoroughly ambivalent; meekness will inherit you the Earth while at the same time it is worryingly close to insipidity and soppiness. Each of these virtues can seem to need its spine, if not its upper-lip, stiffened a little. Only low self-esteem is unambiguously a case for treatment; and that is because the notion was adopted, in its modern currency, to indicate precisely that.

This chapter does not draw a tidy map of self-belief because, in the end, we do not think there is a tidy map to be drawn. If there is indeed a radical lability or instability here, if the words and ideas slip, slide and perish even more than is generally the case, then tidiness is part of the problem. Certainly there are times when philosophy can helpfully undertake the conceptual mapping beloved of the analytical tradition. Sometimes, though, philosophy – or theory, if the reader prefers – undertakes a different and at least as valuable a task, which is to shake the very bedrock on which well-drawn maps and concepts rest. The kind of philosophy (or theory) which, following Jacques Derrida, is called deconstruction, is a way of listening and responding to (and being responsible to, in the name of justice) the subversive, dissident voices from the edges and the margins, opening itself 'not only to the dominant voices of the great masters, but also to other voices that speak more gently, more discretely, more mildly' (Caputo, 1997, p. 57) than those of the canon and the mainstream. It is a kind of philosophy that, like the literary, insists on the necessity of endless re-reading, the impossibility of closure, that refuses to say 'now we have things ordered and tied down', 'now they are manageable'. This philosophy accepts that philosophy, like literature, does not have the last word on the things we care for, because there is no last word (*ibid.*, p. 55). We want our children to be confident *and* diffident, shy *and* full of healthy self-esteem, and what we want for them is not contained by the turbulent and disorderly language of self-belief. What we want for them eludes our attempts to grasp it and pin it down. It is always beyond us, something we seem dimly to perceive, and it disappears as we approach it. It is nameless, and it is unmanageable. It is unforeseeable, because children, like people in general, if we attend to them properly, constantly surprise us. Deconstruction undermines the stabilizing order set up by our best educational and therapeutic endeavours, not out of love of chaos but out of the passion to do justice to what we have not yet understood. None of which means that we cannot help people with their self-belief: only that we need to approach the task, and, as we noted in our Introduction the whole topic of therapy, with a proper diffidence.

# 3
# What Can be Said, What Can be Shown

As Chapters 1 and 2 begin to show, we argue in this book for greater attention to the language that we use – a greater sensitivity to the different ways that language operates and recognition that it is not simply a means of communication but the well-spring of our thought and being. Good counselling is in tune with such an insight, recognizing that the crucial step that enables the client to 'move on' is often the finding of new words, a new way in which to see the situation. This much seems clear and important to us, but we also accept that it can sound too much like 'a solution'. Does there come a time when it is necessary not to speak but to do something more physical and full-bodied?

The lure of the physical is clear, and there are many who promote its benefits. Outdoor, perhaps wilderness, experience, we are told, has important therapeutic effects. On the BBC website 'Inside Out — Surprising Stories, Familiar Places' we are invited to 'Meet Chris and Rosemary':

> They both want to change their lives, but have been told that they must overcome their fears first. Inside Out joins their group therapy session and asks whether all this inner loving really does result in 'a new me'.
>
> As the group in the background chants 'Yes, yes, yes', Chris Raines and Rosemary Dalton stand in front of a pit full of burning coals.
>
> Chris and Rosemary have been told that if they can walk over hot coals, they can do anything. They are the new breed of self-help participants who go to a life coach to change their lives.
>
> Will they walk through fire? Will they change their minds? Will it make any difference?

Walking across burning coals, no doubt empowering to some, has left others with third-degree burns. Such practices take to an extreme the idea that exposure to the elements has therapeutic effects. Try entering 'Wilderness Therapy' into any Internet search engine to see what is available. The Aspen Education Group, for example, confidently declares:

> Outdoor education, also known as wilderness therapy or outdoor therapy, serves as a short-term, high-impact therapeutic alternative to help get troubled teens back on track and develop a sense of personal responsibility. The wilderness serves as the ultimate teacher that teens cannot manipulate. The therapeutic aspect combined with the adventure of the wilderness camping experience has been shown to be highly effective in transforming the attitudes and behaviors of children, teens, and young adults.

For a different sector of the market, the business customer, Karibuni ('a complete package, starting and ending from your office front door') offers team-build and corporate away-days to improve performance, which, we are told, have proved particularly suitable for dynamic smaller teams and organizations. Karibuni's innovative approach allows you to select the 'modules' that you need to achieve your team's strategic objectives and training needs.[1]

What are we to make of this? Is exposure to physical challenge really important to our self-understanding? Does it help us to work with others? Does it build the team? In this chapter we want to address these questions but also to ponder the curious thematizing of the body and its violences. We see, in the Big Brother genre, in the jungle-survival stunts and in the voyeuristic infliction of punitive health and diet regimes, the makings of a what might be called the 'Television of Humiliation'. We see also, in a film such as *Fight Club* (directed by David Fincher, 1999[2]), the violent-therapeutic investigation of who or what we are.

*Fight Club* unsettles, disturbing what is taken for granted in a number of ways. It questions how far words *can* spell things out. The sense of what cannot be said then becomes critical for the recognition and *experience* of embodied relationships and human finitude. Any amount of saying, it seems, any amount of reflection or discussion or talk, is inevitably second-rate to *doing* something. Is the hero here perhaps the Hollywood existentialist, masculine and adventurous with his *acte gratuit*? The therapeutic encounter with pain and the possibility of death – is this the theme the film pursues or rather what it parodies or exploits?

*Fight Club* questions the kind of life we lead. Are we the authors of our own lives, investing them with meaning? The iron necessities of our techno-rational, capitalist world – it is this system that has us by the throats, dictating to us what our needs are. The things you own end up owning you, so that it is only after you have lost everything that you can do anything meaningful. You have to free yourself from the shackles of modern life, which imprison and emasculate you, you men, in particular – and yes, the metaphor is apt. Your therapy is to forget everything you know, or perhaps everything you think you know, to lose hope and find freedom. So, for the moment, we shall follow one possible reading of David Fincher's multi-layered film and call it an investigation into what is real and, above all, into what 'really living' can mean.

What can a film show that philosophy cannot? The film affects us, jolts us and, failing to offer 'a solution', leaves us orphaned and needing to search for ourselves. Its sardonic, testosterone-fuelled science fiction is designed to touch raw nerves, and Finch's angry, perverse, occasionally comic fantasies about what it is to be a man today unfold like a huge phantasmagorical edifice around the search for lost authority, lost masculinity. Asking what we are unsettles what we thought we were, the things we took for granted and never explored. The film shows what can't be said. Punches and blood and scars, then more punches and blood and scars. We want perhaps to avert our eyes.[3] And yet, things are not what they seem. Our very capacity to endure the film is part of what the film is about. We are forced to sort through the ambiguities ourselves. If we want solutions, *we* must provide them. And what the film *shows* and what it means are not things we are going to find through our habitual, discursive, intellectual deliberations.

***

What is it to say, and what is it to show? These questions press on us, and we must change the tone. In the *Tractatus*, Wittgenstein tries to indicate the boundary between what can be said and what can only be shown, and that text famously moves towards the thought: the limits of my language are the limits of my world (Wittgenstein, 1922, #5.6). The human subject does not belong to the world but forms its limit (#5.632). Wittgenstein accepts the idea that the world consists of states of affairs that exist independently of each other. He holds the so-called *picture theory of language*: we make images of facts, and the relationship between a fact and an image is one of similarity. A revelation of a fact's form will give us its logical structure: 'Everything that can be thought at all can be thought clearly. Everything that can be put into words can be put clearly' (#4.116). Every object must have a sign, and signs necessarily refer to objects. If we want to speak about values and meaning, these are to be sought outside of the world: 'What we cannot speak about we must pass over in silence' (#7.7).

Ethics, Wittgenstein says, like aesthetics and religion, is something that cannot be spoken about (#6.421). It belongs to that realm where things cannot be *said* but only *shown* (#4.1212). For Wittgenstein as a person, ethics was extremely important – 'what is the use of studying philosophy ...', he comments to Norman Malcolm, ' if it does not improve your thinking about the important questions of everyday life?' – yet in his philosophy he was virtually silent on these questions. His *Lecture on Ethics*, which brings together ethics and religion once again, more or less reaffirms this ineffability: 'Ethics, if it is anything, is supernatural and our words will only express facts... Ethics, so far as it springs from the desire to say something about the ultimate meaning of life, the absolute good, the absolutely valuable, can be no science. What it says does not add to our knowledge in any sense' (Wittgenstein, 1965, p. 7). It is precisely those things about which one cannot speak (within the strict terms of the *Tractatus*) that are the most important things in life, including ethics.

Yet, as is well known, Wittgenstein later changed his mind about how language works and what it can do. The stark dichotomy of what can be said (the logical structure of the world, logic, mathematics) and 'nonsense' (everything else) is replaced by the variety of 'language games'. Maybe his continuing avoidance of direct talk of ethics, certainly of any kind of ethical system, is a kind of a faithfulness to his earlier intuition: that nothing can be said about ethics. Certainly, his views on ethics were closely aligned with his religious beliefs, about which he was extremely private.

It 'is not certain propositions' striking us immediately as true, i.e. it is not a kind of *seeing* on our part; it is our *acting*, which lies at the bottom of the language-game' (Wittgenstein, 1979, #204). The concept of practice is given shape in the notion of language-games, with their interwovenness of utterances and actions, which find their home within a 'form of life'. Justifications can be given, but justifications come to an end; and then 'I have reached bedrock, and my spade is turned'

(Wittgenstein, 1953, #217). This is simply what I do. Why we do what we do relates our actions to other elements (call this a horizontal analysis), or perhaps it makes explicit what lies beneath (a vertical one). Both have their value, but the kind of analysis they provide is not a matter of justification. So our ability to explain and justify ourselves ethically is limited. If philosophy is a kind of therapy, as Wittgenstein says, the kind of work on the self that helps us get outside certain problems and see them in a new light, then ethics also involves a working on the self. It is about overcoming oneself, about the personal struggle everyone must engage in to find peace in the world. Wittgenstein was surely dealing with his demons: 'Working in philosophy ... is really more a working on oneself. On one's own interpretation. On one's way of seeing things. (And what one expects of them)' (Wittgenstein, 1980, p. 16e – a remark from 1931). Reasons for what we do cannot be exhaustively made explicit; they remain inexpressible. An evocative language may be able to touch upon these reasons: the kind of language he attempted in the *Lecture on Ethics*.

There is a naïve understanding of *Fight Club* that suggests that any kind of doing is better than talking, and there is a similarly naïve understanding of Wittgenstein (fed perhaps by his charismatic taciturnity and the obliqueness of his philosophical style). There is a better understanding of both. *Fight Club* shows us the limits of active therapies better than we could ever *explain* because it shows how seductive therapies can be. It makes it possible for us to distance ourselves from crude criticisms aimed at particular therapies, yet paradoxically it becomes clear how the therapy of the fight club is itself illusory: how, in other words, going beyond saying (see the Club's first two rules, below) may itself go wrong.

What then is the film about? Does it show, say, that risky physical activity in the cause of team-building is attractive and absurd? That the language of film may powerfully impress the mind? That images which hold one's thinking in their grip can enable a process of self-education, of working on the self? Interpretation of a work of art creates an insight into the kinds of human beings we are. It too is a kind of therapy, allowing us to accept what otherwise remains unspoken and in the background. Let us turn more directly to the film.

***

The Rules of Fight Club:

1. You do not talk about Fight Club.
2. You do not talk about Fight Club.

3. When someone says 'Stop' or goes limp, the fight is over.
4. Only two guys to a fight.
5. One fight at a time.
6. No shirts, no shoes.
7. Fights go on as long as they have to.
8. If this is your first night at Fight Club, you have to fight.

There are two central figures: the laconic narrator Jack, played by Edward Norton, and his charismatic, anger-filled crony Tyler Durden, played by Brad Pitt. Here are two young men desensitized by a soulless world of corporate culture and anonymity, vacuous consumerism and self-help platitudes. Jack, the Everyman of the 1990s, has been driven to the edge of his sanity by a dull white-collar job – his work involves travelling around the country investigating crashes for a major car company. He owns a condominium, though it could be said to own him: it gives no respite from the emptiness in his life. He has an empty fondness for material things, wondering what kind of dining furniture defines him as a person. Furniture catalogues become a kind of pornography, the condominium transforming soporifically into a catalogue before our eyes. Nothing makes him feel alive, and he is tormented by insomnia – and when you have insomnia, the narrator tells us, everything is far away, everything is a copy of a copy. He visits a doctor claiming he is in real pain. The doctor refuses him drugs and tells him that really he does not know what pain is. He should seek out those who are truly suffering.

Jack's only relief is in the 12-step support groups for terminally ill people he attends, in particular the one for testicular cancer, where at least he can cry. The first meeting he goes to is, symbolically enough, for post-surgical victims of testicular cancer. He has a meeting lined up for each night of the week, and all are full of men crying, men exploring feelings, men, that is, doing what girls are supposed to do. One of the testicular-cancer patients, a former champion body-builder has, as a result of hormone treatment, developed huge breasts. During one session he weeps openly, clasping Jack to his ample bosom.

Jack is not dying, but when people think you are dying, he tells us, they really listen to you. Crying with the support-group allows him to sleep. What, though, is his problem? He does not know, but he is desperate for something. He finds a fellow 12-step addict in Marla – who is later described as 'the little scratch on the roof of your mouth that would heal if you could only stop tonguing it, but you can't'. Marla, a suicidal junkie, goes to the support group for purely voyeuristic reasons, for entertainment, as she puts it. When Jack confronts her, she explains that the meetings are cheaper than the movies and, what's more, there is free coffee.

The blandness of Jack's days, played out in look-alike aeroplane cabins and hotel rooms, is interrupted when he finds himself in a plane sitting next to Tyler, a macho man who is all loud print shirts, leather jackets and sunglasses. Tyler makes and sells speciality soap at $20 a bar. Later we will learn that the soap is made from human fat, and the bars are sold back to lipo-sucked women. Later too it will be revealed that the bars also contain the ingredients to make explosives. Tyler is also a part-time movie projectionist, who splices single frames of genitalia from pornographic movies into family films just enough to cause subliminal discomfort, as well as being a restaurant waiter (who delights in defiling the food he serves). After his condominium mysteriously blows up, destroying all his possessions (it is the worst day of his life: an airline loses his luggage as well), Jack forsakes his ordered ways and moves into the abandoned wreck near a toxic waste site that is home for Tyler.

It is in a nearby parking lot that Tyler teaches his new lodger to fight – not to prove that he is stronger, but to show his new friend just how good it feels. Seeing himself now as a victim of a feminized consumer culture that accords more worth to furniture and clothes than to strength and power, Jack wants to become a different person. 'Is that what a man looks like?' Jack asks Tyler as they sneer at a Calvin Klein underwear advertisement that displays sculpted, discretely neutered nude male models. 'Of course it isn't... You are not your job. You are not how much you have in the bank. You are not the car you drive. You are not the contents of your wallet.' Men can feel real by fighting, indeed beating each other nearly to death. Soon Jack is going to the office with bleeding gums, black eyes, bruised cheeks, damaged hearing and bloodstained clothes. The tacitly homoerotic bouts between the two men become addictive, as does sex with Marla.

There are plenty of other regular guys who get a real boost to their egos by beating one another up. In order to feel, they battle against each other in bare-knuckle, no-holds-barred fights. Fight Club, born in a bar parking lot, eventually has to move to the huge basement of the bar, so many men are turning up to throw punches. The wild man weekend is relocated in near-primitive circumstances, right in the middle of a modern city. Weekly secret meetings are held now, not to box but to fight with the intent to injure, each man against a new opponent every week, with one badly bloodied man helping his badly injured opponent when the fight is finished. These men, of whatever type and occupation, feel that their regular lives are cocooned. Nothing in their computerized existence feeds the hunger for physical risk, for aggression, for the infliction or suffering of pain. Blood is their warrant of triumph, not over one another, but over torpor, the goal not competitive but co-operative. They wish to spill their own blood as well as others', not just to inflict pain but to have it inflicted upon them. These men feel alive only when they are hurt. When the fight is over nothing is solved, but then nothing mattered, the narrator tells us, we all felt the same. So, if one asks why, Tyler answers: 'Self-improvement is masturbation. Now self-destruction ...' but then his voice trails off. The answer: self-destruction. Men beat each other's heads into a bloody mess so as to reclaim their instincts within a society that has turned them into repressed losers and empty consumers. After fighting, everything else in the world seems muted and smaller – you could handle anything, says Jack. Men crash cars to test the limits of their courage. Tyler, it seems, fears nothing. Clubs start up around the country.

But the Fight Club mutates – as the Hollywood plot progresses – into Project Mayhem, a frighteningly fascist paramilitary organization. More and more men join what has become a don't ask, don't tell, don't think army. What they do escalates, to include vandalism, random brutality toward outsiders and terrorism. Tyler's followers subject themselves to a progressive depersonalization, and the violence they are ready to commit is terrifying. Aiming to bring down civilization, Tyler starts by blowing up the offices of credit card companies, wiping out debt records and letting everyone 'start over'. Who is this Tyler who wants to do this? Who is it who has redefined Jack's life and shown him what life can be? In the final climactic fight between Jack and Tyler, we suddenly see that Jack, in hitting Tyler, is hitting himself. There is no 'Tyler': he is just a dimension of Jack's psyche, a part of his multiple personality. Tyler and Jack are the warring halves of a single mind – one the personification of true belief, the other the niggling voice of honest doubt. And, short of escalating the violence to a suicidal extreme, the two cannot escape each other – the vicious circle they inhabit is absolutely closed. Everything ends in destruction.

***

This then is the self-regarding and self-perpetuating power of our consumer culture. Consumerism equals death, so Jack's job seems to say, and consumer culture is an edifice supported and perpetuated by men.

Contrary to what Tyler says, it is a *masculine* culture. Civilization is not an insidious plan hatched by women, designed for their own protection, but the product of institutions through which weaker men protect themselves. The culture of consumption, the loss of real work, presents men with an identity crisis of unparalleled proportions. The narcissism that drives consumerism becomes incestuous. Caught in that tight loop, we are all infected. The expressionistic twist in the narrative reveals the abiding paradox, the ingenious secret, of this consumer society – its ability to peddle conformity in the guise of individuality. Here is the paradoxical message of today's consumerism: you are as unique and special as everyone else, and so deserve the same material rewards as everyone else. And here is the attendant dilemma that the film presents: if our narcissistic age has turned individuality into conformity, then any attempt to escape the prison of self-involvement – even something as bizarrely self-destructive as the fight club – is doomed to fail. Fight Club is really just another narcissism, an extension of the same trap. As it expands to other cities and recruits its legions of followers, the antisocial impulse grows popular and marketable, dispelling any semblance of liberating power. Anarchy is franchized to the Mayhem brand.

Dictators start with men willing to die for a charismatic leader, men who want to follow the rules. The first rule of *Project Mayhem* is: You do not ask questions. The film's message seems clear. Tyler's Fight Club therapy changes into something much more dangerous. The group's rigorous training and subversive agenda are as disturbing to Jack's mild-mannered character as Tyler's original wild streak was thrilling. Jack is increasingly repulsed by Tyler's commando cruelties and tries to sabotage the sabotage, but even when subversion turns to terrorism he cannot tear himself away. The ironic falseness of Tyler's solution to Jack's problem – that is, to the problem of the American Everyman – becomes clear. Tyler embodies the need to rebel against society, to spit back in the face of authority. He is dangerous because he does what we wish we could do, and because he has followers. It may be that we are all living in a toxic dump, losing ourselves in the kind of society we have to live in. It may be that our life is not a 'real' life anymore. But the person that Tyler turns Jack into isn't a real man either.

\*\*\*

In deference to *Fight Club*, and apart from our reference to Wittgenstein, we have in the above paragraphs tried to withdraw from our 'habitual, discursive, intellectual deliberations'. But let us change the register now to attend to Henry Giroux, whose caustic critique still finds some room for seeing the film as a possible public pedagogy (Giroux, 2000). *Fight Club* is less interested in attacking the broader material relations of power and strategies of domination and exploitation associated with neo-liberal capitalism, he says, than it is in rebelling against a consumerist culture that dissolves the bonds of male sociality and puts in their place an enervating notion of male identity and agency. It has nothing to say about the structural violence of unemployment, job insecurity and cuts in public spending, or about the destruction of such institutions as might be capable of defending social provision and the public good. On the contrary, it defines the violence of capitalism almost exclusively in terms of an attack on traditional notions of masculinity. In so doing it reinscribes white heterosexuality within a dominant logic of stylized brutality and male bonding, which appears predicated on the need to denigrate and wage war against all that is feminine. It mocks new age therapy for men, and it satirizes the 'new man'. It condemns what it sees as the (over-)affective process of feminization that such therapies sanction and put in place. As the embodiment of authoritarian masculinity and hyper-individualism, Tyler could never imagine a democratic politics. He represents the redemption of a masculinity repackaged as the promise of violence in the service of social and political anarchy.

Choice, Giroux continues, appears for Tyler to be an exclusively individual act, a simple matter of personal will, a kind of 'Just do it' ideology that functions outside of existing relations of power and resources, and outside existing social bonds. The freedom this promises does not simply involve preoccupation with the de-politicized self: it also lacks any language for translating private troubles into public anger and thus succumbs to a cult of immediate sensation; freedom degenerates into collective impotence. The body is no longer the privileged space of social citizenship or political agency but the location of violence, crime and aggression. Focusing on bodily pleasure, pain and violence, the film plays dangerously with violence's glamorous, fascistic edge.

The only message consistent with the cynical politics of the film, Giroux claims, is that the ultimate language, referent and state of affairs through which our lives are to be understood is violence itself, and that violence is inevitable. Where then can be its point as public pedagogy? It is to be found, Giroux suggests, to the extent the film plays a role in mobilizing meaning, pleasures and identifications. It has to be understood in terms of a broader network of cultural spheres and institutional formations. In spite of his criticisms, Giroux acknowledges that the film shows that power is never totalizing and that even within an increasingly corporatized social landscape there are always cracks, openings and spaces for resistance. It can remind us of the need to reclaim the discourses of ethics, politics and critical agency as important categories in the struggle against the rising tide of violence, against human suffering and against the spectre of fascism that threatens all vestiges of democratic public life.

Does Giroux get the measure of *Fight Club*? Our question is rather what we are to make of the various therapy settings the movie starts with and of its counter-therapy of violence. How do these things connect with the character-building, bonding wilderness experience, the team-building corporate away-days and the walking on hot coals with which we began? Of course, it is possible that the bonding that occurs through extreme, shared experience really feeds into the character development of managers in just the way that we need. But one also catches glimpses of a rather more curious idea: that it is under such pressure that we discover what we or others are 'really' like. Michael Frayn (1974, sec. 26) points up the absurdity neatly: 'On the surface he has always appeared to be calm and cheerful. But now, after he has spent three days without food, under heavy bombardment, lost his home, and got both shoes full of water, it turns out that *really* – underneath – he is a rather irritable man who lacks the capacity to get pleasure out of life'. Perhaps we should understand the film as showing how bizarre these theories are. None of the therapies, including Fight Club itself, seem to have much value. Perhaps we can defuse *Fight Club's* commercial violence by taking it to show the absurdity of them all.

***

Whether or not we agree with Giroux's interpretation of *Fight Club* is, however, not the issue we find most pressing here. *Fight Club* raises questions of language and representation, and it does this through a fractured narrative structure that plays out what we might think of as a form of schizophrenia. Jack's unnamed character narrates the film, jumping back and forth in time, from dead-pan realism to Hollywood fantasy, and his digressions interrupt the plot's progress. The camera zooms into the ganglia of a man's brain, slides inside walls and kitchen appliances, and catapults out of a trash can filled with junk-food packaging. We see Jack's adventures in the cavern of ice that he feels within him. Searching through various cities, he has only symbolic clues to follow. And so film, the most realistic medium ever devised, gives up representation for semblance, for the non-real, confirming in the process that semblance is itself a real part of our world. Film's illusion is based not on convention, as in the theatre, but on the inalienable realism of what is shown. Certainly what we see is always mediated – a particular lens, a camera angle, filtering, special effects – but the effect of film inevitably goes beyond words and sounds. In one way or another it makes the claim to be 'real'. We said above that the story shown by this film has effects beyond film and touches us in ways beyond discursive, intellectual deliberation. This raises in acute form the question of the part played here by language.

Language is not only an instrument of rational inquiry but a medium of expression, evocation and address. One can express oneself by what one says, by the manner in which one says something. Wittgenstein speaks of the 'feeling of meaning': 'We talk, we utter words, and only *later* get a picture of their life' (Wittgenstein, 1953, II, p. 209e). Any attempt to say something is always partial, it is always one-sided and perspectival. No way of speaking, no doctrine whatsoever can control cultural practices and thus liberate us from the restlessness and incertitudes of human existence, of the search for meaning in our lives. This is not to say that words are arbitrary: they are always embedded in a language and a history, with both bearing the mark of the inter-subjective. But what we do can never be fully transparent. Thus it becomes clear that in what we say we bear witness to what we long for, but it is also clear that the limits of our expression, of our attempts to be coherent, themselves show something about the condition of our lives.

The literary text, for instance the poem, can in its manner of expression be a surrendering or offering in the struggle with oneself. It requires no other material presence; it does not want to explain; it attempts only to see things in a particular way. It seems a means for the lonely individual for a moment to find home. By analogy, the film may enable, therapeutically perhaps, a breakout from the closed viewpoint in which the individual is held captive.

*Fight Club* comments on the absurdity of therapy regimes, unsettling their attempts to get in touch with the real. Faced with questions such as 'What is really happening?', 'Who am I?' and 'What is it to be a real man?', it ends by deflecting the questions or answering 'We do not know'. The film is therapeutic because of its parody of therapy: it challenges therapies of saying *and* showing, questioning how far they can work. It *shows* this and does not argue it, leaving those who would interpret it – the film critics, Giroux, ourselves perhaps – to do so at their peril, imagining no doubt that they have somehow got the better of therapy. If Jack and Tyler turn out in the end to be one and the same person, is this a happy Hollywood ending, the struggle of good and evil resolved? Is it an authorial cop-out, deflecting the issues the film has raised? Does it merely impart the moral lesson that aggression is self-destructive? Or does this uncertainty somehow reveal the limits of showing, of going beyond words?

Literature may also, however, involve something other than the attempt to represent the real, and hence something other than the evocation of sympathy. Here the focus is on the progressive emancipation of literature and language from literality, intensified by the impossibility of closure of meaning and what this means for our lives as a whole. It is in a similar way that images in a film may defy coherence, consistency and unity of interpretation, and confront us with a narrative that is fractured, piece-meal, even schizoid, just as real life at times may be. Of course, we can speak about these things, as we have done in this chapter, and it is to further possibilities of narrative that we turn, albeit with some equivocation, in Chapter 4. But we can never provide a complete picture of what a film shows, any more than we can offer an exhaustive account of any work of art. Good understanding resists spelling everything out. This is a lesson intimated in the *Tractatus*, where it works both reflexively in relation to that text and, by extension, towards the better understanding of life itself. Does *Fight Club* stand up to the implications of such thoughts? Can it stand this analysis?

# 4
# Reading Narrative

Very well, then, I am large, I contain multitudes
(William Carlos Williams)

We found in the previous chapter that one possibility amongst the interpretations that *Fight Club* invites is that the film is therapeutic because of its pastiche of therapy. It incorporates a narrative of forms of therapy in which people tell the story of, or 'restory', their lives, and of a possibly obsessed fascination with such 'storying'; and against what might be the fantasies not only of consumerism but of therapy itself, it offers its own possible story of a reclaiming of masculinity within a society that has turned men into repressed losers and empty consumers; but at the same time this is a story whose grotesqueness allows a teasing equivocation between tranquilized absorption of Hollywood violence and a faltering, deconstructive parody of that genre, including its narrative of masculinity. In this chapter we look more directly at the ways in which narrative itself has come to be self-consciously adopted as a form of therapy and as a method of research, the theorisation of which partly draws upon the widespread acknowledgement within philosophy of the narrative structure of human experience – for example, in Paul Ricoeur, Alasdair MacIntyre and Charles Taylor – but also identifies itself sometimes with deconstruction. We begin by considering accounts of these practices, in therapy and research.

## Narrative therapy

Michael White, of the Dulwich Centre in Adelaide, Australia, explains that the primary emphasis in narrative therapy is on people's expressions of their experiences of life. Expressions of experience are taken to be units of meaning and experience. As White is at pains to stress, however, these are far from being static reproductions of that experience: they are neither 'maps of the territory of life', nor 'reflections of life as it is lived', nor 'mirrors of the world', nor 'perspectives on life' that stand outside what is going on. It is, nevertheless, the structure of narrative that provides the principal frame of intelligibility for people in their day-to-day lives. Through this frame people link together the events of life in sequences that unfold through time according to specific themes, with events understood in terms of linear progressions, and with each event contributing foundations of possibility for what follows. In spite of this linearity, however, narrative analysis brings out the multi-sited and particular nature of the self, deconstructing the pressures of the norm, and reworking dominant notions and practices of self and culture. Experience, on these terms, is construed as actions that are themselves constitutive of life. Seeking to understand 'these expressions of subjective experience', narrative therapy takes it that their effects are to be 'got at' through the consciousness of those engaged in the actions. It is these 'explorations of subjective experience that contribute to "rich" or "thick" description' (White, 2006). Descriptions are thick when they evoke 'people's consciousness in explanations of why they do what they do'. They are rich to the extent that they link alternative stories of people's presents with alternative stories of people's pasts. These in turn are connected with the lives of others, according to shared themes that speak 'to purposes, values, and commitments in common', in such a way as to structure 'contexts for telling and retelling', and with, in consequence, the 'production of meta-texts, and texts that are meta to meta-texts'. Practice of this kind provides options for the 'performance and re-performance' of the 'preferred stories of people's lives' in a 're-engagement and a reproduction of history through the alternative presents of people's lives', a re-engagement and reproduction that are linked by common themes, invoking the 'wisdom of hindsight'.

   In rather less measured terms, the website of the Narrative Therapy Centre of Toronto states that each person 'produces the meaning of their life from the stories that are available in these contexts' (Narrative Therapy Centre of Toronto, 2006). This is said to relate to a 'relatively recent way of thinking about the nature of human life and knowledge which has come to be known as "postmodernism" – which believes there is no one objective "truth" and that there are many multiple possible interpretations of any event. Thus within a narrative approach ... one story is seen as true as another story and our lives are seen as multi-storied.' Therapy involves a 're-authoring' of people's stories and lives.

David M. Boje advances a conception of narrative therapy that is explicitly deconstructive. Methodologically, this involves such steps as: the *duality search*, in which the weaker element within bipolar terms is identified; the *reinterpretation of the hierarchy*, where exploring and reinterpreting the pattern of dominance weaken its grip; attention to *rebel voices*, in which the dominant voice of the narrative is denied in favour of those that are marginalized ('e.g. Who speaks for the trees?'); the acknowledgement of the *other side of the story*, by 'putting the bottom on top, the marginal in control, or the back stage up front' – not, however, with a view to replacing one centre with another but to show the continuous change and disintegration that dominant readings of the story are apt to conceal; the *denial of the plot*, whereby the scenarios, recipes and morals of stories are turned around (from romantic to tragic or comedic to ironic); the *finding of the exception*, which enables the exposure of the rule in a way that makes it extreme or absurd; the *tracing of what is between the lines*, revealing the gaps in the story and 'the context, the back stage, the between, the intertext'; and, on the strength of the preceding steps, a *resituation* of the story 'beyond its dualisms, excluded voices, or singular viewpoint', with the story re-authored so that 'a new balance of views is attained', which becomes a story without centres in order to 'script for new actions' (Boje, 2005a).

Boje offers an example of relevant practice, revealing in the process some of the ways that dysfunctional organizations need narrative just as families and individuals do. In 1995, the Aboriginal Health Council put out a newsletter entitled 'Reclaiming Our Stories, Reclaiming Our Lives' related to an investigation of the pain and suffering of relatives of Aboriginal people who had died in custody:

The idea was to reclaim Aboriginal knowledges about ways to respond to grief and pain, to honor Aboriginal healing knowledge. Narrative therapy was 'identified by Aboriginal health works in different parts of Australia as more appropriate to Aboriginal culture than the more conventional Western mental health approaches' (Aboriginal Health Council, 1995, p. 3). Aboriginal and non-Aboriginal counselors trained in narrative therapy gathered with family groups to hear their stories and recommendations. For five days family groups (26 adults) told their stories of deaths in custody, effects on the family, the healing knowledge of those experiences in Aboriginal culture, and the context most appropriate to further discussion, including recommendations for future counseling services to Aboriginal people. Narrative therapists acted as facilitators for the small group discussions.

Reclaiming our stories, 'the ability to share their own stores and hear other people's stories was identified as a major theme of the five day event' (p. 16). Present deaths are connected to past and present injustices, such that storytelling and hearing allows memories to be sifted to reclaim self-esteem. 'Within the context of the camp, people felt freer to start remembering those things they wanted to remember about the people they had lost, rather than only remembering the loss and the injustice' (p. 16). 'Narrative therapy places a great deal of importance on finding ways in which an audience can be invited to play a part in authenticating and strengthening the preferred stories that are emerging in therapy' (p. 19). This includes finding people to contact who experience us in ways that manifest our preferred stories. (Boje, 2005b)

Our purpose is not to question the kinds of injustice that are at issue here but to attend instead to the terms in which narrative therapy is related to these matters. Narrative therapy, understood in this way, assumes each story to be ideological and each representation of reality ideological. By naming and externalizing dominant stories (as 'put down stories', 'injustice stories'), deconstruction plays a crucial role, so it is claimed, in helping to weaken their grip. Processes of 'authentication and strengthening' in narrative therapy make it possible for stories to be 'restoried and resituated in preferred stories of being', and hence for Aboriginal 'knowledges' to be reclaimed.

More generally, we are told, the assumption is that organizations and people are mired in quite messy problems, against the background of histories of unresolved conflict, inevitably with some players having more voice and power than other more marginal players. Yet people are not the problem; the problem is the problem. Resituation serves to deconstruct the forces that bind the system of oppression in place and to move to a new or resituated set of influences. On the strength of the belief that new stories constructed by network participants are vulnerable to counter-attack by the old notions and by outside influences that want to keep the status quo in place, restorying uses deconstruction in order to break the grip of the dominant story.

Let us, at this point, pause to take stock, considering especially the terms of Boje's account but casting an eye back to the perhaps more circumspect expression of White. What are we to make of the idea of deconstruction here? One thing that this brief gloss shows is the polemical tone of narrative therapy, as a glance at the vocabulary of 'ideology', 'conflict', 'forces', 'oppression', 'vulnerability' and 'counter-attack' in the preceding paragraphs will indicate. A second concerns the orientation of such therapy towards the realizing of 'purposes, values, and commitments in common' and, hence, towards a kind of solidarity; the prominence of group experience here plainly emphasizes this. A third is the way that this supposed deconstruction is tied to the unmasking of power and its operations. Moreover, narrative therapy is connected, a fourth point, with an individual and a collective politics of recognition whose nature is crucially linked with performance, which leads to a fifth point to the effect that, where preferred stories are made manifest to a sympathetic and facilitating audience, this promotes a confessional understanding of the self. Finally, on the strength of the preceding points, and in the light of the more or less deliberate and programmatic methodology that is adopted, it becomes clear that narrative and deconstruction are understood as processes that are predominantly self-conscious.

What narratives are operating here! What is this deconstruction? It will be apparent from the deconstructive aspects of preceding chapters that this is at odds with our own understanding of what that term might mean. Rather than labour the point, however, let us turn to consider the ways in which narrative has come to be understood – usually in more or less methodological terms – within social science.

## The narrative turn in qualitative research

In Norman K. Denzin and Yvonna S. Lincoln's extraordinarily successful and substantial *Handbook of Qualitative Research*, recently published in its third edition (Denzin and Lincoln, 2005), the importance of narrative in research is given renewed emphasis, and once again this is explicitly linked to questions of social justice. The revised book includes such topics as indigenous research, critical and performance ethnography, arts-based inquiry, narrative inquiry, and cultural and investigative poetics. The editors, whose presence and influence are strongly felt in the text as a whole, bring something of a missionary zeal to the project: 'We want a social science that is committed up front to issues of social justice, equity, nonviolence, peace, and universal human rights. We do not want a social science that says it can address these issues if it wants to. For us, that is no longer an option' (p. 13). And this runs together with what appears to be a magisterial overview – in effect, the editors' own narrative – not only of the phases of the research process and of interpretive paradigms (positivist/postpositivist, constructivist, feminist, ethnic, Marxist, cultural studies, queer theory) (pp. 23–4) but also of eight historical moments in the complex historical field of qualitative research that is to be found in North America (p. 3). A footnote warns us of the inherent dangers in any periodization for it is 'never clear to what reality a stage refers, and what divides one stage from another is always debatable'; yet the authors claim that their 'eight moments are meant to mark discernible shifts in style, genre, epistemology, ethics, politics, and aesthetics' (p. 27). Overlapping and simultaneously operating in the present, the moments are defined as:

> the traditional (1900–1950); the modernist, or golden age (1950–1970); blurred genres (1970–1986); the crisis of representation (1986–1990); the postmodern, a period of experimental and new ethnographies (1990–1995); postexperimental inquiry (1995–2000); the methodologically contested present (2000–2004); and the fractured future, which is now (2005–). The future … is concerned with moral discourse, with the development of sacred textualities. The eighth moment asks that the social sciences and the humanities become sites for critical conversations about democracy, race, gender, class, nation-states, globalization, freedom, and community. (p. 3)

Researchers, we are told, have never had so many paradigms, strategies of enquiry and methods of analysis to draw upon and utilize (p. 20). While the editors overtly adopt the image of the bridge to announce both their intentions in the main and sectional introductions and, one presumes, the strategies of reading that they would like to encourage, a range of metaphors is enlisted to indicate the nature of the qualitative researcher's method – quilt-making, jazz improvization, bricolage, montage, pentimento. There is, the book implies, an exuberance about the freedom that now confronts the researcher.

The strong endorsement that is given to the narrative turn, the tendency to accept the crossing of 'the postmodern divide', the rejection of the 'colonialism' of objectivism and the acceptance that this is the age of relativism, all found in the Introduction, are reiterated in different ways in the collection. This is so especially in the prominence that is given to the idea of qualitative research as a kind of writing (to autoethnography, personal narrative and reflexivity). The editors' justification of their listing of historical moments as permitting 'a "performance" of developing ideas' (p. 2) is the opening indication of a thematization of writing in terms of performativity, the most obvious gestures of which are towards Judith Butler's account of gender.

It would be wrong to say that the authors are unaware of the philosophical questions and problems that qualitative research raises, for the text is replete with reference to epistemological, ethical and ontological matters, and there is occasional acknowledgement of the work of philosophers themselves. Philosophy then is seen in friendly terms: in fact, all qualitative researchers are evidently philosophers, because, like all human beings, they are guided by highly abstract principles (p. 22); and not a few philosophers are, it turns out, qualitative researchers themselves. But one cannot get far with these essays, as the above excerpts perhaps begin to show, without coming up against sweeping generalization, false dichotomies, unsupported assertion, non-sequiturs and emotive appeal instead of argument or evidence. Moreover, there is a tendency for the essays to operate at a meta-level to qualitative research itself – to tell its story rather than to do it (which incidentally seems to be the character of some of the most highly rated research). The gaze of the voyeur – the legitimate anxiety of social scientists about the implications of their own empirical practice – is here turned back narcissistically on themselves.

Our suspicions of the grand, sometimes heroic sweep of this endorsement of the narrative turn will lead us, as this chapter unfolds, to suggest that the idea of narrative in various aspects of educational practice and research, as well as in therapy, is itself confused, and that this confusion arises ironically from a failure to take the implications of narrative seriously enough. We want to take issue with readings of narrative that fail to do justice to narrative and reading themselves. In order to set the scene for this more precisely let us provide some more explicit examples of the ways of thinking we have in mind.

## Auto/biographical research and life histories

Against a background of influence from Paulo Freire, Carl Rogers and Malcolm Knowles, research in adult education and lifelong learning has come to set great store by forms of narrative enquiry. A 1998 paper by Nod Miller and Linden West entitled 'Connecting the personal and the social: using auto/biography for interdisciplinary research and learning about experience' both records and is itself indicative of the emergence of this trend. They write:

> Interest in the use of auto/biographical research methods and life histories has developed rapidly in the study of adult learning and in some social scientific disciplines. Feminists and oral historians, in particular, have sought in recent years to give greater space and significance to personal and intimate life. This is partly a matter ... of establishing that culture and psyche are part of the same piece. History can be seen to weave its way into the most intimate aspects of human relationships.

> The current preoccupation with auto/biography may be understood as an aspect of living and learning in the paradoxical postmodern moment. Story-telling, as part of composing an identity within a fragmenting culture, seems to have become essential at a time when the grand narratives may have proved insufficient, but also when local and familial templates have fractured. As tradition loses hold, as male linear biographical certainties – of school, work and retirement – disintegrate, individuals must choose, whether they wish to or not, among a range of options, as well as constructing more of their own meanings and lifestyles without traditional frames of reference. Where, at the collective level, things stayed more or less constant from generation to generation, and where the meanings attached to rites of passage, such as those marking the transition from adolescence to adulthood, were culturally ingrained, psychic reorganisations could be relatively easily accomplished. In present times, in contrast, self and identity have to be constructed and reconstructed without clear parameters or inter-generational templates as part of a reflexive project of self... (Miller and West, 1998)

Once again the authors seem compellingly drawn towards addressing their topic in periodized terms, the rise of narrative being linked to the postmodern moment. What one also finds, as the paper develops, is a self-conscious reflexivity. The value of auto/biographical research is all-purpose – as enquiry into the experience of others, as an element in the educational activities of students and as what researchers do to themselves: Miller's and West's reflections on their own contrasting biographies form the main substance of the text as a whole. Such an approach is by no means isolated (for example, see Greene and Griffiths, 2003, for a discussion of feminism and education structured in this way).

Now it may be that this tendency on the part of researchers to reflect on their own lives originates in legitimate sensitivities: there is the need to acknowledge the positionality of the researcher and the way that this may affect the investigation, and this can be done in ways that avoid the confessional-heroic earnestness from which it sometimes suffers; there is the danger that engaging research subjects or students in autobiographical exercises may itself constitute an appropriation of the other, burdened once again by the voyeurism mentioned above. These then might be reasons for the researcher's turning of the attention onto herself. Is this what she should do? The slash in 'auto/biographical' in Miller and West's title gestures graphically not only to the versatility of narrative enquiry but perhaps also towards this uncertainty or discomfort.

In Valerie-Lee Chapman's engaging paper, 'A woman's life remembered: autoethnographic reflections of an adult/educator', a slash, once again, marks a related equivocation. The paper starts in attractively anecdotal and personal terms:

> For the first time in 10 years I went home to my mother's for Christmas. On Christmas Day my cousin Laurel stopped by for a cup of coffee. Living in a small town in Northern Saskatchewan, where employment is fitful at best, and usually part-time or seasonal, Laurel has become a surprisingly successful entrepreneur. As a saleswoman she is gifted – and remorseless; I clutched my wallet tightly as I asked her what she was doing these days. She has sold Avon, Tupperware, Regal Gifts, Nutrametics, insurance, home made bannock, and Watkins, and she 'helps' her husband sell Electrolux vacuums ... and now?
>
> 'Creative memory, that's the big thing! Parties, and courses, and workshops in it, they come round to your house, and you buy all the supplies and they teach you how to do your life history, you use old photos and letters and all sorts of things. I'm waiting to be trained!' she said, 'It's really big business. Of course, you probably don't get into that kind of thing at that university of yours!'
>
> 'Oh, no', I replied, 'the life story thing is pretty big up there too!' (Chapman, 1999)

Chapman's wry amusement at this commercial exploitation of 'the life story thing', amidst the Avon and the Tupperware, helps to temper her discussion of the ways in which the practice has developed, and she is adept at recognizing the objections that it has tended to invite. She asks,

> Is this new, all part of the postmodern moment, this turn to textuality, this telling of life stories, or is it, simply, an old adult education practice revisioned? Millennial or perennial? Confessional construction of subjectivities? (Usher *et al.*, 1997). Narcissistic and self-indulgent? Or is 'writing a life' about 'getting a life' (Smith and Watson, 1996), is it about writing ourselves back into society ... knowingly? (Chapman, 1999)

Resisting easy assumptions regarding connections between the rise of narrative enquiry and the fragmentation and uncertainty commonly associated with postmodernity, she acknowledges that the postmodern may be neither more nor less unpredictable than any other era. Hence, our storying of ourselves into existence may be a more general feature of human life. Furthermore, and in more Foucauldian terms, she is alert to the ways that something like narrative operates through the forms of discursive practice that construct our identities, sometimes in service of interests other than our own. This is found to be evident, for example, in influential theorizations of learning. She writes:

> I recently taught the last of a series of courses on instructional skills to a group of adults wanting certification for personal or business purposes; I was at first uncomfortable, then perturbed by their self-descriptions, their stories of themselves. 'I am a diverger, I can only learn that way. I am an adult student, I have to learn in groups. I am an adult learner, so I must link my previous experience with new information.' While we can, as good poststructuralists, deconstruct the documenting of the individual and the confessional practices that my cousin Laurel will use in her venture, and even surface our own self-regulating discourses, let's try to re-write our own practice, too. (*ibid.*)

The mildly evangelical note on which she ends is hardly unusual in the practices we are considering. To the extent that it is levelled against the hollow nostrums of current learning theory – seductive as this is to both students seeking alibis for an unchallenging life and educators anxious for quick steps to professional credibility – it is very much to be welcomed. For all the qualifying remarks that are made in Chapman's paper, however, the tide of larger-scale, quasi-philosophical assumptions that attend narrative enquiry is scarcely resisted. There is a weight of expectation here – regarding relativism, constructivism, scepticism and ideology – that itself has a powerful narrative force.

In the 'What is Narrative Research?' Hannu Heikkinen sums up these tendencies:

> The linguistic turn into texts, discourses and narratives has been connected with a paradigm shift from (naïve or scientific) realism toward constructivism... From the constructivist viewpoint, without any narrative of myself or of the world, neither would exist – there is no 'reality' and no 'life' which has not been construed by words, texts and narratives... [T]he move can also be connected to the cultural shift from modernism to postmodernism, which has blurred previously existing distinctions, including the line between scientific reports and artistic expression. (Heikkinen, 2002, p. 14)

While it would be foolish to deny the richness and variety of the turn to narrative in philosophy and elsewhere, and its sophisticated development in the work of some of the leading philosophers of the past fifty years, it does seem that there has emerged a widespread orthodoxy, especially in therapy and social science, that is appropriately expressed by Heikkinen's gloss. Let us phrase our concerns about this more systematically. What assumptions does this adoption of narrative harbour?

In the first place, there are questions of unity and linearity. To be sure advocates of narrative approaches are often at pains to stress the significance of multiple perspectives and intertextuality. These notions tend to be marshalled, however, in service of prior assumptions in such a way that their significance is deeply compromized: rather than providing a more radical challenge to familiar conceptions of identity, the interweaving is made up of strands that remain linear. Sometimes then there comes with this the bland assumption that differences are to be reconciled and harmonized, whether within the group or within the self. Second, we note the ways that it is assumed that we should be the authors of our own stories. The possibility of our being inscribed in others' stories or of our having supporting roles in scenarios other than our own is seen primarily against an ideological background that emphasizes the dangers of colonization. We do not deny that colonization and oppression take place along these lines, but such a way of thinking tends to block the hospitality to the other that is very much a part of poststructuralist thought. 'I am large, I contain multitudes', writes William Carlos Williams, but where this ideological preoccupation dominates our approach, the very sense of this is obstructed. It is important to recognize, as a third point, the ways in which the narrative turn has depended upon the linguistic turn, and to this extent it is to be welcomed. But just as it was Wittgenstein's purpose in his later work to demonstrate the variety of things that we do with language, so too there is a need to acknowledge the multiplicity of narrative forms. The orthodoxy, some of its 'postmodern' forms included, understands narrative in a fairly limited and unproblematic way: a narrative is taken to have unity and internal coherence, and the authority of the narrator's viewpoint is assumed as a matter of convention. Indeed it is precisely in virtue of these qualities that the appeal to narrative is commonly made: to the legitimacy of the individual's re-authoring of the story, to the authenticity of the voice in the telling of the story, to the reflexive project of the self and to the regaining of integrity in the face of postmodern fragmentation.

Against this orthodoxy, our first move is to draw attention to the other forms that narrative can take. The narrative of the omniscient narrator, its authoritative point of view and linear sequencing were challenged especially in the experimental forms of the modernist novel – in James Joyce, Virginia Woolf and William Faulkner, for example. They are also to be contrasted with other forms of storytelling. This in turn needs to be understood, in broader terms, in the light of the other forms that language can take – say, beyond the terms of coherent, sequential narrative, perhaps beyond narrative altogether. Biographical form tends to reinforce the idea of its subject as an atomic, separate individual, whereas, as feminists often urge, our lives are interwoven in textures of dependencies, vulnerabilities, borrowings and lendings, the force of which is seldom captured by those intent on 'using' narrative as a 'method'. Moreover, it is worth considering the possibility that narrative pushes us perhaps towards *knowing* rather than *acknowledging*, a theme that we shall develop in Chapter 5; hence, the contrast might be made with the way that the poem lends itself to something more like sitting alongside, listening to, walking with, or perhaps sojourning. There are multiple differences and possibilities here, but the understandably tempting elasticity in the way that 'narrative' and 'story' are used makes it more difficult to keep these differences in view. We can, nevertheless, at least recognize surely that we are 'language-animals' in more complex ways than conceptions of narrative tend to suggest. Fragmentary forms, even isolated words, may impress us. Think, for example, of the way that a Freudian idea such as 'projection' may, as it were, open a doorway, enabling us to think differently, to *be* different from what we were before. This last example should be sufficient to demonstrate that the wider sensitivity to language that we are emphasizing, with the more varied and in some ways more precisely differentiated idea of narrative that it implies, opens richer possibilities for therapy and education.

One reason why the idea of narrative has been advanced, as, once again, our earlier examples in this chapter show, is as a resistance to instrumentalism and performativity. This, of course, is something that we welcome. But the overenthusiastic and overhasty adoption of the idea has also reinforced problems of other kinds. In the first place, narrative strengthens a conception of the authentic self that is romanticized or sentimentalized. In the second, there is reason to have doubts about the pride of place that is given to reflection. It has become *de rigueur* that we reflect on our teaching and learning, the idea of the reflective practitioner providing the kind of convenient theoretical gloss with which the professional educator can easily relax. We are, it almost seems, only real when we are reflected, as if our actions were continually rehearsed in video playback and, hence, reified, objectified, subjected to the gaze and framed. At a deeper and, we think, more interesting level, however, there are questions to be asked here about the way that the dominant conception of narrative is tied to a historically contingent form – that is, the form of the novel, which came to prominence and flourished in Europe during the 18th and 19th centuries. It is likely that this form of the novel developed with such success partly because of technical advances in printing but also because of the new forms of privacy, and hence the new readership (the burgeoning, literate middle class), that industrialization and demographic change produced. Does not this form of the novel itself hasten the turn to a new theorizing of the self that is steeped in subjectivism, if not solipsism? By contrast with the insistent emphasis on individual identity that remains its legacy, and partly in reaction, Franz Rosenzweig, as we shall see in the next chapter, emphasized early in the 20th century the need not to look for beginnings or endings but for a centring from which to move out.

A further angle on this also warrants consideration. This is that the predominant idea of narrative implies readability, our comprehensibility: the omniscient narrator sees into the hearts of the characters in the novel, just as God does into the hearts of people in the world. Hence, the idea hides from us the ways that we may be strangers to ourselves. If, as Hölderlin had already seen, 'we are a poem that cannot be read', there may be presumptions of reading and readability that can lead us disastrously astray. When we 'read' each other, can we not think instead that we approach what cannot be fully grasped, just as a poem or novel cannot be mastered, comprehended without remainder? It may take an education in reading to teach us this. And such an education may also lead to the recognition that there is, bound up with the implications of transparency in this dominant sense of narrative, a tendency largely to ignore the nature of language and meaning themselves. Thinking of language as a tool – that is, as a means of communication – means failing to see the opacity of language, its thickness, so to speak, its recalcitrance. As Jacques Derrida has extensively shown, words are such that their meaning can never be fully realized but is always endlessly deferred: they are open to new citation, relocation and reinterpretation, in contexts that we cannot possibly foresee; they come to us out of infinite histories of use, the extent of which we cannot possibly recover, operating according to structures that exceed and hence defy history. Insofar as our being as human beings is made up of the thoughts we have and the words we speak – that is, the meanings we find in things – this unknown background and deferral of possibility run to the heart of who we are.

Ironically the dominant idea of the narrative structure of our lives get things wrong even at the level of the phenomenon of reading itself. Reading involves the essentially binary structure of reader and text – of listener and narrative, even of narrator and narrative or writer and script. What this bipolarity of reading figures is a kind of otherness, and it does this in two ways. First, otherness is there in the text, not only in its manner of objectifying whatever is its subject matter, which is objectified or externalized in the words of the text, but also more immediately in the sheer thereness of the page. The written text is quite literally something that the reader faces, just as the oral text is what the listener hears. Second, otherness is there in the way that, even in autobiography, the author cannot fully contain herself in the writing. This is not a quasi-empirical point to the effect that there will always be more to her life than any text can cover, true though this indeed is. It is the more metaphysical point that for any description or narrative formulation that is offered there will always be a relation between this and its author that will remain external to that text. Experimental, sometimes postmodern works that explicitly acknowledge this relation simply push the problem back a stage, leaving intact the question of the relation between the author and this acknowledgement of the relation (or the acknowledgement of the acknowledgement...). They are doomed to fail, and that is part of their point. A camera reveals the camera that has so far been our unacknowledged window on this scene, and then another reveals this camera in turn... But there could never be a final camera, fully in view to itself. This is an analogy for the elusiveness of the first person perspective, and it helps to show that to the extent that we think of ourselves in terms of narratives, we objectify ourselves, render ourselves third person. A further analogy, singly appropriate to this visually dominated conception of representation, is that of the eye's relation to the visual field, as is found in Wittgenstein's critique of solipsism: just as the eye is not a part of the visual field, so the 'I' is not contained within the texts it generates or confronts. In a kind of endless stepping back to try to include oneself in the picture, this robs us of the very ground we imagine we might stand on. 'I am other to myself' robs me of the very location of myself. The formula of thinking of oneself thinking, the solipsist's ultimate ground, denies what is already inevitably a division, a non-integrity, and this non-integrity fundamentally resists subsumption under the narrative expectations we have been considering. The flip-side of this is that this non-integrity becomes an insight to which those ways of thinking are impervious.

Gilles Deleuze says something close to this when he writes:

> A Cogito for a dissolved Self: the Self of 'I think' includes in its essence a receptivity of intuition in relation to which *I* is already an other. It matters little that synthetic identity – and, following that, the morality of practical reason – restore the integrity of the self, of the world and of God, thereby preparing the way for post-Kantian syntheses: for a brief moment we enter into that schizophrenia in principle which characterizes the highest power of thought and opens Being directly onto difference, despite all the mediations, all the reconciliations, of the concept. (Deleuze, 1994, p. 58)

It is important to realize, furthermore, that the dissolution of any capitalized Self depends upon the recognition that what is at stake here cannot be a matter of, as it were, extending the picture or expanding the frame; it cannot be a matter of mere addition, of the adding of a so far unacknowledged aspect of that Self. It is rather the case that the 'I' is 'fractured from one end to the other: by the pure and empty form of time' (p. 86), the very medium of this relation. This is the source of the impossibility of narrative in this respect and the means of showing the reductivism in that project.

This helps to expose the extent to which narrative in therapy and education, burdened with this weight of expectation, requires a focusing on the self that both is incoherent and invites delusion. What it may also reveal is the perhaps paradoxical importance, for the self and its growth, of a turning of the attention away from the self – at least, away from the self as understood in any global sense, say, as capitalized. In education this might be achieved through a focus on the objects of study, provided that these are of sufficient worth to warrant this attention. The proviso here is a clear pointer to the importance of the substance of the curriculum. This is compatible with – perhaps it implies – the need for an initiation into those traditions of thought and understanding characterized by texts that are resistant to reading. It requires us to ask, as we do recurrently in this book: what is reading, and what is it to learn to read?

## Learning to read

> I read the note and was filled with joy and jubilation. 'She can write, she can write!' In these years I had read everything I could lay my hands on to do with illiteracy. I knew about the helplessness in everyday activities, finding one's way or finding an address or choosing a meal in a restaurant, about how illiterates anxiously stick to prescribed patterns and familiar routines, about how much energy it takes to conceal one's inability to read and write, energy lost to actual living. Illiteracy is dependence. By finding the courage to learn to read and write, Hanna had advanced from dependence to independence, a step towards liberation. (Schlink, 1998, p. 186)

In the form of a first-person account of a love affair and its aftermath, Bernhard Schlink's novel *The Reader* is an exploration of Germany's past and its present, examining questions of collective guilt, the relationship between generations, and the uncertainties of individual motivation. At the start of the novel, Michael Berg, the narrator, describes how one day as a teenager he is violently sick on the way home from school. A woman helps him and takes him to her apartment to wash. Later, with his mother's encouragement, he visits the woman to thank her and give her flowers, and he is drawn into a love affair. Their meetings become a ritual of 'reading, showering, making love, and lying beside each other' (p. 49) – he reads to her, at her

request, she always an 'attentive listener' (p. 41). Following a misunderstanding over a note he leaves for her, there is a scene, and when
she disappears, the radiant happiness he has been feeling is turned to a
profound sense of loss. At the start of the novel he is fifteen years old,
and she, Frau Hanna Schmitz, is thirty-six. The year is 1958.

Some years later, as a law student, Michael enrols in a seminar on
the topic of the Nazi past. He initially joins partly 'out of sheer curiosity' and partly because it promises something different from the usual
diet of buyer's rights, Saxon precedents and ancient philosophical
jurisprudence. In spite of the fact that he has no grounds for blaming
his own parents, and almost against his own nature, he becomes
caught up in 'the general passion' (p. 91). It is, so it seems, the general
relationship with that generation that is at issue, and this is to be
addressed by a process of what, in a different idiom, might be called
the re-engagement of history through the alternative presents of
people's lives, a reproduction whose common themes draw young
people together, invoking the wisdom of hindsight. Above all this is a
process in which, in the novel's idiom, air and light are to prevail:

> Exploration! Exploring the past! We students in the camps seminar
> considered ourselves radical explorers. We tore open the windows
> and let in the air, the wind that finally whirled away the dust that
> society had permitted to settle over the horrors of the past. We
> made sure people could breathe and see. (p. 89)

This would-be heroic confrontation with the past carries its own taint,
however, where the quest for justice and the readiness for responsibility cloak a self-righteous, voracious triumphalism: 'The more horri-
ble the events about which we read and heard, the more certain we
became of our responsibility to enlighten and accuse. Even when the
facts took our breath away, we held them up triumphantly. Look at
this!' (p. 91) But is it, for these young Germans in the 1960s, the relationship with *that* generation, the novel seems to ask, rather than the
relationship with the generation that happened to be simply their
*parents*? To be sure, one easily becomes muddled with the other. But
what questions of authority, of freedom and justice, are performatively
addressed in this seminar!

After the sessions have been running for several months, the professor assigns students to attend a court hearing, which becomes the
focus of the seminar's discussions, week by week. It is in the court
that he again sees Hanna: she, a former concentration camp guard,

is charged with Nazi war crimes. It is when she is called, and stands up and steps forward, that he recognizes her and recognizes her body – 'the head with the hair gathered in an unfamiliar knot, the neck, the broad back, and the strong arms' – yet he feels 'nothing. Nothing at all' (p. 93). But his lack of reaction is soon dispelled by a jolt of recognition:

> I realized that I had assumed it was both natural and right that Hanna should be in custody. Not because of the charges, the gravity of the allegations, or the force of the evidence, of which I had no real knowledge, but because in a cell she was out of my world, out of my life. I wanted her far away from me, so unattainable that she could not continue as the mere memory she had become and remained all these years. (pp. 95–6)

Hanna has been arrested because she has ignored all letters and summonses, and has not presented herself to the police, to the prosecutor or to the judge.

Pondering the nature of the charges and his daily presence at the hearing, Michael records conversations he has with his father, an author of books on Kant and Hegel, about freedom, dignity and happiness:

> He instructed me about the individual, about freedom and dignity, about the human being as subject and the fact that one may not turn him into an object. 'Don't you remember how furious you would get as a little boy when Mama knew best what was good for you? Even how far one can act like this with children is a real problem. It is a philosophical problem, but philosophy does not concern itself with children. It leaves them to pedagogy, where they are not in very good hands. Philosophy has forgotten about children.' He smiled at me. 'Forgotten them forever, not just sometimes, the way I forget about you.'
>
> 'But...'
>
> 'But with adults I unfortunately see no justification for setting other people's views of what is good for them above their own ideas of what is good for themselves.'
>
> 'Not even if they themselves would be happy about it later?'
>
> He shook his head. 'We're not talking about happiness, we're talking about dignity and freedom. Even as a little boy, you knew the difference. It was no comfort to you that your mother was always right.' (pp. 140–1)

If it is fair to speak of philosophy's repression of the child, this cannot be separated from its preoccupations with questions of authority. One reason why children are not in good hands when they are left in the hands of pedagogy, we surmise, is that pedagogy, or, let's say, a certain kind of developmental psychology, is apt to read them as if without remainder – these are the pedagogical and psychological enthusiasms that Carl Gustav Jung suspected of 'dishonourable intentions' (Jung, 1954, p. 169).

At the climax of the trial, Hanna confesses to having written an SS report that misrepresented an incident in which women were burned to death. When Hanna and the other defendants are sentenced, she is held to be the one primarily responsible, and she is given eighteen years' imprisonment.

It is in the course of the trial that Michael realizes that she is illiterate. This reveals not only the fact that her 'confession' must be false – however much it may have been preferable to her to the confession of illiteracy – but also the reason for her failure to read the letters summoning her, the details of the charges made against her and the documentary evidence amassed to support them. It shows why, as a prison guard, she had favourites amongst the young girls who were made to spend time with her privately in the evenings, time, in fact, when they read to her. And it enables him to understand also the cause of numerous lesser misunderstandings and puzzles that stretch back through the time he has known her – her reluctance to look at a map, her failure to read a note, her desire not to be promoted in the tram company where she worked. It explains her happiness when he read to her.

At a later stage, when Hanna has been in prison for eight years and when Michael has married and divorced, he becomes a scholar of legal history but suffers from a haunting emotional numbness. Gesina, a girlfriend who is a psychoanalyst, hearing him talk more openly about his experience, suggests he needs to work through his relationship with his mother (Schlink, 1998, p. 172). Another asks about the time before he had met Hanna. To help himself through nights of insomnia he begins to read his favourite books aloud into a tape recorder – Chekhov, Schnitzler, Goethe and Homer, Heine and Mörike, Kafka and Frisch. He sends the tapes to Hanna in prison. He does not write, he simply sends the tapes, and this continues for ten years, until Hanna is to be released. She seems to be facing this with equanimity, but then she is found in her cell: she has hanged herself.

She has left instructions that Michael should be contacted in order that the 7,000 marks she has saved be given to a woman who survived the fire, for her to decide what to do with it. When he goes to the prison, the warden shows him into Hanna's cell, where on a bookshelf he finds Primo Levi, Elie Wiesel, Tadeusz Borowski, Jean Améry, the literature of the victims next to the autobiography of Rudolf Hess, Hannah Arendt's report on Eichmann in Jerusalem and scholarly literature on the camps. 'She learned to read with you', the warden says:

> She borrowed the books you read on tape out of the library, and followed what she heard, word by word and sentence by sentence... She didn't want to tell me at first; when she began also to write, and asked me for a writing manual, she didn't try to hide it any longer. She was also just proud that she had succeeded, and wanted to share her happiness. (p. 204)

But who, in this novel, is the reader? Michael reads to Hanna, and later, in prison, she learns to read and write. She reads his behaviour, all the more attentively in the absence of the kinds of cues that literacy might otherwise provide, all the more 'energy lost to actual living'. At university he reads law and later, as a legal historian, ponders what the law is. Illiteracy, of central importance to the novel's plot, also functions metonymically and thematically for the larger array of questions the novel raises: there is the failure, amongst all their failures, of the Nazis to read the past; there are the blindnesses in the anguish of German guilt and in the attempts of the younger generation to reread or recuperate that past. The novel also implicates the reader *as reader*, forced to retrace the clues to illiteracy threaded through the text, to adjudicate as to the significance of the various courts of enquiry and appeal that the story presents, to feel something like the guilt that Michael feels at his failures in these things. What, finally, of the novelist, in this partly autobiographical story, and of his retrieving through writing of the events and the past that he presents in the text. How does this novel read the past? The persistent doubling of these relationships conveys more than most novels the binary structure, the non-integrity of the self that we have described: it conveys the otherness of words to the author or reader; the impossibility that any text should fully recuperate or contain human lives and human action, meaning, history; the impossibility of the recovery of childhood. In contrast to the settlement that is sought by the earnest students in the camps seminar, this leaves us with the responsibility of a reading that reaches no closure. Does this mean that the human ability to read involves a responsibility that one can never fully answer, a responsibility that always exacts more? Does it imply a power of reading whose object expands the more that power is strengthened? Should we see reading in perfectionist terms, perhaps as the archetypal human perfectionist activity?

Working as a researcher in legal history, Michael finds that it is not the case, as outsiders to history might assume, that whereas one can *participate* in the present, one can merely *observe* the richness of the past. Instead there is a constant trafficking across bridges between past and present. In working on the legal codes and drafts of the Enlightenment, he is impressed by the way that they sustain the belief that a good order is intrinsic to the world. The originators of those laws were striving, paragraph by paragraph, for greater beauty and truth, and thus orientated towards a kind of happiness. But this is juxtaposed against the determined focus on the present and the future of the Third Reich, whose legal history he also reads. The idea of legal history as progress he comes to see as a chimera. There *is* a purpose, he struggles to say, but, after the disruptions, confusions and delusions, that purpose is a refinding of the beginning, a beginning – which for us will end this chapter – from which one must set off again:

> I reread the *Odyssey* at that time, which I had first read in school and remembered as the story of a homecoming. But it is not the story of a homecoming. How could the Greeks, who knew that one never enters the same river twice, believe in homecoming? Odysseus does not return home to stay, but to set off again. The *Odyssey* is the story of motion both purposeful and purposeless, successful and futile. What else is the history of law? (pp. 179–80)

# 5
# Learning to Change

Wie jede Blüte welkt und jede Jugend
Dem Alter weicht, blüht jede Lebensstufe,
Blüht jede Weisheit auch und jede Tugend
Zu ihrer Zeit und darf nicht ewig dauern.
Es muss das Herz bei jedem Lebensrufe
Bereit zum Abschied sein und Neubeginne,
Um sich in Tapferkeit und ohne Trauern
In andre, neue Bindungen zu geben.
Und jedem Anfang wohnt ein Zauber inne,
Der uns beschützt und der uns hilft, zu leben.[1]

(stanza 1 from *Stufen* (Steps) by Hermann Hesse)

We saw at the beginning of this book how the kindly apocalypse both reveals and obscures. Extending across the self-help shelves of our bookstores and libraries, it offers plentiful advice on turning our lives, our schools and our businesses around. It finds its way inexorably into counselling and educational practice. Sometimes this is evident in therapeutic measures addressed to specific problems – to bullying, to stress, to shyness and deficiencies of self-esteem, as we saw. At others the advice is more general in kind: use BrainGym for activation of right and left hemispheres; develop interpersonal skills and emotional literacy to enhance your credibility as a leader of change; give quality time to your children; personalize your learning. Select wilderness therapy as a short-term, high impact alternative. Let narrative therapy help produce the meaning of your life.

What knowledge is presupposed in these various aspirations to self-knowledge? How is knowledge conceived? Educational policy and practice is rightly concerned about the kinds of knowledge that learners should acquire and about how they should acquire it. But here too, so the trend is, knowledge tends to be understood in terms of information and skills. Now there are obvious limitations to knowledge-as-information and well-rehearsed arguments that question the pervasive emphasis on skills. Information is the stuff of trivial pursuits, while data are oddly reified and revered – the dear little animals, as A.J. Ayer said. Skills, rightly considered, are richly characteristic of human life, but they have become transferable, detachable, behaviouristically contained. Against this we can say that knowledge that is worth having is embedded in ways of thinking and understanding; skills are to be acquired within larger conceptions of practice. This much is familiar enough, and it need not be pursued here. More to the point for present purposes are those ways in which our relation to what we know can occasion change in our lives. To put this slightly differently, we are concerned with how the achieving or regaining of a right relation to what we know can lead us to change for the better. Learning is sometimes less a matter of acquiring anything new than of coming to understand the force of what we already know. The expectation that information and skills can solve our problems contributes to a kind of emotional 'stuckness' that is close to the source of our difficulties. Stuckness of this kind is a limit not only on our moral imagination but on our conception of the possibilities of our own lives, including the modes of our happiness. In fact, it helps to hide from us even the fact that there is a problem.

We entertained the thought in the previous chapter that the wrong kind of reliance on narrative – especially where narrative is 'used' as a 'method' – can itself exacerbate these tendencies, presenting the substance of the narrative as something too neatly objectified, simply, that is, to be known. We signalled our concern to reveal in this book possibilities of a language that registers not knowledge but acknowledgement, for part of the problem we are contending with, as we now hope to show, is failure of acknowledgement. In Part II we shall take this thought further, but as an indication of what is at stake here, as a kind of parable, let us consider the following...

***

Dear Sir:

You are, I know, well acquainted with the general features of a case I am referring to your institution in the near future. All the symptoms of acute *apoplexia philosophica* are to be found in it. Word has recently been going the rounds concerning certain outstanding therapeutic successes at your institution and, understandably enough, old practitioner that I am, I immediately recalled what I had heard as soon as the case was brought to my attention. I hope that you will not object to my asking a question on this occasion. My professional curiosity is piqued by your ability to overcome those obstacles which generally confront one in the treatment of such cases.

In the 'professional exchange of letters' from which these words are taken, the concern is with a kind of philosophical sickness. The visit to the sickbed has revealed a patient suffering from a kind of paralysis, preventing attention to the most ordinary aspects of daily life: the patient is silent and immobile, and stares into space. The experience of wonder at things, which emerges and is then dissipated in the course of ordinary life, has here not been allowed to dissipate, in the ordinary flow of life, but has led to a kind of benumbment. In the local geography of the region in which this malady occurs (it is not unique), such benumbment comes about where a patient becomes transfixed by the awesome sight of one of the peaks of the three mountain ranges that surround the valley, ranges named by the trinity of questions: What is man? What is the world? What is God? The doctor-enquirer is well aware of the various quack medicines that have been offered to deal with the condition, including the recent crazes for vaccinations of Criticcin and injections of Mysticol. Such false remedies must be countered, he ventures to suggest, with an 'Environmental treatment'.

The doctor to whom the above letter is addressed replies that the therapy his clinic has developed is perhaps more primitive than the enquirer imagines. It is indeed an 'Environmental' cure, the main reason behind its success lying in the fact that the sanatorium is at the precise geometric centre of the three ranges. Around the building there are numerous roads and pathways that traverse the valley and wind up the hillside, but these always converge, the doctor knows, in a single highway that leads to the summit. The journey to the peaks can be perilous indeed, and there have been fatalities in the ascent.

Of course, there are those healthy mountain-climbers who attempt the journey on foot and with the peaks fully in view. The typical road that the doctor seeks for the patient, in contrast, involves a more roundabout route, a road curving gently around the hillside, on the blind side of the mountain. The scenery on the way is enchanting enough, but these are small-scale vistas that change as the journey proceeds. Only later does the road to one of the peaks open up, revealing between the clouds the other peaks, with intermittent views through the mist of the route that has been taken from the valley below. In the course of the treatment the journey is completed three times – by carriage, on horseback and finally on foot. Following each stage of the treatment the patient is required to complete a written report. It is found that, as the cure takes effect, the language of these reports changes.

The cure has the effect of returning the patient from philosophical apoplexy to the fullness of life – from an excessive preoccupation with the *essence* of things to an ability to cope with the everyday reality of the world, from the preoccupation with 'the Truth' to the truth-in-doing of everyday life, from the 'highest', 'ultimate' questions to the practicality of buying a slab of butter!

\*\*\*

Franz Rosenzweig's 'little book', *Understanding the Sick and the Healthy*, from which the above is loosely drawn, was written in 1921 as a more accessible presentation of ideas he had advanced some five years before in *The Star of Redemption*. In consecutive prefaces at the beginning of the book Rosenzweig addresses, first and with some grudging reluctance, the 'expert', since he knows that he cannot prevent the book from falling into his hands, and second and with warm invitation, *the reader*. Rosenzweig acknowledges that he is, to begin with, hurrying his reader along but with a lightness of tone that marries well with his assurance that he is to avoid the leaden seriousness to which the philosopher has succumbed. At the end, however, in the epilogue to the reader, the author admits that 'contrary to our initial agreement we have dealt with serious matters' (Rosenzweig, 1999, p. 107). We have been led to these unwittingly and, so it seems, from their blind side.

As has been acknowledged above, we are familiar enough today with the suggestion – from Wittgenstein, Nietzsche, Kierkegaard – that a certain kind of philosophical thinking stands in need of therapy.[2] Rosenzweig's patient is depicted in the depressive phases of the illness (silent, immobile, staring), but it also has its other side. Preoccupation with the Truth can assume manic forms, as can an obsessive scepticism or over-concern with 'clear and distinct ideas'. These aspects of the condition can be equally incapacitating. We want to suggest that there is also an *apoplexia pedagogica*, a malady that manifests itself in diverse and usually manic ways in educational theory and practice, the symptoms of which are also to be found in the therapeutic practices we have identified above. Let us consider some examples.

In the first place we group that range of practices connoted by Lyotard's term 'performativity'. Remembering our opening remarks in this chapter about the reduction of knowledge to information and the distorted emphasis on skills, we think here of the competence movement, of the uncritical adoption of ICT, of mechanical procedures of assessment and accountability, and of the box-ticking of systems of quality control. All these are marshalled in what has become the frenzied rhetoric of standards and the faddish enthusiasms of new management.

But we think also of a miscellany of more substantive commitments in education. When we look at the literature of Personal, Social and Health Education, or of multiculturalism or citizenship or self-esteem, and for that matter when we think of the way that these practices spill over into counselling and therapies of various kinds, we are struck by a kind of earnestness, if not an ideological fervour, sometimes a missionary zeal. Of course, we recognize that those who work in these areas are often reacting against the instrumentalization of our lives, an instrumentalization in which performativity colludes. But the humourless excitement of that zeal – its lack above all of any sense of irony – often trades on a kind of ersatz plenitude: this at last is education for the whole child; here at last the person fully in touch with themselves. We are sceptical about whole children, with their lack of the non-integrity we admire, just as we are suspicious about full self-knowledge, that person who has got it all too much 'together'.

It is perhaps ironic then that in spite of the diversity of these kinds of discourse, they have in common this earnestness and zeal. A familiar reaction from critics of these practices and ways of thinking has been critically to examine the clarity and coherence of the claims they make. Others have tried to expose their political ramifications. Again others have called into question their ontological or metaphysical presuppositions or directly attacked their ethics. In contrast, our aim is to identify in them something else and to see this as running through this diversity. It is to find in them a kind of *energy*, to attempt to diagnose where this comes from and to consider how it goes astray. It is to see it as energy perverted. (And – please note – we make no apology, in this book about therapy, for drawing upon an idea and an imagery of good health, however much we may destabilize these from time to time.) If we recognize in this energy a positive force, we begin perhaps to understand something of the power and the allure of these ways of thinking. In order to understand this we need to say something about the socio-symbolic relations within which the energy we identify is generated and expended.

In *The Psychotheology of Everyday Life*, Eric Santner contrasts the 'part-whole logic of socio-symbolic *relations*' with the 'part-part logic of ethical encounter' (Santner, 2001, p. 90). Part-whole logic is evident in the practices enumerated above either in the way that they are conceived atomistically, as components in a composite totality, or in the way they are construed holistically but again in terms of a realizable (totalized) whole. The relations are *socio-symbolic* in that they refer to predicates through the attribution of which our social institutions are constructed; that they are *relations*, a point to which we shall return, implies that they are posited, in third-person terms.

Let us expand on this a little, with the examples of assessment and diagnosis. What needs to be recognized in practices of assessment – whether of purely academic standards, of self-esteem, or of multicultural harmony – is that the attribution necessarily occurs within the logic of what Santner calls symbolic investiture. By this expression he means 'those social acts, often involving a ritualized transferral of a title and mandate, whereby an individual is endowed with a new social status and role within a shared symbolic universe' (p. 47). This applies not only to the acquisition of formal titles such as 'husband', 'professor', 'judge' and so on, but also at the level of the everyday attribution of predicates – to terms of praise and blame, to the awarding of grades and qualifications, to the identification of preferred learning styles or right-brained characteristics, to the naming of behavioural deficiencies or pathologies, to giving a dog a bad name. One never simply 'has' a predicate, whether a source of pride or shame: there is in this symbolic investiture a libidinal component, and this is critical for a proper understanding of attribution. In other words, within socio-symbolic relations attributes come with a performative force. Pierre Bourdieu has called this 'the principle behind *the performative magic of all acts of institution*' (Bourdieu, 1991, p. 122, quoted, with emphasis added, in Santner, 2001, p. 48).

Santner's focus in this book is on both Rosenzweig and Freud. The questions of personal identity and achievement, which are so closely intertwined with academic assessment, with work and professional identity, and with the socio-political and ethical markers that define self-esteem, multiculturalism, citizenship and so on, arise within such contexts of socio-symbolic relations, and it is there that they gain their libidinal charge. This takes them beyond – that is, they function in excess of – the realm of abstract, objective assessment that is reputed to be their purpose. Think for a moment of how pervasive this is of educational (and other) practice and of how opaque this performative force typically remains. As Santner puts this,

> The fundamental restlessness or unsettledness of the human mind that was of primary concern to Freud ... is, in large measure, one pertaining to the constitutive uncertainties that plague identity in a universe of symbolic values; due to just such uncertainties these values are filled with a surplus charge that can never be fully diffused or discharged. (Santner, 2001, p. 51)

On the present account, this surplus charge is manifested in the energy displayed in the performativity or the missionary zeal of educational ideas and practices. If we speak here of the *rhetoric* of these forms of educational discourse, this is to suggest something of the ways in which these kinds of discourse go beyond whatever truth claims they assert – to celebrate those claims, to invoke them or maybe simply to replicate their seeming authority, regardless of their meaningful applicability. Such words demonstrate the problem of *an excess of validity over meaning*, in Gershom Scholem's phrase. This is evident in the way that they lend themselves to increasing, sometimes Kafkaesque elaboration not only in various obsessive behaviourisms but also in the paraphernalia of credentialism – in the display of tokens of achievement, in awards and diplomas framed and hanging on the wall, in league tables of results. As Rosenzweig suggests, this involves a characteristically metaphysical imaginary dominated by part-whole relations, and *Understanding the Sick and the Healthy* is conceived, with mild irony, as a philosophical-theological therapy for such a way of thinking and the life that succumbs to it. Santner shows also that such an imaginary assumes a variety of guises: 'its effectivity is manifest not only in metaphysical thinking but also in the broad spectrum of oedipal fixations that were of primary interest to Freud as well as in the ways in which subjects (fail to) metabolize their experiences of symbolic investiture within this or that institutional context' (p. 55, n. 17). We are susceptible to capture by this metaphysical imaginary, by the 'currency and measure of our predicative being' (p. 97), the pressure of which is such as to define our responsiveness and sense of responsibility in 'the *third person* – as a he, she, or it – rather than in the *first* person, as an *I* (and with respect to a *Thou*)' (p. 104).

That there is a surplus is not to be regretted – it could hardly be otherwise in *human* life – and it is desirable that its energy should not be repressed. But if its presence in these practices can become perverted, as is suggested here, we must ask in what its healthy expression might consist. Let us direct our initial response to this question towards a quite specific aspect of language. One way in which the changed logic that this implies might be understood is by addressing the strange proximity of Lyotard's performativity to the performative, in J.L. Austin's sense, a connection registered only in a footnote in *The Postmodern Condition* (1984). Performative utterances, it will be recalled, do not report an action but instead themselves carry it out – thus, 'I do' in the marriage service, 'I name this ship ...' and, the most familiar example, 'I promise'. But Austin's purpose is, it becomes increasingly clear, not to identify a few exceptional expressions that function in this way but to indicate the extent to which our language works in a manner that goes beyond the constative – beyond statements *about* the world. As the investigation progresses, the attempt to distinguish clearly between the performative and the constative proves to be more difficult than originally imagined, a frustration to which Austin reacts with some delight.

In a felicitous play on Freud's founding distinction, Santner speaks of the 'Ego and the Ibid.'[3] He explains:

> What I mean by this bit of punning is that the *libidinal* component of one's attachment to the predicates securing one's symbolic identity must also be thought of as being 'ibidinal': a symbolic investiture not only endows the subject with new predicates; it calls forth a largely unconscious 'citation' of the authority guaranteeing, legitimating one's rightful enjoyment of those predicates (that is at least in part what it means to 'internalize' a new identity). But because that authority is in some sense 'magical', that is, unsubstantiated, without ultimate foundation in a final ground qua substantive reason, this 'ibidity' is, in the final analysis, a citation of lack, and so never settled once and for all. (p. 50)

It is magical in that sovereign authority is in a sense grounded in itself, in a meta-juridical self-positing that is continually reinforced – in fact, sustained – by repetition. This itself is a function of the 'primordial *ex-citation* of the human subject: its being summoned, called upon to engage in a repetitive and interminable citational praxis' (*ibid.*). This fundamental restlessness of the human mind relates to the uncertainties that plague identity in a world of symbolic values, and 'these fundamental uncertainties are filled with a surplus charge than can never be fully diffused or discharged' (p. 51).

Out of the pressures of ibidity, this returning of everything to the same, there develop different kinds of fantasy: sometimes this will move into the realm of conventional notions of madness; but fantasy can also organize itself around our troubled relationships to power and authority, around our captivation by political ideologies, around siren songs of self-help, and around the routine imperatives of our lives, as for example where we become 'institutionalized' in busy absorption in the place where we work. The 'story' of the institution – its bureau-cratic systems and tacit codes of practice, the earnestness of its strategic plans, the urgency of its 'deadlines' – comes to structure and fill out our lives as a whole, commanding our time in the guise of heroic com-mitment ('This job is 24–7, you know'). As Slavoj Žižek puts this, 'far from simply deranging/distorting the "proper balance of things," fantasy at the same time grounds every notion of the balanced Universe: fantasy is not an idiosyncratic excess that deranges cosmic order, but the violent singular excess that *sustains* every notion of such an order' (Žižek, 2000, p. 86). It is this that constitutes the rigidity and 'stuckness' of our lives where we are too much determined by symbolic relations. In order to name the manic animation that can characterize this stuckness, Santner coins the term 'undeadness', which is to say that this is a vampirized life in which the soul has been sucked dry. Where then is the escape from this existence?

Escape from our capture by this rigidity involves the kind of conver-sion, the rebirth perhaps, that Rosenzweig's parable seeks to convey. The revelation that this involves, it is important to realize, is trans-cendent neither in some kind of other-worldliness nor in a philosoph-ical wonder at things. Regarding the former, our course must be not towards the transcending of social relations, the stuff of this world, but towards converting our mode of capture by them, in the service of more life (Santner, 2001, p. 100); otherwordliness would be an evasion of this. With regard to the latter, the problematic opens, as we shall see, onto a charge against the 'old thinking', with its assumptions of developmental progress and its aspirations towards timelessness, its recuperation of the past and the progressive self-perfection and realiza-tion of culture that Rosenzweig clearly associates with an ideology of *Bildung*. The philosopher, Rosenzweig writes,

is unwilling to accept the process of life and the passing of the numbness wonder has brought. Such relief comes too slowly. He insists on a solution immediately – at the very instance of his being overcome – and at the very place wonder struck him. He stands quiet, motionless. He separates his experience of wonder from the continuous stream of life, isolating it... He does not permit his wonder, stored as it is, to be released into the flow of life. He steps outside the continuity of life and consequently the continuity of thought is broken. And there he begins stubbornly to reflect. (Rosenzweig, 1999, p. 40)

The philosopher's reflection is a barrier to being 'in the midst of life', its stubbornness bearing its own perverse energy. Avoidance of, or the foil to, the philosopher's heroic vision is to be found in the courage to open to being-in-the-midst of life, and the sign of this may be a kind of diffidence (Santner, 2001, p. 138).

Santner closes his book with reference to the famous confrontation between Martin Heidegger and Ernst Cassirer at Davos in 1929, where Cassirer reaffirmed his commitment to the philosophical idealism that seeks to throw off the anxiety of earthly existence. Heidegger's recognition of the singularization of the individual in its being-towards-death, and the possibility of authenticity that this affords, is contrasted with what Hermann Cohen called the 'Learned-Bourgeois-Thought' that 'one must honor the thinker in the soul and accordingly look upon the intellectual transport towards the eternity of culture as the supreme power and the authentic values of the poor individual'.[4]

Rosenzweig opens *The Star of Redemption* with the words: 'All cognition of the All originates in death, in the fear of death. Philosophy takes upon itself to throw off things earthly, to rob death of its poisonous sting and Hades of its pestilential breath. All that is mortal lives in this fear of death; every new birth augments the fear by one new reason, for it augments what is mortal.' (Rosenzweig, 1985, p. 3) Philosophy then occupies itself in an intellectual flight towards the eternity of culture and Truth. By contrast, it is Rosenzweig's view, so Santner implies, that such thoughts of mortality are 'ciphers of the death-driven singularity of human being which can either rob us of our souls – *undeaden our being* – or be taken up in the encounter with the neighbour, thereby becoming the very occasion of our ensoulment. If this is to think *sub specie aeternitatis*, it is to find the eternal in the earthly, opening 'the possibility for new possibilities of being-together, which is, in the end, the very heart of politics' (Santner, 2001, pp. 145–6).

The linking of this part-part logic with the encounter with the neighbour, which so obviously anticipates the thought of Emmanuel

Levinas, recalls us to the point with which this account began: with our capture by socio-symbolic *relations*. The contrast to be made here, already traced in the previous sentence, is between relation and ethical encounter. The third-person character of relations is to be found in their location in terms of predicates and generality, their knowable 'whatness' or 'essence'. They are subsumed under a logic in which difference is marked only by a divergence of characteristics in relation to the same – that is, in a relentless ibidity. This invites possibilities of understanding in relation to a *telos* or an *arche*. Encounter, by contrast, involves not the general but the particular, not mankind but the neighbour, not the timeless but the event: one moves from neighbour to neighbour not in the light of some end point or right beginning but as from the centre of the world. In contrast to a purely linear time, this suggests a time that is always to be rebegun. It is this thinking that is at the heart of the 'germ cell' of *The Star of Redemption*.[5]

The diffidence of this 'new thinking' connects then with the drama of authenticity in the face of mortality but also to the more muted, more deconstructive sensibility that we considered in Chapter 2. Readiness to attend not only to the dominant, canonic voices, the voices of self-possession and self-mastery, but also to those that speak more gently, discretely and mildly, goes with a receptiveness to the ways in which the patterned continuities of our lives can be broken, where there is the possibility, perhaps the urgency, of a new beginning. The troubling force that is the libidinal drive of the symbolic system can become also the source of a decisive break with it or of its irruption: and for Rosenzweig, this can be a breakthrough or opening that, in our escape from our stuckness, is of the order of revelation. Release from the rigidity of our capture by socio-symbolic relations requires a readiness for such a rupture, readiness for what happens to happen, and this openness to the possibility of new possibilities, it turns out, may not be so far from a kind of happiness.

When Jonathan Lear asks how psychoanalysis can promote happiness, given that it is not to provide substantive ethical answers, and when he asks how happiness is to be understood, it is precisely in this direction that he turns:

> Here we need to go back to an older English usage of happenstance: the experience of chance things working out well rather than badly. Happiness, on this interpretation, is not the ultimate goal of our teleologically organized strivings – but the ultimate ateleological moment: a chance event going well for us. Quite literally: a lucky

break. Analysis puts us in a position to take advantage of certain kinds of chance occurrences: those breaks in psychological structure which are caused by too much of too much. This isn't teleological occurrence, but a taking-advantage of the disruption of previous attempts to construct a teleology. If one thinks about it ... one will see that it is in such fleeting moments that we find real happiness. (Lear, 2000, p. 129)

The aversion we have shown to the idea of the whole self, which we expressed in terms of its non-integrity, finds its counterpart in the more dynamic conception of the 'self-interrupting whole', in Santner's phrase, where this rupturing implies in each case the possibility of a new beginning, an openness to the unforeseen that is also an openness to the essential unforeseeability in others. The possibilities of new departure that this new beginning holds can in some ways be figured as an exodus, but this is not an exodus 'from ordinary life into a space beyond but in a sense just the opposite: a release from the fantasies that keep is in thrall of some sort of exceptional "beyond"' (Santner, 2001, pp. 30–1).

The nature of aesthetic experience is powerfully indicative of what is at stake here, and indeed this is central to *The Star of Redemption*. A work of art, essentially a particular, depends upon its reception, and it is in its reception that the individual is singularized. At its best, it can feel that the work of art was intended for me. Such a reception cannot properly be captured in a cumulative, predicative account of the work: the appreciation of the work, like the work itself, is always orientated towards an excess, and this is realized in its performative force. But this will be blocked if I approach the work according to a predetermined agenda of interpretation, if I view it through a grid. It will depend upon a readiness for the possibility of a rupture in my accustomed ways of seeing, and although I can benefit from the interpretations of others, I cannot simply rely on these but must see the work anew, for myself. Every reading of a work of art, Santner writes, is on a certain level a kind of *creatio ex nihilo* (p. 133). The work of art is experienced as event.

So then it is of the nature of ethical encounter that it cannot be reduced to the terms of personal relations. Handbooks for the improvement of personal relations give advice based on generalizations of predicates: they understand all in terms of the logic of the same. Ethical encounter, by contrast, requires a receptivity to the other, that receives the other as a neighbour and that does not seek cumulative understanding, or at least that tempers the acquisition of understanding with the acknowledgement of the unfathomable interiority of the other. It cannot be realized in solely constative terms but depends upon its performative aspect.

No doubt to many good therapists the importance of this performative aspect would scarcely come as news. To teachers and students, however, it may well appear strange. Hence, when Jacques Derrida (2000) makes appeals for a profession of faith in the humanities (and in the teaching of the humanities) of tomorrow, to many of those whose task is to improve teaching and learning in higher education this may seem simply perverse. How far does profession (as of faith) characterize the work in which the professor or the teacher should rightfully be engaged? Derrida explores ways in which the idea of profession requires something tantamount to the performative of a pledge, to the freely accepted responsibility to profess the truth. Is it not the responsibility of the teacher to enact this performative continually in her work. If this is right, the work of teaching must then be something more than the (purely constative) statement of how things are. So too, from the learner's point of view, the reception of teaching – in whatever form of directness or indirectness – must be charged with the quality of the performative, as in the reception of a work of art. But to see teaching in terms of performance is emphatically not to imply the necessity of the charismatic teacher, in a kind of latter-day dead poets' society, with every teacher an aspiring Robin Williams. The good teacher realizes she is singled out by the work. The good lesson, liberated by the intervention of the right word, singularizes the student in a related way. This should, in the process, bring more fully home the fact that a standard cannot be something ready-made, there on the shelf, that is, for anyone casually to use: a standard must be *taken up* and *raised*, by teacher and learner alike. If we register also the fact that the grammatical voice of these verbs is equivocal – that a standard must also be something that *takes us up*, so that we cannot but see things in its light – the post-Nietzschean force of these ways of thinking should become more clear.[6] We cannot remain untouched. The authentic engagement in teaching and learning that is implied by these words, and the sense this might have in the living of our lives, is, hence, absolved of the connotations of idealism or sentimentality that it might otherwise accrue.

We saw how preoccupation with the Truth can assume manic forms, as can an obsessive over-concern with 'clear and distinct ideas', and we believe that these ultimately relate to questions of scepticism that we address later in the book. The scepticist philosopher's compulsion to ask how we know that the world exists or that someone is in pain impels us to think in terms of an axis extending from certainty to doubt. But our relation to the existence of the world or to another's pain is not like this – unless we become stuck within this philosophical fixation. Our relation is one of acknowledgement or denial. It follows, we believe, that our task in teaching and learning, and across many aspects of therapeutic practice, is the achieving or regaining of a right relation to what we know. Knowledge can be made to fit neatly into a totalized conception of what is to be learned, and it submits itself readily to the most mechanical of tests. Acknowledgement, other-regarding, can never be made so subject. It involves an orientation to something other than totalization, carrying with it the sense of something that can never be complete. In acknowledgement the libidinal charge of attribution is in full play. It implies a commitment and attention that largely defy the paralysing structures that the perversion of these energies would otherwise extend.

Can we say this then: that acknowledgement can yet retrieve our lives from their capture by these various forms of *apoplexia pedagogica*, as well as from solutions to our problems that degenerate into *apoplexia therapeutica*? That it can turn the necessary performative magic of institutions towards healthy ends? This has indeed been the direction of our thoughts, but we pause at the impetus of this rhetorical moment, which itself looks like getting stuck, for stuckness has been our concern throughout. We have turned to the aesthetic, but the aesthetic also can be perverted. Philosophy, we are told, begins in wonder. The philosopher is transfixed by wonder. In the ordinary course of life, wonder is experienced too, but there it dissipates; the philosopher's wonder does not dissipate but has been arrested. In contrast to the aesthetic experience that we refer to above, this can become a fixation and benumbment, and these ultimately are forms of anaesthesia. Such anaesthesia is not the preserve of the philosopher alone. There is a need to learn to change, for the philosopher and for us. It is time then to move on.

# Part II
# Coming to Terms

Part C

Coming to Terms

# 6
# Practising Dying

Part I of this book considered a number of practices and aspects of experience that are normally thought of in therapeutic terms: self-esteem, diffidence, masculinity, aggression and self-discovery, one's life as a narrative, and various ways in which we can get stuck, including in philosophy itself. In Part II, *Coming to Terms*, we turn towards a variety of aspects of our ordinary world that may not so commonly be thought of in therapeutic terms. In these we find something that was not evident in the dimensions of education that we considered in Part I. In speaking of 'coming to terms' we have in mind the ways in which the finitude of our lives, spatial and temporal, governs our condition: that we are subject to chance and contingency, and live in an uncertain world. We are interested in the ways in which we can learn to live well, finding happiness of a kind, within these limits. To be sure these are themes that have been traced already, in our discussions in earlier chapters, but here we take a few steps back in order to approach them by a different route.

\*\*\*

In 1995 the British comedian, novelist, actor and polymath, Stephen Fry, underwent a crisis. He had accepted one of the leading roles in Simon Gray's play *Cell Mates*. Three days after the play opened, to rather poor reviews, the actor suddenly walked out on the production, causing a flurry of bad publicity, and the show shut down ten weeks ahead of schedule. His disappearance sparked headlines, with some fearing the actor was dead. When he was found, in Bruges, in Belgium, it seemed that he had undergone a kind of breakdown, and he subsequently underwent psychiatric counseling. In compensation for what he had done, he agreed to pay an undisclosed amount to the producers in an out-of-court financial settlement.

His first public engagement when he returned was to address a university audience.[1] This is how he began:

> King Philip of Macedonia employed a servant in his court who had just one function. I don't know this servant's name so we shall call him Colin. Colin, as I say, had just one duty in life. No matter how busy King Philip was, Colin was required once every day, at any moment he, Colin, chose, to rush forward and tap his master on the shoulder and call out in a loud voice, 'Philip of Macedon, Lord of millions, one day you will be dead and rotting in your grave.' For being, as they say, 'tasked' to discharge this far from strenuous remit, Colin earned a reasonable salary from his wise king and the envy of many in the wide lands of Macedonia.
>
> Now it may be that some of you had already heard that story, which, after all, was pretty well known; it may be that it was new to all of you. Maybe most of you were aware of who Philip of Macedonia was, maybe only a few of you knew; perhaps some of you couldn't give tuppence one way or the other. For Colin was right and Philip of Macedonia did indeed die, thousands of years ago. Colin died too. And Philip's son, Alexander the Great, who many believed actually killed Philip, he too, Great as he was, died. Aristotle, inventor of logic and the young Alexander's teacher, is also dead. Shakespeare, the most perfect poet and dramatist the world has ever known, is dead. Mozart is dead. Michelangelo is dead. Einstein is dead. And as a matter of fact, I'm feeling none too well myself.

So perhaps, when he spoke these words, Stephen Fry was really not feeling too well. In what followed, in trying to say something about education, he spoke of the contrast between discovered truth (what Plato and Socrates were about) and revealed truth (which we get from rigid Christian doctrine).[2] Let's not dwell here on the complexities of discovery and revealing and what these might mean for education and therapy. Let's just take this in Fry's terms, in terms of what this means with regard to death itself: while the Greeks found death a fascinating topic for speculation, he explained, they believed that anybody who claimed to know more about it was either a fool or a confidence trickster. Christianity, in contrast – at least, Christianity without the Renaissance – revealed all the answers and so suddenly everybody knew!

For the moment, as we said, let's avoid more complexities, though they will inevitably return. What we have here is sufficient to lead into the problems of our topic. And, of course, there *are* problems with the topic and problems with the variety of possible approaches, and problems with even talking about such things. It can be embarrassing to raise such matters: people become uncomfortable, shift in their chairs, fold their arms and pull their coats about them, and with unwitting appropriateness consult their diaries; others sit back in a kind of urbane confidence, matter-of-fact, even blasé. The topic can bring out pretentiousness or outright crankiness, even a kind of sensational plundering of other people's lives and deaths. Le Rochefoucauld said that man can no more look at death than he can stare at the sun. Plato, not to be overcome by bedazzlement, devoted much of his considerable efforts to doing just that: to trying to get people to turn towards the sun. So there is a problem with even raising our topic and a problem with where to begin. Let's try beginning in the classroom, where other learning sometimes begins, and ask how death is encountered there.

## Death and the school

It is no great surprise that a trawl through school curricula documents finds few references directly to death. In exploring this matter where does one look? Rather than attempt any systematic account, let us instead identify aspects of the way that the topic is either broached or deflected. We speculate that the salient questions arise in respect of three main facets of recent curriculum development: the ecological, the religious and the existential.

In speaking of the ecological we have in mind those holistic scientific approaches that emphasize the cycles of animal and human life, including birth, growth, maturity and death. Given the basically scientific starting-point of such approaches, it is inevitable that they tend to be naturalistic in orientation – that is, that they see life in terms of health and survival, the avoidance of danger and the seeking of satisfaction, and as part of an ongoing process regulated by a kind of homeostasis or harmony. Such an orientation is widespread. By contrast there are obvious, systematic variations in the extent to which religion is incorporated into schooling, and again marked differences in the substantive forms that religious education can take. The different cosmological claims of particular religions inevitably affect the substance of the beliefs about death that are passed on to children, just as the manner in which the spiritual significance of death is interpreted and engaged in education is diverse. Religious education can be undertaken in more and less critical ways, and with confessional and non-confessional intentions. The idea of a spiritual education overlaps with what we have in mind in speaking of the existential consideration of death within the curriculum. Probably it is in the arts especially that questions of death are addressed – perhaps inevitably so in the study of literature. Here in particular there seems to be the possibility of the imaginative, vicarious confrontation with the experience of death, and the topic of death is something to which young people can readily be drawn. Authenticity of aesthetic experience seems to be of critical importance in arts education, but the possibilities of fantasy and distortion that arise in relation to death are also evident. A wider look at its representation in the flickering images of the mass media is hardly reassuring, and yet this is the adult world that increasingly confronts young people. This is what is taken as 'reality'.

Death comes into the school in other ways, however. Perhaps most readers will recall those occasions during their school days when the routine of assembly was broken for the announcement that a pupil had died. Surely the statistics tell us this must be so. There are, say, eight hundred pupils, perhaps seven years... – how many deaths should one expect? Clearly there is some normal occurrence of death. When children hear the ambulance siren in the suburban housing estate, will they learn that, as Philip Larkin has it, 'All streets in time are visited' (*Ambulances*, in Larkin, 1964)? Aren't all children's lives somehow visited?

Educational literature on death tends to focus primarily on bereavement. In 'Death and Bereavement in School: Are You Prepared?', for example, Tim Gisborne describes his experience, while a student on teaching practice, of being confronted one day by an eleven year old boy whose father had died that night. Deeply disturbed by this, he was at a loss as to what to do, and in the end avoided the subject and said nothing. Yet he was aware of policy documents telling him that teachers had a responsibility to promote the spiritual, moral, cultural, mental and physical development of pupils, and prepare them for the opportunities, responsibilities and experiences of adult life, and finding that his teacher education had given him no clue as to how to deal with death, he decided to do something about it. This led to his involvement in the development of Winston's Wish, a grief support programme established by Julie Stokes following her own experience of counselling a young boy whose mother was dying. The programme provides a combination of individual support, an after-school group and residential experience for children and young people up to the age of 18, as well as working closely with parents or carers 'in a variety of practical and creative ways, to create an atmosphere where they can share their thoughts and feelings and meet others'.[3] Bearing in mind that around forty children a day experience the death of a parent in England and Wales (statistics again), Gisborne argues that schools need to formulate a strategy to respond to death, with a philosophy amongst staff to talk openly to bereaved children and to be sensitive to their needs. Reasonably enough, he emphasizes the importance of talking directly and without euphemism to children about these things, in order to help them to understand that death is permanent; less convincingly, he claims, however, that this will prevent young children worrying about dying themselves (Gisborne, 1995, p. 42).

Reasons why children should not worry about dying are offered in generous measure by Pat Wynnejones and the various books she recommends, and here we find a move away from the naturalistic perspective. In 'Beyond This Life's Outposts: Children's Books, Bereavement and Death' she looks at the potential of 'situation' books, such as *Why Did Grandma Die?* (Madler and Connelly, 1980) and *When Uncle Bob Died* (Althea, 1988) for helping children to talk freely and naturally about death and perhaps to understand the finality of death. But many such books lack warmth and beauty, she complains: they tend to treat death as just a natural process, of the same order as shopping in the supermarket. The Christian view, in contrast, is about 'hope, reunion, seeing face to face, about the survival of the person, about eternal life' (Wynnejones, 1994, p. 18). Thus, children are to be told,

> As soon as one of God's people dies, just as quick as you can blink your eyes, that soul goes to heaven to be with Jesus. There he can think and feel and love and play, and even work. And he is perfectly happy because he is with Jesus. (Luke 16: 19–31; Philippians 1: 21–3) (*ibid.*)

Books in this Christian vein offer three things: first, they provide the language and imagery that make it possible to think about life and death within the spiritual dimension; second, they provide a kind of psychotherapy bringing to the surface and objectifying emotions that might otherwise remain dangerously submerged; third, they lead to the development of a strong personality founded on trust, self-worth and the peace and contentment that religion brings. Wynnejones hopes that teachers will seize the opportunity that changes in policy have now provided to re-establish basic Christian teaching about death and eternal life, including the knowledge that after death we will be reunited with those we have lost.

The above discussions focus primarily on younger children. What happens after this? How do things seem different when we look at adolescence? The theme of loss is also to the fore in a discussion by Susan Hetzel, Victoria Winn and Helen Tolstoshev. They describe the special problems faced by adolescents because of their sense of their own invincibility and immortality. The authors describe their development of an educative programme relevant to a *variety* of losses including death to facilitate a subsequent healthy adjustment to life changes (Hetzel *et al.*, 1991, p. 325). The programme, entitled 'Loss & change', broadly aims: (a) to acknowledge the value and normal loss experiences of childhood and adolescence; (b) to recognize and affirm feelings of grief and loss; (c) to utilize and develop individual and group coping skills; and (d) to develop guidelines that support the school community's response in situations of grief and loss (*ibid.*). In a programme of five sessions students (between the ages of fifteen and eighteen) are asked to discuss and write about how they first became aware of death, to discuss the traumas of loss in breaking up with a boyfriend or moving house, to role play, and to help to formulate a School Disaster Plan and School Bereavement Policy.

What is striking here, however, is the apparent assimilation of bereavement to other kinds of loss. Is this a strategy aimed at those who have not experienced the death of a relative that proceeds by 'starting' with the loss of a boyfriend? What kind of reduction does that involve? The therapeutic aims of counselling of this kind raise all sorts of complex questions. One obvious danger is that the harshness of the truth, its reality, simply gets smoothed over, perhaps providing in the process consolation for the comforter. Recall the infamous advice to the disaster victim: 'You must say to yourself: "Today is the first day of the rest of my life."'

In the face of the vicissitudes of change and loss, the sages of the past have sometimes advocated a detachment from worldly concerns, and Plato is sometimes understood in this way: attachment to finite things fares badly when compared to the contemplation of unchanging forms. A modern version of this is found in the following advice from R.S. Peters:

> To get attached to pets, people or possessions is a bad bet *sub specie aeternitatis*; for there is one thing we know about them – they will

die or become worn out with use and age. No such fate awaits the objects of theoretical activities; for as long as there is an order of the world there will always be further things to find out about it. To love the world under this aspect is to have a permanent object which is safe for ever. (Peters, 1966, p. 157)

If this seems a limited view of relationships with other people, the point is not so much to claim that, when they begin to show signs of wear and tear, it is time to trade in your wife or your toy-boy, as to advance the real attractions, perhaps the seemingly timeless attractions, of theoretical activities. This is an argument mustered in appreciation of such goods, especially in the context of the curriculum. Many, however, have reacted against the implications of this line of thought, usually because of its tendency to eclipse aspects of human experience generally and of the social world in particular. John White, for example, has offered 'a vision of education in which our attachment to the experienced world is placed centre-stage', with social institutions such as the family, the economy and the nation located within a larger natural framework (White, 1995, pp. 17, 19). Peters' remarks seem partly to lose sight of that natural priority of wellbeing that White thinks must be central to education.

It was also within a predominantly naturalistic perspective that Rousseau made the telling observation that, at ten years of age, Emile does not know what death is, and further that priests and doctors unlearn us how to die. But Rousseau took note of an important fact about children's lives in 18th century Europe: that many children died before they became adults. With average life expectancy increasing, any contemporary relevance of this may easily escape us ... until, that is, we think of the conditions of children's lives in the *favelas* of Sao Paulo or the slums of Nairobi or Calcutta, or of the plight of the increasing number of children around the world who suffer from AIDS, in Africa especially.

In one of the earlier books to reflect on AIDS in relation to education, in the very different, vastly more privileged circumstances of the United States, Jonathan Silin discusses his experience of working with child victims of the disease, mounting an all-out assault on our evasion of death in education and culminating in curricular recommendations of a more general, even pervasive kind. The concerns expressed in *Sex, Death, and the Education of Children: our passion for ignorance in the age of AIDS* go beyond the counselling of the bereaved to questions about how to confront those who are dying. Silin's subject is plainly vulnerable to sensationalization, and so it is a matter of no small significance that one of the most telling of the examples he provides relates not to the extreme, if increasingly common circumstances of the child AIDS victim but to the normal occurrence of death and bereavement. He recounts that it was shortly after his work with one such child that he was especially struck by the behaviour of a person who had been bereaved. This was the case of Mrs Greene, an experienced teacher engaged in a mentoring programme:

> I meet Mrs Greene a few minutes before she is to conduct a workshop for new first-grade teachers. She is part of a mentoring program designed to provide ongoing support to inexperienced teachers. Expressing concern that these teachers would need new ideas for activities to conduct with their students, she is busily assembling examples of curriculum materials, charts, and children's artwork. Tense, but controlled, she opens the session by welcoming these teachers and unexpectedly announcing that she has not had time to prepare adequately because of the death of her mother several days earlier. After apologizing for the introduction of this personal note into the work setting, she launches into an extended presentation of an array of projects that can be thematically linked to the changing seasons and holiday celebrations. Emphasis is placed on how to present eye-catching products that may be attractively displayed. Neatness, order, and conformity are given high priority, with many of the art activities requiring students to follow a teacher-made pattern. Room for individual expression is often left only to the choice of colors employed by individual students. (Silin, 1995, pp. 41–2)

This is a master teacher reluctantly accepting that a personal crisis has interfered with professional duties. Her acknowledgement is thoughtful and correct, yet it has created a wall between her and her students, and has undermined the purpose of the meeting – which was to help them to gain confidence in their practical endeavours as teachers. Silin sees this scene, with its recovery of apparent order and reflecting, as it does, the school's commitment to keeping the children busy, as demonstrating the very evasion that is his concern:

> A vision of schools as places where people search after meaning, and enrich that search through increasing access to the wisdom of the past as encoded in the disciplines, has become buried under mountains of photocopies, pre-packaged materials, and curriculum guides. (Silin, 1995, p. 41)

Silin's complaint that the rich diet of a liberal education has here become reduced to a kind of educational fast-food is powerful enough, but a different imagery is also suggested. 'Buried' under its mountains of paper, with its soporific curriculum guides and its nostrums for good practice, schooling of this kind has been stifled or tranquilized. Its cheery emphasis on 'active learning' betokens the frenetic busyness of the 'undead', in Santner's mordant phrase (see Chapter 5).

Silin speaks of this as a death-defying curriculum, but surely 'death-denying' is the more apt term. To defy death is to draw the sting of death, to deny the grave its victory. This can be the claim of a Christianity that is nobler and more realistic than the saccharine comforts of Wynnejones's professed faith, while contemporary existentialist heroic engagement is more bracing than the philosophical ambitions of the timeless reason that, as we saw in Chapter 5, Cassirer hoped would throw off the anxiety of earthly existence. The naturalistic turn is welcome to the extent that it resists the otherwordliness, ultimately the nihilism, as Nietzsche saw, in some of these responses to death. It is, nevertheless, what may be suppressed or repressed by this naturalism that we now need to consider. What we have to say is going to mean little or nothing, we realize, to religious believers such as Wynnejones, just as it is scarcely likely to appeal to science's 'true believers', such as Richard Dawkins. Reductive points of view of these kinds blind us to the depth of ethics, and they scarcely do justice to religious belief.

What then, for all its acknowledgement of human pain and pleasure, of the conditions of desire and satisfaction, are the limits of this naturalistic perspective? Heidegger suggests that what is pushed aside is still death itself:

> If we make a problem of 'life', *and then just occasionally* have regard for death *too, our view is too short-sighted.* The object we have taken as our theme is *artificially and dogmatically curtailed* if 'in the first instance' we restrict ourselves to a 'theoretical subject', in order that we may then round it out 'on the practical side' by tacking on an 'ethic'. (Heidegger, 1962, pp. 363–4)

Death is crucial to our lived experience, and losing sight of death stands in the way of that larger perspective. In a sense, as Silin begins to show, it stands in the way of education itself. Our earlier examples generally took as their concern the death of others – his death, her death, your death. These are facts within my world. I can measure out those lives; I can hear the words at the crematorium, read the obituaries. But what about my death? My death is not a fact within my world. It is the cessation of that world wherein I can talk of facts. To say, perhaps with a certain heroic flourish, that one thing I am certain of is that I will die can be, paradoxical as it may seem, to screen from myself the awesome nature of this cessation by speaking of it as a fact, albeit a special one, within that world.

Our first steps in Sartrean existentialism tell us that man is the sum of his acts and that existence precedes essence. In a different register Wittgenstein acknowledges the tension between our sense of the wholeness of someone's life at his death and the sense of incompleteness that characterized the living of that life:

> After someone has died we see his life in a conciliatory light. His life appears to us with outlines softened by a haze. There was no softening for *him* though, his life was jagged and incomplete. For him there is no reconciliation; his life is naked and wretched. (Wittgenstein, 1980, p. 46e)

What that softening hides is elusive outside the first person perspective. And this is not something relevant solely to death, for this relation to mortality is crucial for ethics itself. But how is this to be explicated? We propose to move forward through two stages, the first of which involves drawing a distinction between 'metaphysical time' and 'ethical time', which in turn involves a high redefinition of ethics that accentuates experience and disparages systematicity and axiology as metaphysical (and hence false to experience). The guiding thought here is Heidegger's *being-towards-death* (*Sein zum Tode*).

## Metaphysical time and ethical time

Metaphysical time is clock time, the time of the others that I can measure out. Abstract, linear and infinite: it belongs to a totalizable field, in which ethics understands itself systematically; it is the time of the deaths of others, which I can mark with obituaries. The economy of metaphysical time contrasts with the *aneconomy* of lived time. Thus, ethical time is *my* lived time: as the immeasurable time of the absolute, it is perspectival, relational and finite. This necessarily incomplete time has an ethical depth that exceeds the rule and the system but that is unthinkable without the relation to death. As Joanna Hodge puts this,

> The metaphysical model of time is one of life viewed after death by other people. The processes are complete and definitive judgments are made. The ethical model is that of the living process itself, as marked by the irrecuperable moment of death. The former is a disowned model, where the stance from which the construction takes place is not taken up into the model constructed. The death is the death of the other... The former acquires completeness by not attempting to account for its own possibility; the latter is emphatically incomplete and incompletable, but does address the question of its possibility. (Hodge, 1995, p. 12)

'*Moribundus sum*', Heidegger writes: I myself am in that I will die (Heidegger, 1992, pp. 316–17). We live, we might say, in the *not-yet*, and in the finitude that is determined by our death. And this bleak fact is the very condition, so it seems, for meaning in our lives. Imagine that life were to go on forever. Meet me for coffee at three o'clock. But if time is infinite, this, like all our other projects, simply loses significance.

Heidegger, it is sometimes said, has no ethics, but such a criticism wholly fails to register the weight given to the ethical by this acknowledgement of death and by the authentic engagement it exacts. In fact, both in the suspicion of systematic ethics and in the emphasis on singular authentic engagement, Heidegger is not so far from Wittgenstein:

> A hero looks death in the face, real death, not just the image of death. Behaving honourably in a crisis doesn't mean being able to act the part of a hero well, as in the theatre, it means rather being able to look death *itself* in the eye.
>
> For an actor may play lots of different roles, but at the end of it all *he himself*, the human being, is the one who has to die. (Wittgenstein, 1980, p. 50e)

Courage in the face of hardship and, especially, resolution in the face of death stand as supreme moments of human dignity. Far from reflecting a deficit with regard to the ethical, these are examples of the unacknowledged conditions that would give point to more systematic ethical reasoning.

Let's try to fill out this picture by considering how ethical time, non-metaphysical and lived, is to be understood. We are apt to lose touch with this kind of understanding – more strongly, we are in *flight* – not least because it implicates us in our movement towards our own deaths. We fall into our everyday roles, and these keep us busy. They 'occupy' us, we are inclined to say – and a second glance at this apparently benign word perhaps reveals the way that our potential for being is tranquilized and our space usurped by institutional expectations and routine. We subside into the mass of information that daily swamps us. Numbers and more numbers, values expressible as numbers, numbers to be reckoned up, counted and accounted for – these lull us into a quasi-aesthetic security. Think of the dutiful school principal or the over-zealous head of department busily absorbing and disseminating information, managing timetables, making the required returns, keeping things moving, chasing *dead*lines. Think also of the way that we can be swept along with the tide of our involvements with others – 'what they do, what they say'. We can become tranquilized even where we seem most alert. In reasoning something out, in arguing the case, the structuring of the argument can overdetermine our thinking. Think of Hamlet, in soliloquy, carefully working out the reasons why he should not take vengeance and kill Claudius, not now while Claudius is praying – praying, at least, so it seems. These are all kinds of flight.

To see through this, try remembering an occasion when a colleague at work has died and the glimpse that this gives you, the education you receive, as it tears the veil of that daily busy world. Consider the reaction this can prompt in the following more or less schematic, Heideggerian terms. First, facing up to death, perhaps even just glimpsing our impending nothingness, makes possible our *authenticity* (*Eigentlichkeit*). It strips away our acquiescence in that common sense world of 'what they say, what they do'. Second, this experience *individuates* us by isolating us from those networks of concern in which we are otherwise caught up. No-one else can die my death. Yes, someone can step up to face the firing squad in place of me, but this will not be *my* death. My death remains *for me*. And this takes us to our third point: that death remains a *permanent possibility*. This is not the possibility of an occurrence about which we might have quite specific fears, that we might hope to get around or avoid, something *within* our world. The constant, ineliminable threat of non-being is understood only in anxiety. This is not a matter of expectation (*Erwarten*), of things that will become present like those that are now present, but of anticipation (*Vorlaufen*) – an orientation to the future that acknowledges our necessary futurality, that we are always still to come, that we are always *not yet*. If we are asked, 'How would you like to die? How would you like to be remembered?', in the manner of Sunday newspaper profiles, and if we wonder what our death will be like, we are again displacing the possibility of our death with the scenario of some future actual event, with ourselves looking on as bystanders. The pure possibility of our death is nothing we can stand by. As nothing I can know, my death *remains* for me. So, fourth, we need to face up to its inevitability, its *certainty*. And finally, as the preceding sentences show, we need to recognize the *indefiniteness* of when and how it will occur.

In *Tess of the D'Urbervilles* Thomas Hardy grimly remarks that there is a date that we silently and unwittingly pass each year – not our recorded birthday or wedding day but the day when we shall die. Children, following curricular recommendations, read records of births and marriages, and death notices in newspapers, measuring out human lives with wall charts. Is this ethical or metaphysical? Perhaps this measuring of lives is a sensible step in a child's learning, and perhaps Hardy's exploitation of the idea of our 'deathday' merely occasions the kind of recoil the adolescent savours. We are tempted, to be sure, to move to safer, less theatrical ground. But it turns out that the idea of a liberal education, of philosophy itself, is not so easily separated from stories of death.

Without death does a liberal education lose its point? The modern understanding of a liberal education has tended to foreground the ideal of systematic understanding and autonomy, the freedom rationally to choose the way one lives one's life. In the classical roots of the idea, by contrast, it is a freedom-*from* that is emphasized, the freedom from illusion in order to see things truly. The allegory of the Cave theatricalizes this, as the benighted prisoners turn from the flickering images that are their world towards truth and goodness, the wonder of the sun. But the experience of wonder is more subtle and this drama more complex than we might at first have expected. *Paideia*, as Heidegger shows, is to be understood in terms of the continual overcoming of lack of education – that is, in the repeated return to the common 'reality' that the Cave represents. He writes:

> Hence the telling of the story does not end, as is often supposed, with the description of the highest level attained in the ascent out of the cave. On the contrary, the 'allegory' includes the story of the descent of the freed person back into the cave, back to those who are still in chains. The one who has been freed is supposed to lead

these people too away from what is unhidden for them and to bring them face to face with the most unhidden. But the would-be liberator no longer knows his or her way around the cave and risks the danger of succumbing to the overwhelming power of the kind of truth that is normative there, the danger of being overcome by the claim of the common 'reality' to be the only reality. The liberator is threatened with the possibility of being put to death, a possibility that became a reality in the fate of Socrates, who was Plato's 'teacher'. (Heidegger, 1998, p. 171)

Western philosophy understands itself in the context of a heroic in which there is played out this facing of death for the sake of education, for the passage, that is, to truth and goodness, with the death of Socrates providing its inaugural moment.

Condemned to death by the court, Socrates declines to plead for banishment (a worse fate) and, in spite of pressure from his friends, refuses to attempt to escape. With remarkable equanimity and quiet resolve, he accepts his fate. We can, however, be impressed by the principled stand yet lose sight of Socrates' confrontation with the imminence of death. Not prepared to avoid execution, he judges that it is not worth stringing life out a little longer: he knows that his death is inevitable and this is what he must accept. As he says at his trial, 'I have often noticed that some people of this type, for all their high standing, go to extraordinary lengths when they come up for trial, which shows that they think it will be a dreadful thing to lose their lives; as though they would be immortal if you did not put them to death!' (*Apology*, 34d–36b) Accepting death, it now seems, allows a kind of integrity, the wholeness that the hero's life can attain. Socrates' life demonstrates the way that authenticity may be attained, and it shows the impossibility of this without acknowledging the unfathomability in a person's life that death confers. It shows also how this authenticity is of a piece with the kind of liberal education that philosophy exemplifies. For, in Socrates' words, 'those who engage in philosophy aright are practising nothing other than dying and being dead' (*Phaedo*, 64a): philosophy is learning to die.

In many ways it would be tidy to leave the matter there, but we are not happy with this conclusion and with the kind of perspective on a life as a whole, a life viewed from outside, that it seems to countenance. Our reservations extend back through this argument, from the reassurance found in the figure of the hero to various strategies of consolation. To see things must be more complicated than this we can perhaps look again at Socrates. Let us then qualify the presentation of the heroic that has just been entertained. We have shown already how the anticipation of a satisfying wholeness indulges a fantasy that fails to face up to the non-integrity of the self or the need for self-interruption. We have our doubts too about the existentialist's resolute facing up to death that is the condition for authenticity. While the former (at least) gives itself up to a thinking of human life in third person terms, the latter also tends towards a reflexive thematizing of itself. Both succumb to the siren voices of narrative. Lives seen in this way are viewed as spectacles, and they become a further barrier to understanding the conditions of our being.

Socrates's life, nearing its end, takes on a complication that compromises its expected unity. Consider his last words, his request to his friend Crito:

> 'Crito,' he said, 'we owe a cock to Asclepius; please pay the debt and don't neglect it.'
>
> 'It shall be done,' said Crito; 'have you anything else to say?'
>
> To this question he made no answer, but after a short interval he stirred, and when the man uncovered him his eyes were fixed; when he saw this, Crito closed his mouth and eyes.
>
> And that, Echecrates, was the end of our companion, a man who, among those of his time we knew, was – so we should say – the best, the wisest too, and the most just. (*Phaedo*, 118a)

Asclepius is a minor deity connected, by association with Apollo, with healing. Is this a proposed sacrifice, a symbolic expression of the settling of one's debts, acknowledgement perhaps of a need always still to be healed? Or is this, more prosaically, an actual debt, muddled in Socrates' drugged and fading mind? The question is undecidable. And this undecidability, opening onto Plato's recurrent play on the imagery of drugs,[4] connects with some surprising things that Socrates does near the end.

In several dialogues Socrates' fine arguments give way to the presentation of myths, which Socrates refers to as charms. The *Phaedrus*, for example, a dialogue that in a variety of ways ponders the possibilities of wholeness, ends not with a tidy conclusion but with a prayer. In spite of the dialogue's arguments, wholeness becomes something less to be achieved than to be prayed for: we live in the condition of its not being achieved. Having in the past banished the arts, Socrates responds to a dream that calls him to write: he writes a hymn to Apollo and a fictional verse that is an adaptation of Aesop. He writes, and he writes in private. And remember that in the *Phaedrus* writing itself has been condemned: writing is like a dangerous drug, a cure or a poison; cut off from its author, it has no-one to safeguard its interpretation; it can fall into the wrong hands; it survives the death of its author. Yet Socrates now commits himself to the undecidable terms that art and print provide. Death itself remains an undecidable term.

Yet, as Socrates faces death, there is in this scene, depicted in several dialogues, a certain stoical lightness of touch: 'Now if there is no consciousness but only a dreamless sleep, death must be a marvellous gain… If on the other hand death is a removal from here to some other place, and if what we are told is true, that all the dead are there, what greater blessing can there be than this, gentlemen?' (*Apology*, 39d–41b) On receiving news of the arrival of the boat from Delos, which signals his imminent execution, Socrates says: 'Well, Crito, I hope that it will be for the best; if the gods will it so, so be it.' (*Crito*, 43c–44a) The debt to Asclepius draws back from the final closure that the pathos of the scene might otherwise achieve. It is finished, and it is not finished – a debt always still to be paid.

This founding event in the light of which philosophy understands itself is then complicated by a non-integrity, by a wholeness aspired to but interrupted by itself. These are thoughts that work reflexively in the present chapter towards a further deconstruction, and this opens the way to the second stage of our considerations. This will involve turning our attention towards the immemorial.

## Time and the immemorial

It is worth recalling the way that the clock and the calendar encourage us to think of time. The line of time whose stages they mark provides a convenient spatial metaphor for our temporal experience, as well as for the understanding of time in more technological ways. The future is conceived as a present that is yet to come and the past as a present that was. Past, present and future are then brought together in a kind of common, uniform time or *synchrony*, a protension of the present. Perhaps historically the development of chronological devices and their application throughout the realm of technology have reinforced our tendency to take such an understanding of time as given, indeed as natural.

Against the idea of time, however, what can clearly be seen is that any sense of context – a condition for meaning itself – necessarily incorporates a relation to the past and the future such that they have a bearing on the present. Heidegger puts this in terms of the necessity of understanding *Dasein's* being-in-the-world in terms of the *ecstases* of past and future, our always having come from ... and being on the way to...[5] This implies the paradox that we are always outside ourselves, once again destabilizing facile notions of identity. Past and future are then not a present that once was and a present that will be but dimensions of our current being. The reality of this escapes the understanding of time in terms of synchrony.

Important though the shift of understanding expressed in Heidegger's thought is, however, it retains a referencing to the self, a kind of egocentricity. My always having come from ... and being on the way to ... preserves some connection with the idea of a present that has been or will be mine. But there is a time that exceeds anything that could be mine – the time before my birth and after my death, and the time beyond what can be recuperated and recovered. Hence memory is bounded by an immemorial time. The following words of Levinas echo but subtly disrupt the anticipation of death in Heidegger:

> For a thought moving continuously amidst interdependent notions, death is the hole which undoes the system, the disturbance of every order, the dismantling of every totality. You go toward death, you 'learn to die', you 'prepare' yourself for the final event; but in the last quarter of an hour – or the last second – death is there, travelling its part of the route alone and ready to surprise. (Levinas, 2001, p. 122)

There is an ethical depth to this displacement of the self that altogether escapes Heidegger's insights.

The point can be made more far-reaching still with the suggestion that past and future are not empty spaces waiting subsequently to be charged with meaningful content. This would be to claim that the very idea of past and future are derivative of human possibilities: only a being that remembers and has regrets, that hopes and seeks redemption, can have a past and a future in this sense. Hence, there can be no *natural* history.[6] Past and future are constructed out of these human possibilities, the very ground for responsibility and justice. And our present, which inevitably tremors with, or is traumatized by, this other time of responsibility and justice is conditioned not only by the synchronic but by a *diachrony* that continually cuts across it, putting it in crisis.

Heidegger's understanding of time, as we saw, is critically determined by death itself, and in the end this becomes a totalized way of thinking. Levinas writes: 'If death completes *Dasein*, *Eigentlichkeit* [what is one's most proper] and the totality go together. We can see here, in ridding ourselves of any reified notions, the coincidence of the total and the proper.' (Levinas, 2000, p. 41, translator's parenthesis[7]). With diachrony there is a shift. Here what is crucial is the death in question, for now it is as if the gravity of my death is displaced by a force that draws me, as it were, upwards, towards the other's vulnerability, a force that calls me to responsibility. Levinas explains the ethical charge of this:

> Heidegger deduces all thinkable signification from the attitude of man in regard to his own death. He thinks to the end, in both senses of the term. He takes his thought to its final consequences, and he thinks that my death can only be, for me, the ultimate 'of-itself'. I ask myself whether that is truly the limit of thinking. Is there no thinking that goes beyond my own death, toward the death of the other man, and does the human not consist precisely in thinking beyond its own death? In affirming this, I am not trying to adopt the stance of some sort of beautiful soul. What I mean is that the death of the other can constitute a central experience for me, whatever be the resources of our perseverance in our own being... But in every death to which one attends, and in each approach of someone who is mortal, the resonances of this extraordinary unknown are heard. We apprehend this unknown irresistible in the other man's encounter with death. An event the significance of which is infinite, and the emotion of which is thoroughly ethical. (p. 126)

This displacement of the first person is emphatically not a return to the third-person awareness of death that was considered earlier in this chapter. It is a move beyond heroic being-towards-death. The bracing acknowledgement of one's mortality, which figured so prominently as a condition of authenticity, now responds to the different tension of a humility that attends to the other. 'We encounter death in the face of the other' (Levinas, 2000, p. 103).

The charge that Heidegger has no ethics rests on the assumption that to have an ethics must mean having some kind of systematic account. But plainly the phenomenology developed in *Being and Time* shows values to go 'all the way down', just as it is evident that the ideas in that book of authenticity, resoluteness and destiny, for example, carry immense ethical import and power. What is to be noticed, however, is the nature of Heidegger's conception of the relation to others (*Mitsein*), for this exerts a severely constraining influence on the idea of the ethical that emerges. Heidegger's being-with is a relation of adjacency, commonality or solidarity, suggestive, as Levinas says, of marching together. What is absent is what we referred to in Chapter 5 as the encounter with the other, which is to say the relation to the face. What Levinas means by the face is crucial to understanding the claim that 'the death of the other can constitute a central experience for me', for it implies a sense of the other as having a depth I cannot fathom and a vulnerability for which I am responsible. The asymmetry of this relation is such as to preclude all synthesis of I and the other, whether of common identity or reciprocity or complementarity. Hence: 'The impossibility of settling on the same terrain, of composing in the world, the impossibility in the form of a slippage of the earth beneath my feet.' (Levinas, 2000, p. 111) Consider the following as an indication of the primacy of place this has in Levinas's phenomenology:

> when Heidegger teaches us that tools, like the knife, the fork, and also, for example, the street, 'fall into my hands', and are ready-to-hand for me before I objectify them, it is not because this possibility is based on knowledge. The possibility is not grounded in a meaning either, because meaning itself is grounded 'in the hands'. I think the face in exactly this manner. The face is face not because I see it, nor because I recognize the color of your eyes, or the form of your lips. That wouldn't be seeing the face or approaching the face... In the West, this is certainly the way we *regard* a person. But I think that to approach the face of the other is to worry directly about his death, and this means to regard him straightaway as mortal, finite. The directness of death *is* the face of the other because the face is being looked on by death. It is like the origin of the straight line. One can neither prove the origin, nor define it. It is directness in itself, the directness of death. And his death, your death, is immediately present to me, even though I do everything possible in order to forget it. What nonetheless remains behind the scenes is the ethical, an original being delivered over to the other – love. (Levinas, 1986, pp. 135–6)

Love thy neighbour. Thou shalt not kill. These commandments speak to this fundamental responsibility – to which, of course, we make ourselves insensitive through various forms of evasion, doing everything possible in order to forget it.

What 'remains behind the scenes' requires us to acknowledge a number of things that we cannot fully fathom or know. The other has an interiority that remains a mystery to me, and the forgetting of this – any attempt to override it – will be a kind of violence. This shows us something about other things too. For I need to see in myself also a depth of unknowability. I come from a past that I can never fully remember and recover: call it childhood perhaps. And the attempt to recuperate this past, to haul it up into present consciousness – in a certain kind of psychoanalysis, say, or perhaps in the overview of childhood of a developmental psychology, or again in writing one's narrative or life history – is both violent and self-deceptive. And this violence extends to the very operation of language and thought themselves. The events that confront or befall me are subject to the sensible measures of justice, to recording in a narrative or history, but the subjection these categorizations of our thought effect overrides and represses their particularity – and, that is, their character as event.

What am I to do? Do I jettison the past, ignore the unfathomability of the other as, by definition, beyond my ken? Do I consign what I cannot recover to oblivion? The point of the immemorial is to acknowledge what cannot be remembered but what must not be forgotten either. The point is not-to-forget the forgetting, and this involves the maintaining of a space for what cannot become the object of a representation. Our lives with other people are inevitably subjected to measure – laws, classifications, comparisons, identities, narratives and number – without which systems of justice and the machinery of society simply could not function. These must be renewed and maintained. But this can only happen well if there is also retained a sense of what is other to them, of the event as event, of the event as other to their capacities for representation. Experience is diachronous, out of synch, discordant, out of key. The immemorial haunts us.

Suspicious of the heroic, we have tried to reveal the hubris that taints fortitude in the face of death, the savouring of the pathos of one's mortality. We are suspicions of the consolations of the comic too. When King Philip of Macedonia employed Colin to remind him each day that he would die, he was, we suppose, seeking therapy or education. Why did he, King Philip, need this, and what did it achieve? To employ someone for this purpose you must have time and money, and with time and money comes self-indulgence, however it may dissemble. Perhaps we need the *memento mori*. But can the *memento mori* remember the immemorial?

# 7
# Room for Thought

'Where does our investigation get its importance from, since it seems only to destroy everything interesting, that is, all that is great and important? (As it were all the buildings, leaving behind only bits of stone and rubble.) What we are destroying is nothing but houses of cards and we are clearing up the ground of language on which they stand.'

(Wittgenstein, 1953, # 118)

Just as it is as well to keep a careful eye on those leaders with a taste for writing poetry, so an enthusiasm for architecture is a characteristic that should ring alarm bells when present in a certain kind of political figure. This wry observation by architecture critic Deyan Sudjic is made in the course of his recent diagnosis of the 'Edifice Complex', a psychological condition said to have afflicted most of the 20th century's totalitarians, but not to be limited to dictators, with perfectly respectable software tycoons, presidents, museum directors, bishops and fashion designers all infected too (Sudjic, 2006). Such building can be aggressively competitive, and it is motivated in more than a few cases by the desire to memorialize oneself, whether in the form of the 'Mother of all Mosques' or – Sudjic's particular *bête noir* – in that of a Frank Gehry house. It is not just that the victims of the condition want things built in their name, Sudjic complains: they suffer from the delusion that they can design architecture themselves.

We begin with monuments; we shall end with huts. But what is at the heart of this chapter's concerns is the way that the built environment within which we live has important effects on the way we think, feel and interact, and on how we perceive ourselves. The rebuilding of our cities in the 1960s introduced into the urban landscape heartless tower blocks, themselves pale imitations of Le Corbusier's 'machines for living' or of the sublime austerity of the glass towers of Mies van der Rohe. We now have buildings that are acutely sensitive to the phenomenology of ordinary human interaction – sound-proofed, climate-controlled and ergonomic, and offering flexible space. At the same time, and in humbler terms, we find in the IKEA catalogue the ideal forms of modestly priced interior design, while discount furniture and DIY stores on the edge of towns, seemingly indifferent to their own ugliness, attract us in our hordes: we are eager to enhance our own living space, to defend it with tokens of difference (for so they seem) against the anonymous architecture of the suburban housing estates that sprawl around us. Or, conscious of the significance of clutter around our homes, of the need for space, of light, of colour, we can turn to Feng Shui Solutions, whose website explains:

> Feng Shui is the ancient art and science of placement. It is an Eastern philosophy that determines how you can live in harmony with your environment, creating auspicious personal living and working space... Feng Shui is used by experts to re-balance the Chi (energy) of a home or business to obtain maximum benefit in well-being, prosperity and success.

It is then a 'profoundly creative and intuitive art', bringing benefits in terms of health, financial success, mental peace, job satisfaction and spiritual fulfilment. As such, it is clearly one that interior designers must need. But in case this sounds too fanciful, we are reassured by the fact that it is 'also a science with diagnostic equipment, mathematical formulas and specialized terminology'.[1]

Feng Shui may not yet have reached our schools, colleges and universities, yet there is change there too. That there is a substantial literature on the changing nature of the classroom – from its early development with the influential practices of the monasteries and churches, to its rapid transformation during the 19th century with simultaneous instruction and the advent of the monitorial system – is familiar enough. Such changes are not independent of the ways in which learning and the relationships associated with it are understood, nor of deeper questions concerning the kind of life we should lead. The high windows of the Victorian school prevented children from being distracted from their work, while simultaneously directing their attention upwards, towards God; in contrast, the picture windows of the progressive elementary school of the 1960s invited the children to look at the world outside, underlining their connection with the natural environment and the larger community, and making them feel at ease. The creation of a number of new universities in the UK in that decade, following the Robbins Report into higher education, opened new possibilities for architects, with the exciting brief of creating a campus from scratch. At the University of Lancaster the architects designed confined stairways that caused people to rub shoulders with one another, creating community, so they imagined, even as the bull-dozers and cement mixers were rumbling away laying the foundations of adjacent buildings. The less privileged students who, forty years later, enter our further and community colleges find newly smartened entrances and designer reception areas, before being swallowed into the drab concrete towers, the factory-like extensions and squatting Nissen nuts of the former technical colleges that these makeovers front; or in the best cases they find themselves in the glassy structures of pristine new-builds, with wide-open walkways designed to simulate shopping malls.

Yet when we acknowledge these sensitivities, how far do we escape the earlier, more utilitarian, even philistine ways of thought that have so often constructed our environment differently or that have reduced our natural environment to mere resources? To put this in somewhat exaggerated terms, how far is the new sensitivity overlaid on what is still a fundamentally Cartesian outlook? Our bodies are, of course, inti-mately connected with our minds, with how we feel and think. We are *not* dualists, we protest, we have learned from the East – or this at least is what we may imagine. But the self-consciousness of this recognition is something that almost inevitably invalidates the experience to which it presumes to relate. We expect to 'obtain maximum benefit in well-being, prosperity and success' through adopting various tech-niques: we build quality time into our day, and night; we ensure we exercise and relax. So, at the level of our lived experience we are still minds contingently related to bodies: however cerebrally we may have come to learn that we must treat our bodies well, our gut feeling still is that we are still not them.

Hence – let us press deeper – if we ask ourselves about *how* space and place relate to our minds, whether causally or analogously, the reach of these questions is fixed in advance by these metaphysical strictures. 'I need my space.' 'Room for thought.' 'You need to open your mind.' Are these metaphors or actualities? There is, let us be clear, a difference between the measurements of your room and the measure of your mind, but which is first? The literal is prior to the metaphorical meaning, you say. But could there be a measured room that was not also the measure of a mind? What would a mind be like without that measuring? We shall return to this place before the end of the chapter. What we want to maintain for now is the emphasis on embodiment. We want to consider a range of ways in which places and spaces, the most ordinary aspects of our lives, influence the way we live and learn, the way we think. How are we to orientate ourselves here, how find our bearings? And what after all is a bearing?

Let us begin first by turning back to what has come to be seen as a classic discussion of the problems of space and place, a discussion found in the later essays of Martin Heidegger. As we shall see, the scenes that Heidegger calls to mind in his elaboration of these themes may seem to have only a limited bearing on the lives of many people today. How are we to read Heidegger's descriptions without the nostalgia they too easily invite? We shall consider the problems this raises, especially in a postmodern, globalized world dominated by new technology. If we now wait to see where these thoughts lead, this 'where', we shall remember, returns those thoughts to questions of place.

## The measure of language

What is the sense of 'space', 'place' and 'site'? What is Heidegger looking for in his exploration of these matters? To address these questions it will be necessary to change the idiom and to adjust to a Heideggerian language that, though it may alienate some, is critical to his purpose. The extraordinary titles of his 1951 lectures, 'Building Dwelling Thinking' and '... Poetically Man Dwells...', make clear Heidegger's desire to resist the tide of Western philosophy and, especially, any entry of Cartesian thinking into these matters. The ostentatious linking of building, dwelling and thinking by the omission of commas or conjunctions blurs the boundaries between what are commonly supposed to be discrete activities – that is, between terms in quite different registers. To build is not to think, and the idea of dwelling carries a poignancy or evocativeness that typically escapes the other terms, resonant though these at times can be. What Heidegger wants to emphasize with this unpunctuated series of terms is not some kind of metaphorical connection but rather the fact that each of these is not properly thinkable without the others. This is not only a matter of describing the way that we live but of saying how we can live well. And we cannot live well without a relation to a particular place, the homeland of our thought.

To see how these terms can be linked together we need, perhaps not surprisingly, to attend to the richness of the Greek idea of *poiesis*. This incorporates, within a generalized idea of production, the production that is language, and this accentuates the specifically creative meaning-making of poetry. As Heidegger puts this in his 1936 address 'Hölderlin and the Essence of Poetry',

> The poet names all things with respect to what they are. This naming does not merely come about when something already previously known is furnished with a name; rather, by speaking the essential word, the poet's naming first nominates the beings as what they are. Thus they become *as* beings. Poetry is the founding of being in the word. (Heidegger, 2000, p. 59)

Man is precisely the being who attests to his own existence, to his belonging to the earth as the 'inheritor, and the learner of all things', in what Hölderlin calls their 'intimacy' (p. 54). Heidegger's title phrase, '... Poetically Man Dwells...', is quoted from a Hölderlin poem that also contains the lines:

> ... man
> Not unhappily measures himself
> Against the godhead. Is God unknown?
> Is he manifest like the sky? I'd sooner
> Believe the latter. It's the measure of man.
>                     (Hölderlin, in Heidegger, 1971a, p. 219)

And man is, Hölderlin reminds us, an image of the godhead. God is manifest like the sky, and this somehow is our measure. But how can this be so? In the first place it is necessary to think of height and of things being raised up, where 'raise', we need to see, is an evaluative word. Looking up to the sky is not a movement to which a symbolic meaning comes to be attached. It is rather an original exaltation from which a Cartesian separation into physical movement and value added can occur only as a kind of abstraction. This is a draining of meaning, ultimately a kind of nihilism.

In his later essays Heidegger turns away from the project of fundamental ontology – that is, from the attempt directly to examine the nature of being – more or less on the grounds that too direct an approach risks turning this into something that it is not. It risks a kind of idolatry. That being is neither to be directly named nor simply to be avoided becomes marked by the graphic gesture of crossing it through, twice, with intersecting diagonal lines. That is to say, it is placed *sous râture* (under erasure). The manner of address now takes up these four points of the crossing out of being – that is, its cross – in what Heidegger calls 'the Fourfold' of 'earth', 'sky', 'gods' and 'mortals'. The relation between the forces or conditions of this quaternity is to be understood in terms of the intersecting of the lines of this cross, in the necessary tensions of which human lives are lived out and human practices constituted. 'Earth' implies the fruitful yet retiring source of sustenance, 'sky' the cycles of time and changes in atmosphere and mood, 'gods' our orientation by aspiration and vocation, while 'mortals' suggests the flickering awareness of our own finitude as the place of revelation. They are dimensions without which things as things cannot be understood. For what is a place? Is it whatever is marked by the co-ordinates of a grid, within a space that is uniform and universal. Or is it the location, the particular locale in which lives unfold? And what for that matter is a thing? Heidegger takes as an example something as apparently simple as a jug. The jug is a three dimensional object, it is inert matter, of a certain weight and shape. This is how the jug is understood in abstraction, and there is no doubt that we can and do use languages of abstraction – rightly so in many spheres of our lives. But the reduction that this effects, especially if the abstraction is imagined to be somehow fundamental, can obscure more than it reveals. This is not the jug of lived experience. For the jug holds the water that slakes the thirst after the day's work; it pours the wine shared at the family meal. The jug focuses a practice in such a way that what it means must be something more than can possibly be conveyed by the purely physical description offered above: that physical description drains the thing of its part in human practices, in a human world. What the jug means, the way it is understood, is tied to the practices of which it is a part, in all their fourfold richness.

The richness of Heidegger's thought in these later essays is to be found especially in the way they make vivid the possibilities of a receptivity – that is, the kind of letting-be intimated in the cognate terms *Gehörenlassen*, *Seinlassen* and *Gelassenheit*. These are other-regarding virtues that are necessary to the mirroring relationship between the fourfold: 'The round dance of the world' constitutes the 'ringing mirror-play' from which 'the thinging of the thing takes place' (Heidegger 1971a, p. 180). That is to realize things not as static but always in the making, in the mutual appropriation through language of human being and world: it is to think the thing in a verbal sense – that is, as verb-making. In contrast to the reductiveness that threatens to deny this richness, the language of poet and prophet, which we find in proximity here, suggests a way of thinking beyond rational ontology or rational theology, and beyond, as we saw, the idolatrous deification of being: a responsibility is realized to what cannot be directly named or represented, and this is a responsibility also to what *may be*. The poetic is implied to have consequences that affect our ordinary lives – and, that is, let us make no mistake, the morality of our ordinary lives. But the sensibility or response in question in these words has less to do with a heightened sense of *being* than with the *responsibility* of remembering the extraordinariness of ordinary things – of their otherness to us and ultimate unfathomability even as they are part of our ordinary world. Such things are discovered, Heidegger shows us, not as items amongst the innumerable 'objects' in the world, or amidst the 'measureless mass of men as living beings'. They depend upon a dwelling with things. And this dwelling is characterized by a reverence for things that is poetic in kind, where the poetic implies, obviously, something both about language itself (and the dangers of an excessive emphasis on the indicative or representational), and about the *poeisis* of bringing things forth into being. The practice of teacher and learner then must be to read meaning but not to rest in it: to make the same expressive objects exponents of continually new thought.

Language comes to be understood then as being intimately connected with measure-taking, without which there can be neither building, as is plain, nor dwelling, as is less plain; but that this is so can be seen in the way that in our learning we must gradually come to be able to take the measure of things, extending that measuring in new and unforeseen ways. As Wittgenstein might say, we learn to follow a rule. This measure-taking is to be understood less as the application of a preexisting measure to an already existing thing, than as an instituting of the very possibility of measuring, and hence as a measure-making. To ask how our measure-taking gets going is akin to the familiar question of how language gets going. In important respects these are indeed the same thing:

> This measure-taking is itself an authentic measure-taking, no mere gauging with ready-made measuring rods to the making of buildings. But poetry, as the authentic gauging of the dimension of dwelling, is the primal form of building. Poetry first of all admits man's dwelling into its very nature, its presencing being. Poetry is the original admission of dwelling. (Heidegger 1971a, p. 227)

It is not just the nature of our measuring, of what is to count as criteria for us, but the very possibility of such criteria that is the heart of the matter here. The 'house of being' that such a poetic thinking constructs, for this is how Heidegger will put the matter, must also be the institution of education, its instauration and building of our world. Poetry is then, though the expression will surely seem inflated, the 'founding of being in the word'. In the beginning was the word.

The account of the poetic as *poiesis*, and of language as revealing possibilities of being, is critical not only for our lives and learning; it is necessarily and integrally entwined with ontological reflection on the very possibilities of that *poiesis*. The importance of Heidegger's work for education and other practices is rightly celebrated in terms of its critique of the totalizing effects of technology. But this negative critique needs to be seen in conjunction with the affirmation of value found in the account of the poetic. The restoring of the sense of truth as the revealing of the worth, the reality, of the objects of knowledge, as opposed to the understanding of truth as a property of propositions – in other words, as *aletheia* rather than *adequatio* – should be at the heart of the overcoming of nihilism. This indicates something of the task that besets the teacher. The force of the German word *Dichte*, with its connotations of spiritual leader and teacher, implies the capacity not so much to represent or describe, or to inculcate or pass on, as to institute something new. Realizing the criteria of what is to count, finding, let's say, the measure of things, this is an edification that is a building too, as the Latin *aedificare* surely tells us.

Heidegger and Hölderlin are not alone in saying these things, and it is important to see that they can be said in a different way. In his essay 'The Poet' of 1844 Ralph Waldo Emerson presents a conception of the poetic that is not too far away from what is being said here. He writes:

> For it is not metres, but a metre-making argument that makes a poem, – a thought so passionate and alive that like the spirit of a plant or an animal it has an architecture of its own, and adorns nature with a new thing... Every one has some interest in the advent of the poet, and no one knows how much it may concern him. We know that the secret of the world is profound but who or what shall be our interpreter, we know not. (Emerson, 1982, pp. 263–4)

The poet's role is to announce and to affirm. For what nature offers is to be understood not as something fixed or permanent – in terms of raw data or sensory impressions. Rather it is to be seen semiologically: 'Nature offers all her creatures to him as a picture-language. Being used as a type, a second wonderful value appears in the object, far better than its old value; as the carpenter's cord, if you hold your ear close enough, is musical in the breeze' (p. 266). And in the essay 'Nature' Emerson writes: 'The world is emblematic. Parts of speech are metaphors, because the whole of nature is a metaphor of the human mind... The axioms of physics translate the laws of ethics' (p. 53). Recall the measurement of your room and the measure of your mind.

Far from any naming of a pre-given and fixed world of things, the creative nature of language emphasizes fluidity, and this fluidity, as we shall see, is linked in Emerson with something that runs away from Heidegger's concerns with hearth and home, and with land and belonging:

> But the quality of the imagination is to flow, and not to freeze. The poet did not stop at the color of the form, but read their meaning; neither may he rest in this meaning, but he makes the same objects exponents of his new thought. Here is the difference between the poet and the mystic, that the last nails a symbol to one sense, which was a true sense for a moment, but soon becomes old and false. For all symbols are old and fluxional; all language is vehicular and transitive, and is good, as ferries and horses are, for conveyance, not as farms and houses are, for homestead. (p. 279)

The abundant flow of the imagination, and of the words of the poet, is not to be understood in terms of home and settlement. It seeks for new ways to actualize its energy, releasing and realizing new intensities of experience. The poet, the thinker, the person who lives in this way is 'the conductor of the whole river of electricity' (p. 283). Emerson points towards an intensity of thought and being, and lays the way for Nietzsche's Dionysian thought. We shall have reason to ponder what happens to this American thought.

## Heidegger in California

As various remarks above have indicated, Heidegger sees language as connected with particular places, and the German language, with its extraordinary resources, as intimately tied to the German land, with its farms and houses, and the ways of life it generates. In Chapter 8 we shall consider the particular burdens this conception of belonging places on his idea of thinking, an idea that the vision of rural life in the Black Forest helps to promote. To say that this is tainted with nostalgia is at once to accuse it of the unrealism of a longing for the past and to recognize in it the savouring of the pain of home. But these ideas have had a powerful influence on contemporary thought – not least, in architecture – and it is pertinent, therefore, before we move on to consider the particular problems they raise in a post-industrial, post-modern and globalized world. What of the measure of language when things are changed in this way? Let us begin to address these matters by considering what we take to be the Californian Heidegger that is found in the influential work of Hubert Dreyfus.

Dreyfus's claim to credibility as an interpreter of Heidegger rests most obviously, though far from exclusively, on *Being-in-the-World* (1991), his clear and systematic study of Division I of *Being and Time*. His purpose in that text was in part to demonstrate (and celebrate) Heidegger's shifting of the philosophical tradition's emphasis 'on getting our descriptions of objects right to Dasein's absorption in unimpeded coping with equipment' (Dreyfus, 2000, p. 313). The roughly pragmatist reading towards which Dreyfus was then inclined tended to see this coping as in service of yet more ongoing coping. This was the product of 'more or less ignoring Division II of Heidegger's book as something of an existentialist embarrassment' (*ibid.*) – ignoring, that is, the part of that book where Heidegger examines being-towards-death, as we saw in Chapter 6. The subsequent correction of this neglect has led Dreyfus to the view that Dasein 'copes with equipment and pursues truth not merely for the sake of understanding entities but ultimately for the sake of taking a stand on *its own* being' (p. 314). Admirably clear though *Being-in-the-World* is, this later realignment suggests a deeper reading. But how is ongoing coping to be *placed* with regard to the 'fantastic exaction' (*ibid.*) of being-towards-death that Division II identifies?

The question of this placing should also be raised in connection with Dreyfus's equally clear but still somewhat secularized reading of the later Heidegger. Here his emphasis is on what he calls 'focal practices', as, for example, where the jug of wine on the table focuses the family meal. In 'Highway Bridges and Feasts: Heidegger and Borgmann on how to affirm technology', Dreyfus and Charles Spinosa ponder the kinds of focal practices that can exist in conditions of contemporary technology, seeking to understand such practices in terms of Heidegger's Fourfold of earth, sky, gods and mortals. Of the gods they write:

When a focal event such as a family meal is working to the point where it has its particular integrity, one feels extraordinarily in tune with all that is happening, a special graceful ease, and events seem to unfold of their own momentum – all combining to make the moment more centered and more a gift. A reverential sentiment arises; one feels thankful or grateful for receiving all that is brought out by this particular situation. (Dreyfus and Spinosa, 1997, p. 167)

These are moments that are constantly threatened by the dispersal of modern technological practices through which we are converted into nothing more than flexible resources. Dreyfus and Spinosa's response to this threat is to suggest that we see ourselves as mortal disclosers of plural worlds, finding our integrity in our openness to dwelling in many worlds, with the capacity to move among them. Moreover, as they make clear, such attunement can extend through our technological lives – say, while driving in fluid traffic around the clover-leaf intersections of city highways, or perhaps, at a lower ebb, in the seamless flow of writing at a word-processor. For many people such experience may extend to what truly are heightened moments in their lives, and one should be cautious about casting doubt on their value. But in Dreyfus and Spinosa's emphasis on attunement and sentiment, and in the general dampening of the religious (including the Christian) resonances of Heidegger's vocabulary (the intersecting lines are of a cross), it is difficult not see once again a naturalizing movement – one that might contain these thoughts within a harmony or homeostasis in which the anticipation of death is contained and the sky closer to our reach.

For Heidegger, early in *Being and Time*, a vivid example of the ongoing coping to which Dreyfus refers is supplied in terms of the action of hammering a nail into wood. But can such a practice, understood holistically, in terms of the 'micropractice' of which it is inevitably a part, make sense without taking in, full-blown, as it were, the social world of the building of the house or the barn, or, for that matter, the building of the church itself – its social philosophy, its theology?[2] Dreyfus's partially secularized updating of Heidegger, with its emphasis on attunement and its economy of satisfaction, inclines him away from ways of thinking – including Heidegger's thinking about skilled coping – that exceed the bounds of this underlying ethical naturalism. It is this that we think of as a Californian Heidegger, and, as these remarks suggest, we see it as partly conditioned by a culture of therapy.[3]

## Places and virtual space

Dreyfus's powerful critique of the excessive claims that have been made for new technology has been richly informed by his reading of Heidegger, mostly with the focus on what computers cannot do, and especially with regard to the relationship between human and artificial intelligence. In order to consider the ways in which Heidegger's thought can cast light on virtual space, however, we turn to an essay by David Kolb whose title 'Learning Places: Building Dwelling Thinking Online' plainly signals its orientation. Kolb is interested in the question of how far the resonance of experience in relation to places in Heidegger's account can apply to the virtual space of websites. Kolb is well aware of the ways in which the idea of the Fourfold may seem to many to block from the start any possibility of application online. But he suggests a different way of looking at this:

> Heidegger's four dimensions do suggest ways in which truer places might be constructed online. For an online site to be a place, it needs to be more than a static block of data. It needs 'earth', objects to interact with that have some independence and thickness of their own; it needs 'sky', times and changes, so that it is not always the same but varies according to its own rhythms; it needs 'gods', ideals and aspirations and calls to what we might become; it needs 'mortals', a sense that choices are meaningful in finite careers, that time makes demands and is not unlimited in amount. This sense of opening possibilities and an identity being offered and forwarded puts more 'there' there. (Kolb, 2000, p. 124)

While it is a different constellation of possibilities and roles that is revealed through modern technology, and while in many ways these will be less than those that are possible in the traditional world of the wine jug, there is, so it seems, no other, deeper dwelling available to us: hence, we need to attune ourselves better to the processes of revelation of our contemporary world. Crucial to the positive account that Kolb goes on to provide are practical questions – concerning the kinds of conversations that people can have online, the constraints and possibilities of the visual world that websites provide and other aspects of the phenomenology of online experience. It is open to us, Kolb speculates, to try to develop and use the technology in such a way that websites become places with the fourfold richness indicated above. Building such places may enable us to think and to dwell in better ways.

Kolb anticipates many potential problems – not least to do with a kind of Disneyfication of online experience and with over-emphasis on the development of simulation – but his suggestions take an interesting turn when he considers what he calls 'the Thoreau strategy': withdrawal for the sake of achieving perspective and in order to get in touch with deeper values. He relates this to broader debates in architecture, in the context of which Michael Benedikt has urged the need to create '"real" places outside the bustle of style and image' (p. 131). Benedikt writes:

> The urge is strong to make a building complete in itself and finished, a totally encompassing, dazzling, climate-controlled and conditioned experience. But totality and completeness are too often achieved at the expense of reality.... much contemporary architecture lacks emptiness, by being quite literally full. Full, if not of people and goods and pushy displays, then of Design. (Benedikt, 1987, p. 60; quoted in Kolb, 2000, p. 131)

The need, Benedikt suggests, is to get away from places that try to mean too much – and, one might add, from the constant reinforcement of the idea that this is how things must be. Kolb elaborates on the idea of such an escape in terms of the ideas of Ann Cline (1998), who writes of the attraction many feel, in the face of this architectural complexity, towards dwelling in simple huts. She sees this in explicitly therapeutic terms: the hut is a healing refuge.

While Kolb concedes that Cline and Benedikt would probably deny this possibility, their ideas lead him to speculate about whether, given the conditions of this technology, something like the refuge of the hut might be realized online:

> In a physical hut you can share silent presence as you serve tea, or watch the moon rise. Online, you can't do that, at least until VR becomes infinitely better. But don't essentialize the technology; it may be used in more than busy ways. Imagine quietly composing a jointly written poem together, or listening to haiku. Imagine an online place where works of art are shared peacefully but intensely, where discussion evolves slowly. The technology and methods currently used do not favour such places, but they are not impossible. (p. 132)

Perhaps, he suggests, this is happening already. Surely this is so. While email, for example, can be the site of frenetic activity, it can also open possibilities of communication of a different, more agreeable order, where relative immediacy and ease of use combine with its textual form to enable a subtle combination of spontaneity and reflection. In modest terms, does this not realize a new way of being in the world?

Whatever virtual places are, they are very different from non-virtual places. They are derivative both in the way that they are conceived or imagined and in the fact that the user is always in a non-virtual place. The website in principle, is accessible from anywhere (in non-virtual space), and so the website itself has no geographical location. It belongs to another realm and opens another order of experience. At least, this is how it would seem at first blush. In fact the difference identified here uncannily resembles what is commonly thought of as the relation between idea and reality – between 'table' as an idea, which has no geographical location, and the table in front of you, which plainly does. But though these things do indeed suggest different realms, they are not separated in quite the way we might imagine, here the idea (or word), there the physical thing: the table that you use is dependent upon the *poeisis* of language that brings things forth into being. So perhaps the distinction the virtual and the non-virtual is not so secure as it seemed. Kolb's sense of responsibility towards real and educational life online is readily apparent, but he too is eager to deconstruct the kind of tidy contrast between the supposed reality of our ordinary lives and the non-reality of our virtual experience that tends to dominate consideration of these things.

In the 1950s Heidegger was already expressing concern about the rise of computers, with the calculative rationality they reinforced and the new kind of subjectivity they were creating (see, for example, Heidegger, 1991). In the 1980s, well before the creation of the World Wide Web, and under the title of 'cyberfeminism' Donna Haraway embarked on a tentative utopian exploration of the new forms of relationship and being that might be afforded by the connectivity of computers (Haraway, 1990). Today, in a more globalized world, there are those who ponder the possibilities of a nomad identity, unconnected to particular places, at home, wireless, perhaps anywhere. There are questions here regarding location and settlement, belonging and departure, and the economies of thinking these imply. These are thoughts that we revisit in the chapter to come.

We have explored aspects of the relationship between the places where we dwell and the thinking that these enable, with language seen as critical to all of these. Realizing the measure of language helps to reveal the poverty of our attempts to calculate a place for 'quality' experience in our lives, just as it exposes the technicist fantasies of 'experts' who 'use' Feng Shui to re-balance the Chi. These are counterfeit currencies that circulate where there has been a dulling of the sense of worth that standards should otherwise sustain. The sustaining of standards cannot be simply a matter of reading off assessments from a pre-given scale ('a mere gauging with ready-made measuring rods') any more than living 'in harmony with your environment' can be a primarily technical matter. Our criteria stand in need of application – that is, judgement – and in our judgements we exercise our words; therapy depends upon the sensitive exercise of practical reason, not least in the words that we use. Success in these matters involves an 'authentic guaging', the metre-making movement of the poetic, and this is a responsibility to language.

# 8
# The Thoreau Strategy

Wir sollen heiter Raum um Raum durchschreiten,
An keinem wie an einer Heimat hängen,
Der Weltgeist will nicht fesseln uns und engen,
Er will uns Stuf' um Stufe heben, weiten.
Kaum sind wir heimisch einem Lebenskreise
Und traulich eingewohnt, so droht Erschlaffen,
Nur wer bereit zu Aufbruch ist und Reise,
Mag lähmender Gewöhnung sich entraffen.
Es wird vielleicht auch noch die Todesstunde
Uns neuen Räumen jung entgegen senden,
Des Lebens Ruf an uns wird niemals enden...
Wohlan denn, Herz, nimm Abschied und gesunde![1]
(stanzas 2–3 from *Stufen* (Steps) by Hermann Hesse)

To imagine quietly composing a poem together or listening to haiku, to imagine an online place where works of art are shared peacefully but intensely, where discussion evolves slowly... These are the kinds of experiences, as we have just seen, that David Kolb evokes in considering the online possibilities of what, with mild humour, he names 'the Thoreau strategy': withdrawal for the sake of achieving perspective and in order to get in touch with deeper values.

Thoreau has been an attractive figure to therapists of various kinds, and the causes for which his name has been enlisted range from 'existential therapy' and 'harp therapy' to the more predictable kinds of wilderness experience that we considered in Chapter 3.[2] Writing of the journey of discovery that is wilderness treatment, Mary Allen and David M. Edwards are characteristically robust about what this means:

When Henry David Thoreau took up residence at Walden Pond, he went in search of an antidote to the pressures of modern living, which caused people to lead 'lives of quiet desperation'. Since Thoreau's time, the problems associated with life in our society have grown beyond anything he is likely to have imagined. For many people, however, the solution to those problems lies in the combination of personal responsibility, physical challenge and communion with nature that was so productive for Thoreau. (Allen and Edwards, 2006)

Wilderness treatment of this type, based on the experiential education movement pioneered by Kurt Hahn, founder of Outward Bound, is said by Allen and Edwards to provide a unique kind of healing. Offering such peak experiences as challenge courses, rock-climbing, climbing wall therapy and day-hike canyoneering, this is not 'talk' but 'reality' therapy. It provides those who take part – typically, troubled young people – with the chance to rethink themselves, to redefine their self-image. This, we are told, is at the core of almost every form of therapy. The climbing experience is, of course, made as safe as possible, but it is the perception by the climbers that they are doing something life-threatening that seems to elicit the trauma response. The truly amazing thing, according to Daniel Meyers, a nationally recognized authority on wilderness treatment, is that the majority of people 'are so tired of feeling not in control that they say no, I want to keep climbing and get this over with. They want to get the trauma behind them.' The 'sacred state' that is achieved through facing pain and accepting responsibility is such that 'all of a sudden a sense of self-acceptance is so much greater – the sense of timelessness, where they really feel that they have done something that is absolutely incredible, very vital in their life.' The historic idea of the hermit, as someone who secludes himself from the external world in order to ask vital questions, is revived in the 'solo experience' that is also offered, and here, as for Thoreau, journal writing is important. But just as Thoreau's stay at Walden came to an end after a couple of years, so these young people, after these day-long therapies, must return to their communities. The challenge then becomes one of how to take the sacred state back with them, how to transfer the learning.

Thoreau's experience of living at Walden Pond and the journal in which he recorded that experience constitute part of the American imaginary in complex ways and at multiple levels, as the above examples of 'the Thoreau strategy' begin to indicate. It is not just to the questions of self and community, of the nature of responsibility and of the return to nature, gestured therapeutically in the text above, it is to the place of these things in relation to the idea of America – with its possibilities of democracy, philosophy and education – that we need to turn. Let us for the moment ignore any question of 'strategy' and ask rather: what is *Walden*? For asking this will lead us to question its place in the American imaginary – that is, to question how far it is well represented or understood there, and how far it is confined, which is to say repressed by America and American philosophy.[3] To do this we draw also upon *The Senses of Walden*, Stanley Cavell's study of Thoreau's book. This will help us to show the way that there are ideas here about therapy of a kind – the therapy that, as Wittgenstein later saw, our philosophy and our lives recurrently stand in need of – and that to come to understand this is itself a kind of education. Let us begin by saying something about the book's genesis and reception.

Thoreau's *Walden*, published in 1854, is his account of the period of nearly two years that he spent living at Walden Pond, not a remote place but a place in the woods away from the town. Compressing the two years into one, it provides an account of the time he spent there, of the hut he built, the beans he planted, the birds and animals he saw in the woods, the people who visited him and the pond itself. It is written – allegedly – in order to respond to the kinds of questions that the townsfolk asked of him: what did he eat, was he lonely, was he afraid, how many children did he maintain, what did he give to charity? These questions may seem innocent enough and perhaps they were, but they sketch the territory of the economy of living that it is the book's purpose to explore and elaborate. It is, Thoreau says, his experiment in living. But what is this *it* that is his experiment in living? While, to be sure, it involves the two years spent at Walden in conditions not exactly of self-sufficiency but of making a living simply, it is also the writing of *Walden* – the realizing of a language (or of the possibilities of language) that can provide the conditions for the economy he seeks. Hence, a major concern of the text is with language itself.

This more subtle and complex purpose, as our opening example crudely shows, has not always been recognized, and the book's reception since 1854 has, in fact, been uneven. While it has been celebrated as a key work in the establishment of an American consciousness and literature, it has commonly been read as a kind of rural idyll, and a rejection of society to boot. In 1917, in an edition of *The Seven Arts* marking the centenary of Thoreau's birth, the editors comment that it was through living close to 'the elements, the forest, the sea, the soil' that Thoreau was able to discover the perfect integrity that he exacted from living things: 'It was this that led him to look with the aloofness of an immortal upon the world out of which he had grown'; it was this that made him 'solitary and disdainful', a man 'whose imagination never compassed the gelatinous mass of human kind' (Editors of *The Seven Arts*, in Paul, 1962, p. 9). The sense of the demanding individualism of Thoreau's thought is there too in what Max Lerner, in 1939, described as the uncompromising nature of Thoreau's social criticism – 'a taut, astringent rejection of everything, that could not pass the most exacting tests of the individual life. In that sense there was something of the nihilist about Thoreau, and his thought effected an almost Nietzschean transvaluation of values' (in Paul, 1962, p. 21). Lerner counteracts these rather heavily weighted remarks with the suggestion that Thoreau's hermit-like individualism should not be overemphasized. But it is still a revulsion against society that is understood to motivate his retreat – and indeed it is significant that it is seen as a retreat. In the popular imagination, this amounts to the idea of the escape to the woods, the healing refuge of a solitary life lived close to nature, with Thoreau cast as a kind of environmentalist *avant la lettre*. In the more literary, more philosophical imagination, yet in a still compatible way, Thoreau's text is read as a homely version of the realignment with nature that was the Romantics' preoccupation.

But there are good reasons, as we have indicated, for contesting this picture. In the first place, the book is not without its reflections on matters of a quite different kind – on slavery, the Mexican war, factory labour, business, charity, neighbours, health and wealth – reflections that in effect answer to the innocent questions of the townsfolk. Above all its experiment involves living not in the remote countryside but *within about a mile* of his nearest neighbours – which is to say, at a distance where they will see what he is doing, in such a way that his experiment can serve as a kind of example. It is something from which he expects to learn, and it may teach others also: 'I went to the woods because I wished to live deliberately, to front only the essential facts of life, and see if I could not learn what it had to teach, and not, when I came to die, discover that I had not lived' (Thoreau, 1986, p. 135). Yes, he went searching for what the woods had to teach, but this is not, it turns out, the only place to go for lessons of this kind, for there will come a time when he will move on, seeking edification in a different direction: 'I left the woods for as good a reason as I went there.

Perhaps it seemed to me that I had several more lives to live, and could not spare any more time for that one' (p. 371).

If the book is his record or account of his time at Walden, it is also the means by which he accounts for himself, showing in the process what counts for him. He even goes so far as to present the odd page of accounts, where columns of figures detail what he spent on the materials for his house, what profit he made from his beans, what his food cost him – inviting the reader to be, as it were, the auditor not only of this balance sheet but of his account as a whole. In order to set our economy straight, the auditing that is needed, this seems to say, is something other than the accountancy procedures that preoccupy the busy townsfolk with their enterprise and their expanding businesses. Indeed a good economy cannot be confined to columns of figures, for it must relate to our language as a whole.

If it is Thoreau's aim to present us with a holistic vision of an economy of living, it becomes possible to see the book as a kind of utopian text – albeit that Thoreau's concerns are painstakingly practical (planting beans, building a shelter) and doggedly realistic. But even in these most practical tasks the suggestion of their larger significance is made through a kind of mock-heroic imagery: when he hoes his bean-field, his battle with the 'Trojan' weeds casts him as Achilles overcoming '[m]any a lusty crest-waving Hector' (p. 207). The book that remains open on Thoreau's table as he goes about his daily tasks is none other than *The Iliad*, though – the humour may seem deflating but it works both ways – sometimes he preferred to read the scraps of newspaper in which for convenience he had wrapped his lunch. It is not the sensational in the news, about which Thoreau is predictably scathing, but the epic in the ordinary that this implies. The suggestion of epic importance is more grave, as Cavell demonstrates, in the numerous ways in which Thoreau's language takes on the expressions, rhythms and imagery of the Old Testament prophets, Ezekiel and Jeremiah. It was prophets such as these who had warned of the dire consequences of failing to heed the word of a just but wrathful God, and it is worth noting some details of their message here. The God of Ezekiel, who is severe and just, is eternally the same, but the ways in which he can be apprehended by the people change. In consequence, it falls to each generation to think of God in new ways. The destruction of Jerusalem and exile to Babylon had left the people to whom Ezekiel ministered traumatized and manifesting anger and denial. Ezekiel responded to this by exposing the people's responsibility for the disaster that had afflicted them, castigating them for their worship of idols, and their acceptance of the words of false prophets. He implored them to see that their only hope for recovery was to change. Ezekiel is the prophet who affirms the continued presence of God amongst the people but of God's withdrawal under certain conditions and who ponders the question of legitimate religious and political leadership in the restored community. The withdrawals and approaches of God, Cavell suggests, can be looked upon as tracing the history of our attempts to overtake and absorb acknowledgement by knowledge; God would be the name of that impossibility. Jeremiah's task was to show the moral necessity of the destruction of Jerusalem and to proclaim this in the ears of the people to be the inevitable result of their moral guilt. In order to arouse the people from their moral lethargy, he preached repentance until it became monotonous. He had not only 'to root up, and to pull down,' but also to undertake the positive work of salvation, 'to build, and to plant' (Jeremiah, i, 10). The sense of visionary purpose that is reinforced by such connections helps us to see *Walden* as a kind of perfectionist writing that stands in line with Rousseau's *Emile* and Plato's *The Republic*. Just as Rousseau's purpose is not to provide tips for teachers but rather to offer a substantive social philosophy in which a good education will play a critical role, so here Thoreau's experiment enacts a possibility of living that is tantamount to a kind of lifelong learning. 'We have', he tells us, 'a comparatively decent system of common schools, schools for infants only... It is time that we had uncommon schools, that we did not leave off our education when we begin to be men and women' (p. 154).

We shall shortly ask what such an (uncommon) education might amount to, but first let us test out the significance of prophecy here. The Old Testament prophets were charged with the responsibility of alerting the people to the ways in which their lives had become corrupt, and of insisting on the ways in which they had, as it were, become blind or deaf to this. They foretold of a world-to-come. The former function is symbolized in Thoreau's book by the figure of the cockerel: the author must brag as loudly as a morning cockerel in order to wake his fellow citizens up, for they have gone to sleep in their lives. The latter is accomplished not in specific predictions but in the demonstration of a possibility of living, in which the idea of experiment is itself a motif. For this is no recipe for the good life but an illustration of the need for each of us not to copy Thoreau but to engage in our own experiment, to live as experiment: we should not settle down complacently, like the townsfolk, but should regard our lives as opportunity at every point, with neither established foundation nor final settlement, but with every occasion an occasion for new departure.

The proto-Nietzschean affirmation that is evident here is also pointed up in the denial that precedes Thoreau's commitment to this 'bragging', a denial made first in the epigraph to the first chapter, 'Economy', and repeated later in the book: 'I do not propose to write an ode to dejection, but to brag as lustily as chanticleer [the cockerel] in the morning standing on his roost, if only to wake my neighbours up' (p. 45). But one reason that Thoreau will not write an ode to dejection is that Coleridge has already done that. Hence, this remark helps to place *Walden* in relation to Romantic thought and achievement. Yet the association with Coleridge's poem, and the repeated denial of dejection, means that, for all the affirmative emphasis of Thoreau's claim, melancholy is never far away. As Cavell points out, Thoreau allows space to something like desperation or despair in the book in the kind of irritability – and actually boredom – that creeps into some of its pages. The robust affirmation symbolized by the cockerel is also complicated by various forms of indirectness in the text – a stealthy approach that wrong-foots the reader, at times even the deviousness and unpredictability of the trickster, symbolized by the cockerel's adversary, the fox. The inconsistency of Thoreau's voice, the wilful ambiguity of the rhythms of his sentences, serve to put the reader in the position of *having to read*: of being faced constantly with the decision of how to take a phrase, how to react to it, what to understand by it, whether to assent. This condition of reading – which is treated directly in a chapter by that name – tells us something of how we should address ourselves to the occasions that life presents.

But – the question from earlier chapters is revived – what exactly is reading, and what is its importance here? The indirectness of the relationship between reader and writer is associated at one point with the bent arm's length, the elbow support, that separates book from reader, implying the bearing the reader must gain on the text. While reading a book is metonymic of the more pervasive reading of the world that is required of us, the written word carries a special significance in terms of our education as adults – that is, our education *into* adulthood, *through* adulthood. Indeed it represents a crucial aspect of our ongoing acquisition of language, the condition of continual rebirth. As we grow up we inevitably learn to speak: we acquire our mother-tongue. This is our common schooling, our schooling into community. But we need later to acquire the 'father-tongue' – a 'reserved and select expression, too significant to be heard by the ear, which we must be born again in order to speak' (p. 146). The father-tongue is associated by Thoreau crucially with the written word. The learning of the father-tongue stands in contrast to the naturalness of our initial and conventional acquisition of language and learning, at our mother's knee. That the phrase is not intended to suggest anything authoritarian or doctrinal is made clear: 'I desire that there may be as many different persons in the world as possible; but I would have each one be careful to find out and pursue *his own* way, and not his father's or his mother's or his neighbour's instead' (Thoreau, 1986, p. 114). Neither is it intended to suggest that these are simply developmental stages, so that we must be initiated into the mother tongue before we acquire the father tongue, the latter being a kind of sophisticated accretion to the former. The language to which the child gains access is language full-blown, albeit that this access is initially tentative, rudimentary and inchoate; so too, the adult – complacent and comfortable perhaps – whose speech is confined within the mother tongue remains in a kind of denial of the father. The point is to keep faith at once with the mother and the father. The union of the mother and father is not a unification, but a union that has issue: the birth that is the potential renewal of language and culture, and thereby of the self.

In Thoreau's own withholding of meaning in his text – in its ambiguities and ruses and unsettling of the reader – the book repeatedly foregoes its claims to direct the reader in substantive ways. The reserved and select expression that we confront in reading well requires us to return to words as through a condition of estrangement, to choose our words and see how their meaning measures us. Cavell writes: '[F]or a child to grow he requires family and familiarity, but for a grownup to grow he requires strangeness and transformation, i.e., birth' (Cavell, 1981, p. 60).

That the question of America, of its creation and inauguration, is never far from the preoccupations of *Walden* is made plain enough by the fact that Thoreau began to build his house on the 4th July. Writing in New England in the 19th century, Thoreau could hardly have understood the measure of the words that confronted him without some sense that, with the burgeoning culture of business and individualism, the Pilgrim Fathers' promise of a new land had *not* been fulfilled, and that the promise of America had *not* been realized – that, in a sense, America was still to be created. Writing in 1971 – *The Senses of Walden* was written in an intense period of some seven weeks when the Vietnam War was at its height, at a time when American identity, and what America represents, was exposed in an especially painful way – Cavell's judgement on this point is unlikely to have been more sanguine, nor could it be so today. Perhaps like Jacques Derrida's *Specters of Marx* (1994), written defiantly against the backdrop of triumphalism over the demise of communism and the 'end of history', *The Senses* is also an 'untimely' book. Cavell focuses philosophically on a philosophical work that has come to be denied and reads this in a way that challenges both what has become the conventional reception and celebration of this work, with its convenient placement within the genre of the pastoral, and the received understanding of what philosophy itself is. He reads it as a book about politics and education, and about what has gone wrong with the American dream: allusions to the visceral precision of Thoreau's remarks regarding the Mexican war leave little doubt as to Cavell's concerns about American encroachments on East Asia, while the Eastern influences acknowledged in *Walden* – its references to Buddhist stories and to the *Bhagavad Gita*, for example – reflect a hospitality to thought that America has learned to deny. The sense of America's failure in Thoreau's own text is sustained in its repeated pondering of questions of gain and loss and of the kinds of investments that it is right to make, with the rightful ordering of the home that is economy[4] and with the relations of labour and neighbourliness that this implies. The book asks what work is and what it is to be housed, and what indeed possessions are: 'For whosoever will save his life shall lose it... For what shall it profit a man, if he gain the whole world, and lose his own soul?' (Mark, 8, 35–6)

Not to lose one's soul, for Thoreau, cannot be understood in purely negative terms – say, as the avoidance of sin – because in such a life of avoidance the human being goes to sleep! On the contrary, there is an increasing demand to take up the occasions of one's experience in such a way that one departs from one's settled and accustomed ways of understanding them, in order that one should seek possibilities of new departure – and this not only at the level of one's larger decisions in life but also in one's daily engagement with language and life, epitomized by the process of reading. Of course, we begin by acquiring a language, and to a large extent our use of this language requires our obedience to convention. But words that are just repeated or passed along down the line go dead on us and on the culture; the culture is deadened by them. 'It is difficult to begin without borrowing', Thoreau writes, but, as with an axe that you borrow, you can return words sharper than you received them (Thoreau, 1986, p. 83). The salience of the vocabulary of counting and accounting in fact extends into a constant use of words that relate to money ('borrow', 'interest', 'invest', 'return', 'economy', 'currency'). But there is a responsibility in using words so that they do not devalue, so that you return them, sharpened, with interest. That this is a condition to be achieved, and always still to be worked at, is, so Cavell suggests, not only a question of our personal fulfilment, or of our saving of our souls, but the condition of seeing the world aright: 'Until we can speak again, our lives and our language betray one another; we can grant neither of them their full range and autonomy; they mistake their definitions of one another' (Cavell, 1981, p. 34).

One thing this requires of us is our readiness to be affected. Thoreau makes fun of conventional Christian notions of rebirth – as if rebirth were something that must happen just once. On the contrary, it is a process that must recur. It is not, as must be conceded, something we can simply decide to do, but we can make ourselves open to its possibility. In *Walden* rebirth is symbolized in various ways. It is there in the proximity of Walden pond and the daily bathing that this affords ('I got up early and bathed in the pond; that was a religious exercise, and one of the best things which I did', Thoreau, 1986, p. 132). It is there in the various processes of moulting or shedding feathers or skin that Thoreau describes in the animals he observes, processes paralleled in the discarding of surplus clothing. It is there in the idea of giving up unnecessary possessions. The religious resonances of these symbols connect also with a powerful indication of what it is that our receptiveness or openness requires and of why this might involve a kind of death of the existing self, a departure from any existing settlement with the world. You are required to allow yourself *to be struck* by something new: 'If you stand right [and face a fact], you will see the sun glimmer on both its surfaces, as if it were a cimeter,[5] and feel its sweet edge dividing you through the heart and marrow' (Thoreau, 1986; *Walden*, II).[6] In sum, it requires being ready to leave what you think is yours (your possessions, *you*), and so a readiness for departure, where readiness is not something for which you consciously prepare but more like a receptiveness to the new and a release from the hold of the past. And so, with Thoreau's celebrated pun, morning (the orientation towards the future) is close to mourning (loss, departure): mourning becomes morning.

Thoreau's economy of living is to be distanced also from two further currents of thought. In some ways the emphasis here on departure and newness seems to bring us close to some of the siren pressures of postmodernity. But in Thoreau the individual's exposure to experience is to be attuned not to the ephemera of the postmodern world, in which image displaces substance, but doggedly to the real. For the learner to be at stake in what is undertaken is a matter of words, but not *merely* of words. To foreground language is to sanction not some kind of free spinning of words but rather an answerability or responsiveness to the possibilities of thought and being that language realizes. And the idea of continual rebirth and departure has little to do, say, with the self-reinventions and makeovers that the media constantly entice us towards or with the itinerant, skill-bearing, anonymous, flexible learners that are, it is imagined, the requisites of a globalized know-ledge-economy, any more that it has to do with the therapy of rebirthing. It is more like a call towards becoming, orientated less by any substantive end than by a strengthening sense of the fakery of the identities that proffer themselves – from the outside and from within. It is departure from these things and a refusal to acquiesce in fixed identities and the values they enshrine, whether the result of custom or the object of (perhaps commercially constructed) desire, that opens the way to these possibilities.

But, in the same manner, Thoreau's economy of living is not to be understood in terms of what might at this point offer itself, inspired perhaps by the later Heidegger, as a kind of salvation from ephemeral-ity: a fidelity to one's steady sense of place and history. Thoreau's building of his house in the woods is tantamount to an enacted medi-tation on the building-dwelling-thinking that Heidegger a century later will thematize (Heidegger, 1975). It involves a fidelity to the way things are, here, at this time, which requires the observance of a daily regime that is something other than dull mechanical routine. The vibrancy and validity of this are born not only of familiarity but also out of an acceptance of and receptivity to strangeness. In the end, however, and contrary to popular readings of Thoreau, it is not this particular place that is the heart of the matter: what is more important is the possibility, or perhaps the principle, of this combination of par-ticular attachments (the regimes of living attuned to them, the com-mitment appropriate to them) with a readiness for departure – before, as it were, they fossilize or perhaps come to be romanticized or to parody themselves. Moreover, as Cavell puts this in a recent essay, the manner of Thoreau's leaving of Walden demonstrates

> what Freud calls the work of mourning, letting the past go, giving it up, giving it over, giving away the Walden it was time for him to leave, without nostalgia, without a disabling elegiacism. Nostalgia is

the inability to open the past to the future, as if the strangers who
will replace you will never find what you have found. Such a negative heritage would be a poor thing to leave to *Walden's* readers,
whom its writer identifies, among many ways, precisely as strangers.
(Cavell, 2005a, pp. 217–18)

The idea of the stranger, alien to *Dasein's* being-with-others, also points
up a contrast between the journeying home or being homebound that
exerts so strong a gravitational force in Heidegger's thought and the
*sojourning* emphasized in Thoreau, where one is to live 'each day,
everywhere and nowhere, as a task and an event'.

But Thoreau's 'everywhere and nowhere' must be something other than
the purely transitory, placeless existence, eased no doubt by Blackberries
and Ipods, and eked out in airless airport lounges, or the online virtual
existence that busy so many people today. Herman Hesse tells us that
when a circle of our life presents itself as 'home', we grow weary: 'only she
who is ready to journey forth/will escape habit's paralysis'. And Emerson:
that, around every circle another circle can be drawn. So, for Thoreau, to
sojourn – physically and psychologically – is neither to be rooted perma-
nently in one place nor to pursue the kind of nomad identity mentioned
at the end of Chapter 7 (though Thoreau occasionally speaks favourably of
nomads). It is to stay in a place for a while and then to be ready to move
on. This would be a better dwelling, but its possibilities are also suggested
by the taking of steps to find a way – in short, by walking itself, where the
foot, grounded on the earth, is the *point d'appui*, the place from which one
moves forward, the place that one leaves. Thoreau was an inveterate
walker, in long afternoons and through the night, and the various references to this in his writings include the celebrated essay simply entitled
'Walking'. Early in this essay he thinks of the 'art of Walking' especially in
relation to those who have 'a genius, so to speak, for *sauntering*'. In a paragraph that plainly delights in the nuances and ambiguities of the words in
question, he comments on the way that the word 'sauntering' is

beautifully derived 'from idle people who roved about the country,
in the middle ages, and asked charity, under pretence of going à la
Sainte Terre' – to the holy land, till the children exclaimed, 'There
goes a *Sainte-Terre*r', a saunterer – a holy-lander. They who never go
to the holy land in their walks, as they pretend, are indeed mere
idlers and vagabonds, but they who do go there are saunterers in the
good sense, such as I mean. Some, however, would derive the word
from *sans terre*, without land or a home, which, therefore, in the

good sense, will mean, having no particular home, but equally at home everywhere. For this is the secret of successful sauntering. He who sits still in a house all the time may be the greatest vagrant of all, but the Saunterer, in the good sense, is no more vagrant than the meandering river, which is all the while sedulously seeking the shortest course to the sea. But I prefer the first, which indeed is the most probable derivation. For every walk is a sort of crusade, preached by some Peter the Hermit in us, to go forth and reconquer this holy land from the hands of the Infidels. (Thoreau, 2002, pp. 149–50)

Thoreau is indeed on a crusade, but the Holy Land that needs to be reconquered is none other than the world itself, and for the Infidels who are the townsfolk of Concord, Massachussetts – call this America (call this ourselves) – that world has been not only lost in their avaricious plundering of its resources but rendered invisible through the acquisitive modes of their understanding and the etiolated forms of their social life. Later in the essay (p. 151), Thoreau declares: 'In my walks I would fain return to my senses.' For his life has lost sense, he has lost his senses, and the way to restore them is through a proper attention to what is around him: 'You only need sit still long enough in some attractive spot in the woods that all its inhabitants may exhibit them to you by turns' (Thoreau, 1986, p. 275).

Unlike the ideas of 'mineness' and belonging, the *Eigentlichkeit*, that recur in Heidegger, as we saw in Chapter 6, there is here some sense of what Cavell thinks of as the essential immigrancy of the human, a further formulation of the self's non-integrity. Reading well, the essentially binary structure of which was elaborated in Chapter 4, requires us to return to words as through a condition of estrangement, as though we have still to arrive at our words. Education, the education of grownups as Cavell famously puts this in *The Claim of Reason*,[7] requires our discovery of our immigrancy to ourselves. Thoreau's figure for this non-transparency and non-identity is that we are persistently outside ourselves. Being 'beside oneself' – *ek-stasis*, ecstasy – can mean being mad. But it can also take less dramatic, more ordinary forms. Thoreau speaks in *Walden* of 'being beside ourselves in a sane sense' (Thoreau, 1986, Ch. 5). In the responsible use of our words, in our making and shaping of things, we project something beyond the way we are, projecting new conditions within which we may serve as examples to one another, within which we may (mutually and continually) find ourselves; this would be a condition of friendship towards which aspirations of community might rightly be directed. Such things are, as it were, *next* to us: '*Next* to us the grandest laws are continually being executed. *Next* to us is not the workman whom we have hired, with whom we love so well to talk, but the workman whose work we are' (Thoreau, 1986, p. 179). We are less the author than the work. The workman with whom we love to talk is scarcely other than language itself, and it is this to which we are progressively attuned.[8] We find our pitch in the address by the stranger. That this is the restoring of a correct relationship between inner and outer is borne out by Cavell's remark:

> Our first resolve should be toward the nextness of the self to the self; it is the capacity not to deny either of its positions or attitudes – that it is the watchman or guardian of itself, and hence demands of itself transparence, settling, clearing, constancy; and that it is the workman, whose eye cannot see to the end of its labors, but whose answerability is endless for the constructions in which it houses itself. The answerability of the self to itself is its possibility of awakening. (Cavell, 1982, p. 109)

A right relation to our words and work, including our response to those of others, awakens us from the spell of psychology and from the disenchantment of the world at philosophy's hands. It depsychologizes psychology (Cavell, 1976, pp. 91, 93). Correcting the relation of the public and the private, it restores the ordinary world as one of nextness and neighbourhood, of an internal alterity where we are strangers to ourselves, and of an essential immigrancy of the self.

Can someone who has not woken up to this strangeness within himself really relate to what is different in others? He assesses what sense he can make of them. The better direction of thought – from the other – is the means of my finding sense in myself. 'Here one is taking the problem of the other', Cavell writes, 'in rather the reverse direction from the way philosophers tend to conceive the matter, letting it provoke him to learn something else from the encounter: it is not the other that poses the first barrier to my knowledge of him or her, but myself' (Cavell, 2005a, p. 233). It is in the mature relationship to language, which the father-tongue represents, that this learning can come to pervade the ordinary, uncommon experience that can and should be ours. This, as we shall show further in the final chapters of this book, is not the actual ordinary from which we start but the eventual ordinary towards which our education can lead. Such experience depends upon education and upon the kind of uncommon schooling that can recur through our lives. This perhaps is the teaching of *Walden*.

Near the start of this chapter we spoke of the way that *Walden* and Thoreau, and for that matter Emerson too, had been repressed by America, conveniently placed within the genre of the pastoral, and even, in a further ruse of containment, monumentalized as essential to the American literary heritage (whence 'recuperated', as a therapeutic strategy, in wilderness and other treatments). American Philosophy Departments collude in this insofar as Thoreau is not read there, and this exclusion says something about what philosophy is now taken to be. Cavell claims this as a characteristically American form of repression, a failure to acknowledge what is most original about itself, which denial of what is most near is paralleled by the sceptic's anxiety for still more secure foundations. The consequences of this we might reasonably look for in the acquisitive and totalizing forms of understanding that extend around the world in processes of Americanization, the current names for which might also be 'neoliberalism' and 'globalization'. That this is something that America itself suffers from, and something with which we must all come to terms, is on the above analysis made all too clear.

The understanding that is suggested by walking, where the foot finds its *point d'appui* in extending forwards and down, back to the rough ground below, contrasts with the over-confident, too busy thinking of the person who never looks down, whose feet have, as it were, lost contact with the earth. There are ancient origins to this way of thinking, and it is to these that we turn in the chapter to come.[9]

# 9
# A State of Abstraction: Knowledge and Contingency

'Imagine abstract man, without the guidance of myth – abstract education, abstract morality, abstract justice, the abstract state...'

(Friedrich Nietzsche, *The Birth of Tragedy* § 23)

## I   Abstract education

It is conventional to start with an Abstract; perhaps some readers never get beyond it. Sometimes it seems we need little more: after all, the Abstract gives you the essence, the gist, filleted of examples, allusions and other distractions. We start here not with an Abstract but with the idea of abstraction in a different but related sense, and connect it with the way that a kind of knowingness has come to take over education, at least in the contexts with which we are personally familiar. It seems it is not enough to know, in many of the educational systems of the west: we are also to know that we know. Pupils and students are enjoined not merely to learn, but to learn how to learn: to reflect on their own processes of learning, and develop metacognitive skills and strategies.[1] The following statement, from a Teaching and Learning Research Programme under the auspices of the ESRC (Economic and Social Research Council) is symptomatic:

As knowledge now advances rapidly, raising educational standards means that at school pupils need not only to learn but also to learn how to learn as an essential preparation for lifelong learning. To support this, teachers need to know what they can do in their class-room practice to help pupils acquire the knowledge and skills of learning how to learn.

A review of the curriculum and qualifications for 14–19 year-olds in the UK speaks the same kind of language. Young people are to be prepared with the 'skills and self-awareness to exercise their choices effectively' (para. 22);[2] 'All learners must be taught and supported to review their learning and achievement, understand the pathways open to them, and make well-informed choices' (para. 51). In Further Education students are encouraged to identify their own personal learning style – kinaesthetic, inter-personal, linguistic, iconic – with the result that it appears to be possible for them to know themselves as learners before they have yet come to learning anything: a remarkable achievement. Universities in the UK are now to require their students to engage in Personal Development Programmes (PDPs). Students will be encouraged to review the key skills and competences associated with their studies, in order to be clear which they have acquired (the better to sell themselves to potential employers, perhaps) and which they still need to learn. Thus a student facing her third year of study, say, will be able to select modules that will add missing skills to her portfolio (because of course these modules will spell out unambiguously the skills they offer).

There is something extraordinary here. Such skills and metaknowledge will indeed be abstracted from richer contexts – the books, lectures and seminars – in which learning is engaged, as if the books and so on were merely incidental vehicles for their delivery. It is, furthermore, as if the Cartesian ego had never been challenged: as if our highest image of humankind were still individuals transparent to themselves, entirely confident of being neither robot nor replicant, their thoughts and feelings not conceivably the result of mischievous demons or of alien scientists conducting brain-in-vat experiments in some distant galaxy. The learners of this new utopia seem to stand miraculously above all the literary, historical and philosophical streams that might have seeped into their souls, able to survey all that has gone into them, judiciously in control of themselves. They are, in Nietzsche's way of putting it, abstract men (and women). They will presumably never be overcome, overwhelmed by Shakespeare or Keats; never find themselves obsessively arguing with Wittgenstein. They will be altogether too coolly rational, too well equipped with metacognitive skills, to be thus distracted and unbalanced. They will speak language; it will never speak them.

Of course there are good reasons for this interest in learning how to learn. Not so many years ago it seemed that a university course was there for no other reason apparently than that it always had been, its rationale and point – and thus what you were supposed to get out of it and how you were supposed to approach it – largely obscure. Who would want to go back to those days? Yet the insistent emphasis on these skills moves education away from a matter of rich and complex subjects and disciplines (mathematics, history, the poems of Keats) in which we can immerse ourselves and lose ourselves and towards being a closed system where everything can be transparent only because everything has been reduced to what can be abstracted, mapped out and made explicit.

It is a familiar point too that education has in many countries become subjected to regimes of inspection and audit: where everything must be representable, on pain of being held not to exist. In this education is like other services in what Vattimo (1992) calls the 'transparent society' and Power (1997) the 'audit society', characterized by what Power calls 'rituals of verification' rather than trust. One way of understanding these developments is as an effect of the way in which education has been conceived more and more in economic and industrial terms. Skills and competency approaches to education derive from Taylorist models of production. In neo-liberal thinking all human transactions are conceived as economic forms of exchange. In such a regime education is re-shaped to follow the logic of the market, and educational policy becomes ever more subject to economic policy. The result is that education is transformed into the acquisition of instrumental knowledge and marketable skills.

One of the many effects of this insistence on seeing education in purely economic terms, we suggest, is a kind of amnesia with respect to contingency and finitude. That our lives are subject to chance and that they are circumscribed by all sorts of eventualities over which we have little or no control, including of course the eventuality of our own death, seems somewhat neglected, set on one side, by the perfectionist drive for thoroughly effective teaching methods, schools that are totally reliable organizations, state programmes in which there is Nothing Left to Chance,[3] Every Child Matters,[4] programmes so panoptic and all-embracing that the result will be No Child Left Behind.[5] This must be the tendency of a philosophy derived from Taylorism, for the whole drive of that industrial movement is to make production into a smooth process from which chance has been eliminated, eventually by automated assembly lines which do away with the unreliability of human beings altogether. Such a conception of education is indeed abstract in treating it as if it were removed – abstracted – from the most characteristic condition of human life.

There are, we suggest, two worrying outcomes in particular of this abstraction. One, which we return to in the next section, is the difficulty of finding the language for, let alone practising, a kind of education that is respectful of, and shaped by the demands of, human contingency. The second, which is related to the first, concerns what we are not alone in finding a disturbing trend among the young people we teach, university students mainly between the ages of eighteen and twenty-two. The number of anxious and depressed students – seriously so enough to seek advice, medication or counseling – seems to be rising at a most alarming rate. Many of these students express the fear that while they have been successful in education so far, they are now about to come unstuck. The knowledge, skills and determination that have hitherto served them well have run out. Disaster looms. The word 'perfection' comes up frequently in these conversations.

A recent article by Sara Rimer (6 April 2004) in the *New York Times* is concerned with the same trend. It begins: 'It was intended as a statement against the kind of perfectionism that drives some Bowdoin College students to spend two hours a day on the treadmill'. The College is concerned about the 'rising number of students seeking help for stress-related conditions on campus and the expectations of consumer-minded parents'. They are aware that there is a 'contradiction inherent in their new efforts to offset stress and encourage the joys of reflection and unstructured time. After all, it was multitasking, hyper-organized, résumé building behavior that helped some students get admitted to their schools in the first place'. Parents are seen as a major part of the problem: rather than regarding late adolescence as a time of learning by trial and error 'many parents put great energy into trying to eliminate the error'. A College spokesperson suggested that parents 'were creating a generation of students afraid to take risks'.[6]

A culture of knowingness, then; of a one-dimensional self-awareness that posits transparency as a ready ideal; of a dangerous kind of perfectionism; of education that neglects or falsifies the human condition of contingency. Yet our culture offers us enough guidance to the perils lurking here.

## II    The guidance of myth

In an infant school in one of the more deprived parts of the United Kingdom the Literacy Hour was in progress. The English language spells similar-sounding syllables in different ways: – *er* and – *ur* are a case in point, and children must learn how to spell the words containing these sounds. *Father*, but *blur*. *Further*, but a *herd* of cattle. *Murder*. Outside the windows, meanwhile, along the road that passes the school, a rival scene competed for the children's attention: a funeral. In front of the slowly-moving hearse walked a diminutive undertaker, carrying a stick, and wearing a tall black hat ('A wizard!' gasped the children). Behind the hearse a procession of fire-engines, their red paint and brass fittings almost painful to the eye. The funeral of a firefighter, then, or fireman as he used to be known. And behind the fire-engines moving more slowly than you have ever seen them move before, a procession of lesser vehicles. Teacher was quick to call the children away from the windows and a spectacle that struck her as morbid. Besides, the Literacy Hour has to be taught. *Stern, turn, burn*.

The point is not to criticize the teacher. She is simply a person of her time, and her time, which is the United Kingdom of the present day, is not comfortable with the scene outside the windows. It is disturbing. It has an almost elemental force: it seems to come from an older world – that of Charles Dickens, perhaps. The children certainly respond to it, rapt in their attention and in the awed, barely-comprehending respect that the scene compels from them. You will observe the same absorption if you tell them the story of the Snow Queen ('... and she told Kay that if he could move the blocks of ice to spell the word "eternity" she would give him the world, and a pair of skates') or if you read them a straightforward version of *Little Red Riding Hood*, or tell them the story of what happened to Odysseus on his long way home from Troy.

We need myth, Nietzsche thinks, because a culture that has ready recourse to myth will be less prone to what he calls Socratism, that is the ruinous tendency to rationalise, to rely on reason too much and in contexts where reason should not be our only guide. Even more than that, myth is at the heart of our sense of the tragic, and tragedy – the tragic genre – has the vital function of reminding us that not everything is in our power to achieve. It is the most natural thing in the world that we strive to progress, to build bulwarks against the unkindness of fate (our possessions, our *curriculum vitae*, even our relationships), but the sense of the tragic can rescue us from the dangerous supposition that we can make ourselves perfect. We discuss below why this is particularly relevant to western cultures today.

The classical Greeks in particular thought that tragedy keeps alive our sense of the sheer contingency of things: of the propensity of chance to intervene in apparently well-ordered human affairs, of the ground on which we build our achievements to reveal itself as thin as paper, to open up before our feet often at the very point where it seems most solid. It is not just that disaster can happen, the simple matter of being in the wrong place at the wrong time. It is rather that we are prone to over-confidence, the Greek *hubris*, in our own capacities: our intellectual prowess, our capacity to make the world respond to our will. We can sail ships across the seas in the face of storms and waves, harness horses to plough the ever-fruitful earth, snare the birds of the air, build cities, learn speech and reason (thus Sophocles, *Antigone*, ll. 332 ff.). We can do all kinds of wonderful things, awe-inspiring, even awful things (the Greek word *deina*, which Sophocles uses here, has all these meanings). The contingency of the world lies in its power to show our confidence as misplaced even, or perhaps especially, where it is most firmly held, and held on the most rational basis.

Sophocles' play *Oedipus Tyrannus*, often regarded as the quintessential Greek tragedy for other reasons – such as its propensity to inspire pity and awe, and produce catharsis – exemplifies the workings of contingency, as described above, to a high degree. The plot is the well-known one of how Laius and Jocasta, King and Queen of Thebes, left their baby son to die on a hillside, his ankles pinned together, because of a prophecy that the child would kill his father and lie with his mother. A shepherd found the baby, christened him 'Oedipus' which means 'swollen-foot', and gave him to the King and Queen of Corinth who brought the child up as their own. When the child grew to adulthood rumours circulated in Corinth about his parentage. Oedipus visited the oracle at Delphi in search of the truth. The oracle confirmed the prophecy that Laius and Jocasta had heard before: Oedipus was fated to kill his father and lie with his mother. Appalled at this prospect, and now perhaps forgetting that the rumours in Corinth had given him reason to doubt his parentage, Oedipus resolved never to return to Corinth. As he made his way near Thebes he fell into an altercation with a man travelling by chariot. The man struck him and Oedipus killed him – a man old enough to be his father – in the brawl that ensued. Continuing now to Thebes, Oedipus discovered that the city was afflicted by the monstrous sphinx with a plague that could not be removed until someone solved the sphinx's riddle: what goes on four legs at dawn, on two at midday, and on three in the evening? Oedipus, thoroughly rational or as we might now say quick on the uptake, saw the answer: humankind, crawling on four limbs, walking on two legs, leaning on a stick. The hero who had rid Thebes of sphinx and plague won its recently bereaved queen in marriage: a woman old enough to be his mother.

The contingency here lies in Oedipus being at that particular cross-road, of all the cross-roads in Greece, at that particular time. Of course, there is a kind of rashness here as well. To fulfill the prophecy while you are making good your escape from the likelihood of it coming to pass takes a kind of single-mindedness cultivated to the point of stupidity: thus over-confidence – the kind of excessive confidence that seems to spring from insecurity and its denial – appears to be both the cause and effect of Oedipus' tragedy. His good sense, as it seemed, in putting distance between himself and Corinth, is his undoing. There are modern variations on the same theme. We recall a television drama some thirty years ago which turned on the idea that an apparently normal person was in fact a robot carrying a nuclear device. The robot, it was known, would detonate if it uttered particular words that had been programmed. The first task then appeared to be to convince the 'person' that he was a robot (the logic of this is not entirely clear, or our memory may be at fault). Finally convinced, the robot-person declared, 'But if I'm not...then I must be...' at which the screen flashed white, and went blank. One element of the underlying theme here is reminiscent of Rick Decard, the replicant-hunter of *Blade Runner*, to whom finally the thought seems to occur that he may be a replicant himself.

At any rate Oedipus' mixture of cleverness and stupidity repays study. Not just to kill and marry people of his parents' generation: looking up and about himself, as any street-wise person would do, he never seems to have looked *down*, not just to what was before his feet but to what his feet themselves could tell him. For Oedipus, almost uniquely, did not walk on four legs in the morning, since his feet were pinned together when he was left to die as a baby and had borne the marks ever since. His stupidity and a kind of knowingness – the cleverness that solved the riddle and won the throne – are of a piece. It is of this knowingness that Oedipus is an emblem, if we only attend to the story rightly.

> Sophocles is offering a diagnosis of 'knowingness': both a critique of its thinness as a way of being in the world, and an account of how it comes to take over a culture...*Oedipus Tyrannus* is a tale of abandonment. Oedipus is abandoned by his parents, and in response he abandons himself to thinking...He acts as though thinking could compensate him for his loss, but since there can be no compensation, the thinking has to become so enthusiastic, and so thin, that it blinds him to any recognition of loss. (Lear, 1998, pp. 47–8)

## III   The evasion of contingency

How have we come to this, this culture of knowingness in education that we described in the first section of this chapter? We have not learned from the thinkers who told us that contingency and finitude is our natural condition. We have interpreted Sophocles' play as if Oedipus was oedipal – as if Oedipus was acting out the Freudian unconscious desire to kill his father and sleep with his mother, when there is no evidence of oedipal wishes in the play (Lear, 1998, pp. 39–40), and as if oedipal wishes were themselves invariable laws of development. As if Freud himself proposed psychoanalysis as a certain cure, whose techniques could reliably be taught and learned. Adam Phillips (2002) convincingly argues that Freud is wholly ambivalent about the proposition that psychoanalysis has techniques, a possibility that seems subverted by the very idea of the unconscious, that 'saboteur of the ego's world of rules and methodological procedures. Indeed, from a psychoanalytical point of view following a rule could be re-described as obsessional neurosis' (p. xx). Phillips gives us a Freud very different from that of his biographers, who depict a resolute man of science, in control to the end, even in the matter of his own death. Like Darwin, Freud can be understood rather as reminding us of, even as celebrating, contingency and impermanence. Freud writes that psychoanalysis begins with 'a chance observation' (1981, *Studies on Hysteria*, II.3). He asks just how life can be lived 'with what remains', just as Darwin can be understood as asking 'How should we live if we take unredeemable transience seriously?' (Phillips 1999, p. 46).

> In Darwin's and Freud's view it was our relentless, unforgiving attachment to the available varieties of perfectionism – to idealizing our ideals – that consistently humiliated us. There was a will to pessimism in our choosing spurious, impossible ideals for ourselves; as though we had somehow become addicted to looking disappointing in our own eyes. (*ibid.*, p. 129)

Yet the Darwin too that has come down to our age has been turned into a proponent of certainty: the certainty that evolution guarantees optimality because anything less than optimality would be eliminated in the process of natural selection. Darwin himself, by contrast, emphasizes the oddities and blind alleys of evolution – the flightless birds and sightless moles (and, we might add, *homo sapiens* busily proceeding to make the planet uninhabitable) – and reminds himself never to say of a species that it is higher, ie more perfect, or lower. This is the Darwin who famously wrote of nature as 'clumsy' and 'blundering' rather than as embodying inexorable laws: 'What a book a devil's chaplain might write on the clumsy, wasteful, blundering, low and horridly cruel works of nature'.[7]

> For Darwin, imperfections were the mark of a historical progress. A perfect artificer could create a perfect human being, but an organism that was a layer of accretions and adaptations each of which has to make do with the material at hand, could only be the result of a historical process rife with contingencies and unforeseen changes. (Morson, p. 301)

So much for intelligent design. As Richard Rorty (1989) has suggested, our ability to accept the contingency of things might have been greater had Darwin, rather than Newton, been taken as the model scientific thinker and guide to 'Nature, and nature's laws'.

Philosophy too has tried to evade contingency. Much of Richard Rorty's book *Contingency, Irony, and Solidarity* (1989) can be read as an argument to this effect. The error of this evasion can also be read very satisfactorily from the reception of the texts that are usually taken to inaugurate systematic western philosophy, the Platonic dialogues. Consider for example how these have so often been taken to express Platonic doctrines, such as that of the Forms,[8] somewhat mysteriously dressed up with badinage between the interlocutors, biographical details about them (such as at the beginning of *Theaetetus*) or even descriptions of the location of the dialogue (*Phaedrus*). As for education, it is a minor scandal how many writers have been content to identify Plato's views on education with the conclusions that emerge from the *Republic*, eugenic infanticide (*Republic* 460), the abolition of the family and the establishment of communal nurseries included.

The literal, abstract or what might be called authoritarian reading here craves the universal and metaphysical and fails to register the particular and physical. Yet it is this latter which offers us much from which we can learn. For example, the teaching that occurs in the early dialogues is presented as occurring as the result of chance meetings with certain individuals, whose characters – Theaetetus', for instance – are sketched with some care.[9] The *Republic* only takes place because Polemarchus the son of Cephalus catches sight of Socrates and Glaucon on their way back from the Piraeus and insists they accompany him back to his house. The *Euthyphro* starts with a chance meeting between Socrates and Euthyphro in the porch of the Archon. The *Phaedrus* has as its opening words Socrates's greeting to Phaedrus whom he has come upon as the latter is making his way out of Athens to learn by heart a speech from the sophist Lysias: 'My dear Phaedrus, where are you coming from, and where are you going?' (Fancy trying to teach someone when you don't know where they're coming from! Really Socrates should acquaint himself with Phaedrus' learning style and establish, before proceeding further, what skills and competences he has already acquired.) Similar points could be made about many of the other dialogues.

The difference here is not between charming but philosophically slight earlier dialogues on the one hand and fully developed epistemological and metaphysical thesis in the later works such as *Republic, Laws* and *Timaeus* on the other. The difference is rather between two ways of thinking of and practising philosophy. In one, philosophy is conceived as a timeless curriculum of puzzles concerning for example the nature of knowledge, whether others' experiences are like our own, and whether we have free will. In the other, philosophy is the name of the lively process by which embodied, realistic and perhaps real people are challenged to examine their ideas and prejudices and to think more carefully and richly. They are often thrown into confusion, *aporia*, and seldom offered any answers. Many of the dialogues, as is well-known, fail to end 'satisfactorily'. In this conception the dialogues 'awaken and enliven the soul, arousing it to rational activity rather than lulling it into drugged passivity' (Nussbaum, 1986, p. 127) and Plato is to be credited less with eternal doctrines than what Seery (1996, p. 76) calls 'a slyly self-deprecating pedagogy'.

There are in turn two roughly corresponding conceptions of education – philosophy being, in Dewey's words (Dewey 1916, ch. 24), 'the theory of education in its most general phases' – and in particular of higher education. The first insists on the live contact between individuals that implies some minimal knowledge of a person. It is nicely caught in Newman's insistence in *The Idea of the University* (I.vi.8) that the university should 'know her children one by one'.[10] It underlies the Oxbridge tutorial system and other arrangements that take this as their model, and is thus easily caricatured as outdated and elitist. The second conception derives in part from the German idealist tradition, in which universities are seen as 'state institutions, supplying cadres that could assist the development of the state, and [as] ...sites of systematic research, particularly in science' (Barnett, 2003, p. 146). In this conception there is more interest in research than in teaching, and teaching tends to be conceived largely in terms of techniques for the dissemination of information (the internet, distance learning, interactive whiteboards, online discussion groups). The contrast here is somewhat crude, but we suspect it is recognizable to anyone who has worked in a British or North American university in recent years.

In short, the modernist – some would say Enlightenment – quest for equity and efficiency drives contingency from the university. Along with contingency much else disappears: principally the possibility of a relationship between a particular teacher and a particular pupil of the kind that Plato presents so carefully and movingly in the early dialogues. Such a relationship is, as Rorty writes, a matter of 'the sparks that leap back and forth between teacher and student' (1999, p. 126).[11] Such sparks are the source of the realisation of forms of human freedom that otherwise cannot be imagined. Live and autonomous teachers, instead of interactive learning packages (*ibid.*, p. 125: Rorty writes 'computer terminals', but of course technology makes progress), enact that freedom by teaching what they know intimately and care for passionately, 'without regard to any larger end, much less any institutional plan' (*ibid.*). And that of course involves a considerable risk – that of exposing what you love to scrutiny and perhaps rejection.[12]

## IV   The abstract state

Recall again the unhappy condition of education as we described it in Section I. Young people driven by a kind of perfectionism, fear of failure, haunted by the thought that anything less than straight 'A' grades will entail disaster and dissolution. Their teachers, meanwhile, not permitted to rest satisfied with what might be called ordinary knowledge of their pupils' and students' performance, but constantly required to show evidence, display their criteria – and no doubt the criteria for *those* criteria, to minute meetings, log conversations, record and account. And all in the name of that very reasonable transparency which, demanding that everything be shown and open to audit and inspection, becomes obsessed with the anxiety that it is *merely* being shown, so that the whole process constantly feeds its own neurosis.

This, it seems to us, is a manifestation of scepticism, understood as the concern that our experience is not properly secured to the world, that what we seem to perceive is not the truth out there but a fabrication in here, within ourselves: that what we take for real may merely be replicated. Perhaps we ourselves are replicants replete with false memories, as from the film *Blade Runner*, creatures who like Oedipus conceal their fear of not belonging with a veil of knowingness. This scepticism is a recipe for what Cavell (1990) calls 'despair'. It is there in the madness of King Lear who cannot respond to ordinary love but must have it quantified and audited. Unlike the blinded Gloucester and the self-blinded Oedipus after his tragedy has unfolded, who both discover a kind of wisdom in their lack of literal sight (Gloucester memorably says 'I stumbled when I saw': *King Lear* Act IV, Sc I), Lear imagines that an auditor's perspective will give him insight. (See below, Chapter 12, Narrative and number.) As Eagleton (2003) notes, this is connected with Lear's longing for abstraction, his fantasy of dis-embodiment.[13] It is there in the neurosis that to one degree or other runs through contemporary formal education in the west.

There are perhaps three broad ways of responding to this scepticism and what it brings along with it. The first is continually to show how scepticism is unwarranted: that our ordinary knowledge of the world and of other people will in general do perfectly well in the sense that we add nothing to it by adducing grounds or criteria. To yearn for such grounds or criteria, as Raimond Gaita (2003, p. 52) puts it, makes us spectators in the world. It thus raises us reassuringly above it and its attendant risks rather than making us part of it, wholly and inex-tricably caught up in its contingencies. This response takes a familiar enough Wittgensteinian form, perhaps as developed by Stanley Cavell, and it is a continual task because scepticism is a constant temptation and so the urge to solve it tends only to re-instate it. It is the dissolu-tion, rather, of scepticism that we should undertake, accepting that our ordinary knowledge of the world is born and ends in finitude; it is bumpy and ultimately unsecured. This will not cease to be the case however many meta-analyses we make or however many millions of students we study (cp. *n*.1).

The second response is to regard the search for certainty and for an end to doubt as characteristic symptoms of modernity and thus as potentially curable, or at least open to amelioration, by the treatments offered by writers who have explored the costs and contradictions of the modernist project. If for instance meaning can never be tied down but is always subject to deferral, if signs only ever point to other signs, then we must learn to live without the possibility of ultimate appeal to the knowledge of origins, or to self-authenticating truths, that con-stitute what has been called the 'metaphysics of presence'. It is worth recalling here that one issue at stake between more and less radical versions of 'postmodernism' – to use that loose term for convenience – is whether we truly must and can live with unreason (and uncertainty) or whether our attempts to do so only end up admitting it in a domesticated form. This second response, then, has the power to address scepticism and despair in a particularly far-reaching way.

A third response begins from the acknowledgement that we are indeed obscure to ourselves and will continue to be so. We shall never wholly understand the meaning of our desires. To see human beings like this is to depart from the prevalent vision of democracy in the west. This vision, writes Lear (1998, pp. 28–9):

> Treats humans as preference-expressing political atoms, and pays little attention to subatomic structure. Professional pollsters, political scientists, and pundits portray society as an agglomeration of these atoms. The only irrationality they recognize is the failure of these preference-expressing monads to conform to the rules of rational-choice theory.

Neo-liberal democracies that foreground choice and the satisfaction of the voter-as-consumer offer a profoundly limited conception of rationality, and this flaw is perhaps most worrying in the context of education. For education, perhaps uniquely among social practices, has the role of forming preferences and not simply of satisfying them (Jonathan, 1997).

Nietzsche believed that the rise of democracy and tragedy at the same time in Greece was not a coincidence. He writes (*Birth of Tragedy: attempt at a self-criticism*, § 4) that the 'good, rigid resolve of the older Greeks for pessimism, for the tragic myth, for the image of everything terrible, evil, cryptic, destructive and deadly' gave birth to the 'Dionysiac madness', the dithyramb, dance and chorus out of which Attic tragedy developed. As the *polis* became more democratic, rational and philosophical, with violence replaced by argument, tragic drama was the countervailing force, the echo of an older and more mythic age. Lear (1998, p. 30) comments that Sophocles' message to the Athenian citizens who came to the theatre was that, like Oedipus, they ignored the realm of unconscious meaning at their peril. 'From this perspective, democratic citizens need to maintain a certain humility in the face of meanings which remain opaque to human reason. We need to be wary that what we take to be an exercise of reason will both hide and express an irrationality of which we remain unaware'.

In short, a culture that is rational, calculative and utilitarian, that associates value with choice and the measurable satisfaction of preferences, that is obsessed by audit and accountability, whose most significant rituals now seem to be, in Power's (1997) subtitle, those of verification, seems to stand in need of something like myth, or tragedy, to recall it to a different order of things and remind it of the contingency and finitude of human affairs. Democracy, Cavell (1990, p. 52) suggests, might usefully be thought of as 'the public manifestation of the individual situation of adolescence, the time of possibilities under pressure to consent to actualities'. That is to say, one of the most vivid and significant features of democracy is not its capacity to maximise any particular condition such as freedom, or individual happiness. It is rather its willingness to allow a society to pause and even haver at the crossroads (p. 52) wondering which of its so to speak youthful aspirations it wishes to realise. And that, we would say, is not simply a rational process, still less a knowing one. It is one where we need to listen to other voices, speaking an older and less abstract language. If Oedipus had paused and listened thus, less streetwise and more cross-roads – thoughtful, things might have gone better for him. And in the same way so might they for us.

# 10
## Unfinished Business: Education Without Necessity

> You enter; they are waiting for you. You have nothing in particular, nothing set to say, which is the general condition of philosophical discourse. But here, in addition, you have no long- or short-range aim set by an institutional function...There you are, given over to indeterminate requirements.
>
> Does this mean that each teacher in your department speaks of what he or she likes? – No, it means that no one is protected, and above all in his or her own eyes, by prescribed rules. And all must give their names to what they say, without pleading necessity; and all, like stutterers, must head toward what they want in order to say it.
>
> (Jean-François Lyotard, 1993, pp. 70, 71)

## I

Education itself from time to time stands in need of therapy, as we noted in the Introduction. One current sign of this is that the various kinds of language that we use for talking and writing about teaching and education show signs of strain. In the UK for instance there is a technical language largely spawned by the National Curriculum for schools and all its works: Key Stage 3, benchmarking, value-added, baseline assessment – a mechanistic language which seems to long to be put into bullet-points. Higher education has been less affected than schooling, but there are ominous signs: the language of aims and learning outcomes that regimes of quality assurance have brought with them, and the very idea of quality as something that might be controlled as if a seminar were an item on a production line. Then there is the language of management: empowerment, ownership, account-ability, targets going forward. The urge to control and to eliminate contingency seems central here, as we have noticed elsewhere (cp. Chapter 9), and the argot of 'risk management', a new discipline and a new career for the bureaucrats, has consequently evolved as if to ensure that nothing, not even chance, is left to chance.

We say these languages show signs of strain because they completely fail to speak to our experience of being teachers, at any of the various levels and in any of the contexts in which we have taught, and we know from our many conversations with colleagues that this sense is widespread. Worse still, these languages do a kind of violence to our experience, silencing the voice that tries to articulate the business of being a teacher and learner more richly, sensitively and truly. There is something deeply alienating about listening to – and joining in – talk of 'performance indicators' or 'module delivery' as if they are the edu-cational reality to which one's professional and personal being must accommodate itself. And we think that talk of therapy is appropriate here because these languages and the forms of rationality – scientistic, performative, managerial – that they express have the characteristics of *compulsions*. Their fascination comes perhaps partly from the way that they appeal to our deep longing to be in control, and our terror of chaos and personal responsibility (cp. Chapter 13).

There is yet another problem in writing about teaching in a standard journal article or book chapter. Respectable academic prose can also fail to do justice to the experience of teaching and learning, as the many students and teachers who have recoiled from educational literature in despair can attest. The tropes of academic research, in particular, do not necessarily make for readability: the more scholarly the book is, the more footnotes the article lists, perhaps the more tenuous the connection may seem to be with the complexities and felt particulars of daily experience. Then too there is the danger of seeming to privilege research over teaching: as if teaching (generally less esteemed in the university than research) is all very well, but much better if it leads to the kind of thing that counts for the latest Research Assessment Exercise. We can only say that we are uncom-fortably aware of these difficulties. It is interesting to reflect that this book is unlikely to be seen as good academic research: for the gold standard of educational research is the international, peer-reviewed journal article, on the spurious grounds that since cutting-edge research in physics or psychology appears in such outlets, so must research in every other subject. As if research always consisted in making fresh discoveries, always something new to be advertised to a world greedy for novelties.

The difficulty of this chapter, and indeed of the book as a whole, is that of offering general philosophical reflection while at the same doing justice to reality as we know it in our lives, or as Martha Nussbaum more elegantly writes (1986, p. 227), 'combining the rigour of speculative argument with sensitive responses to the particulars of human experience'. At the very beginning of western philosophy Plato felt the force of this acutely. On some interpretations (eg Hadot, 1995, Fendt and Rozema, 1998) he attempted in his early work at least to explore philosophical questions without losing sight of their essentially embodied nature. That is to say, they are questions for real individuals, living historically and socially contextualised lives, subject to frailties and contingencies particular to them while at the same time familiar to us. Accordingly Plato wrote his early work in dialogue form (the later work too, but there the dialogue is more of a formality), presenting Socrates as the philosophical *educator* of Euthyphro, Phaedrus, Theaetetus and the rest. Euthyphro for example is a self-righteous young man: his proposal to prosecute his own father for wrong-doing (complicity in the death of a slave) displays philosophical wrong-headedness about the nature of the right and the good, but this is motivated wrong-headedness. It springs from the kind of person Euthyphro is, so that to lead him to a kind of self-knowledge and to increase his philosophical acumen are just different dimensions of the same thing. In the dialogue that bears his name, then, we do not find timeless philosophical topics dressed up in dialogue form in order to make them more palatable to the reader.

It is worth quoting Fendt and Rozema at some length. They write that the early dialogues are

> A shaping falsity into which the reader's desire for truth (and perhaps many other things) is poured... As a medicine, the dialogic arguments make the reader stronger, for rather than learning what the argument is and remembering the conclusion, the reader must figure out...what has gone wrong in the arguments, and how. And since the last argument is not the right answer, or its conclusion does not exactly follow from the argument, the answer is never clearly given in the back of the book, to be remembered for the exam while the rest is forgotten. Any answer must be worked out in thought and worked out in life...All of this is done under the aegis of plot and character, in particular places and times, with peripeties and recognitions that open into Humour and Irony: Joy's children... (Fendt and Rozema, 1998, pp. 163–4)

For these kinds of reasons we take in what follows what might be called a Platonic approach to thinking about our own teaching, its successes, failures and values. The seminar depicted is something of a collage of real and concocted episodes from various seminars that 'George' teaches on the theory of social science. George is both ourselves and not ourselves. (Teaching is often a strange business of being yourself and not being yourself, in any case.) The students are combined, in a sense that they, if any of them read this, will recognize, and their names are changed. This chapter is not held up as evidence of anything whatsoever, of what works or doesn't, of good, mediocre or disastrous practice. It is best thought of as a work of fiction in any case. It does not so much represent reality as remember the humour and irony, and the joy, that George has found in teaching like this, if this is teaching. The reader puzzled by any of this will find some more conventional, abstract reflections at the end of the chapter. But the thinking is *in* the dialogue as much as in what appears in Section III.

## II

*George*: Hello, everybody. Sorry I'm late. I was stopped in the street by one of the Registrar's department, anxious to remind me that I should have submitted a revised version of this degree's aims and outcomes ahead of the forthcoming Faculty Review...

(*Merry laughter around the room*)
*Matthew*: You mean we have aims? But you don't believe in them!
*Tom*: I thought you were just going to put down that quotation from Lyotard, what is it, 'to go there without knowing where?'[1]

(*More laughter*)
*Tom*: And then the outcome would be, well –
*Sally*: 'Here we are, wherever that is!'
*Vaz*: It could be the title of that Gauguin picture on the front of the Course Outline last year, 'Where have we been? Who are we? Whatever next?!!'[2] Or, as we used to call it, 'Where the fuck are we?'

(*Still more laughter*)
*Matthew*: Seriously, though, why do you have to do that, why do we have to have aims and stuff all the time? Like with today's session, if we knew exactly where we were supposed to end up at eleven o'clock there couldn't be any exploration. Or it would be 'to understand the

social implications of Darwin's theory of evolution' or something as bland as that.

*Hinna*: Or the lack of implications.

*George*: Nobody checked the website to see the aims of this seminar, then?

*Vaz*: Can't catch us that way. We don't have aims, we have Foreword and Afterword!

*(Jane, who started the module several weeks late after an unfortunate vacation incident that required her to assist the Thailand police with their enquiries, is manifestly baffled.)*

*George*: Can anyone bring Jane up to speed on why we don't have Aims and Outcomes?

*Sally (reading from Course Outline)*: 'There is a school of thought that believes all teaching should be characterized by a clear statement of aims on the one hand and of outcomes on the other (and naturally the outcomes should reflect the aims). Some would say that this conception of education is simply commonsense. However this module takes a critical view (aims to take a critical view, if you like) of this conception (the outcome is that you will learn that such a conception of teaching and education can be challenged). Indeed, the critique of performativity (one dimension of such a conception) is at the heart of the module (if modules can have hearts: we shall wonder about the easy use of metaphors). It is not therefore possible to indicate clear aims (the very notion of clarity is suspect, we shall discover) and outcomes without self-contradiction or bad faith. However there is much to be said for some preliminary indication of the scope of each session of this module, and of where we might be at the end of it. These are therefore supplied, as Foreword and Afterword respectively. Those who crave aims and outcomes can substitute those titles, and rest content'.

*George*: How does that sound to you, Jane?

*Jane*: Oh yes. Like when I was travelling this summer, I didn't have *aims*, did I? What I wanted could only emerge when I got to know a place or people, I couldn't know what there was to want in, say, China until I got to know it a bit. I was travelling to see *what there was to want*. Does that make sense?

*Tom*: Certainly does. And what (*affects ironic voice*) are the outcomes of your travel?

*Jane (makes rude gesture at Tom and ignores his question)*: Why is clarity suspect, though? Is there something wrong with being clear about things?

*Hinna*: We talked about that last week. Clear language suggests language that you can see right through to what's beneath, to the reality it so to speak labels –

*Tom*: It suggests language takes its meaning from the reality it represents, while a lot of language actually *creates* reality, poetry does this, and the meaning of 'Tuesday' is largely that it isn't 'Wednesday' or 'Thursday'.

*Jane*: Tuesday is Tuesday because it isn't Wednesday. I can see this module is going to teach me a lot!

(*laughter*)

*George*: But we do have a Foreword for this session...

*Andrew*: 'Evolution doesn't have an aim: evolution evolves. So will this seminar's discussion, if you all make sure you've read the newspaper article, "The arts of seduction".'[3]

(*groans*)

*George*: Do these groans mean that none of you have read the article?

*Penny*: No, it means that the idea of a seminar on evolution evolving is a bit too –

(*various cries of* 'Neat', 'Glib', 'Yuk')

*George*: Point taken, sorry. Look, we haven't done what we generally do, go round the room and utter a few sentences. Carol?

*Carol*: (*after a pause*) Feeling knackered already, and only a few weeks into term!

*Sam*: The slugs in our house have made it up to the first floor. There was an enormous one in the bath this morning. (*Sympathetic laughter: Sam's slugs have become legendary.*)

*Michelle*: Pass.

*Chris*: I've got three essay deadlines on the same day next week, I shall go mental.

*Katie* (*who has been shifting in her seat through this, interrupts*): Look, why do we do this every time? I mean, I don't mind, and we can always pass, but we all know each other by now and we get on with each other...why do we do it?

*George*: To be honest, I don't really know. Something about having the chance to put down any baggage we've brought with us. I was going to say my car's having its service and MOT today, I'm waiting for a phone call to say the cost is going to be monstrous. Once I've said that – now I've said that! – perhaps it won't clutter up my head so much. Something about being here in this seminar in person, and not bringing just the academic part of yourself.

*Katie*: Well, ok. Perhaps we might cut to the chase a bit quicker, that's all.

*Matthew*: Get to the outcomes quicker, you mean!

*Katie*: Ok, ok, piss off.

*Tom*: I've suddenly seen why there's all this scene-setting at the beginning of the *Phaedrus* – all that stuff about the river and the plane tree and so on. It's the same kind of thing, isn't it: Socrates doesn't just touch Phaedrus intellectually, he touches him –

(*bawdy laughter*)

*Carol*: You know what I'm going to say: Jean Brodie, *Dead Poets' Society*…

*George*: The dangers of education being more than academic, more than just intellectual stuff. Yes, very dangerous stuff, this education. Is that alright, Katie?

*Katie*: Yes. The *Phaedrus* point helps. I can't stop expecting more of a classic seminar, though, know what I mean?

*George*: Let's finish the round, then, and then we'll go classic. Or as classic as we're ever likely to go.

(*The round takes its course: there are worries about next year after graduation, a tribute to a lecturer who proved more flexible over a missed tutorial than expected, complaints about library opening hours. No solutions are offered, or expected.*)

*George*: Right then. Would someone like to give us a brief summary –

*Vaz*: Just a minute. 'Evolution doesn't have an aim'. That's not quite right, is it? Despite all we've been saying about performativity – about the dangers of effectiveness taking over all other values – that's exactly what evolution aims at. It aims at maximum effectiveness: the survival of the fittest!

*Matthew*: Of course that's right. A species or an animal that isn't effective, isn't an effective hunter or grazer or whatever, just won't survive.

*George*: True enough. But what about those species that do very well by sitting around quietly for millions of years? Cockroaches would be a good example. If the planet goes up in nuclear smoke apparently the cockroaches are most likely to survive.

*Matthew*: Well, then, they're very effective, aren't they?

*George*: It's just that talk of effectiveness carries overtones of dog-eat-dog aggression, the kind of thing that leads to social Darwinism and the idea that the poor shouldn't be helped and public services shouldn't be subsidized. The cockroach is hardly an example of effectiveness in that sense.

*Sam*: Or the case in that book we were looking at, *Almost Like a Whale*.[4] The AIDS virus: how millions of Americans deny Darwinian evolution and believe in Creationism even though the evidence of evolution is staring them in the face...

*Penny*: Because the Aids virus has learned to kill people slowly, because this means its host lives longer and so can infect more people and spread the virus more widely. Yes: seems strange to think of killing people more slowly as a matter of improved *effectiveness*.

*George*: At the very least, being less effective turns out to be more effective here. Which suggests the notion of 'effectiveness' isn't very helpful. It's more of a rhetorical term that people reach for when they want to argue for social Darwinism.

*Chris*: That makes me think. You know, I went down to those interviews for Harold Henderson Consulting. And they got us into teams to solve problems together. What they were looking for wasn't the kind of person who tried to take the team over and tell everyone else what to do. They wanted people who could genuinely work as part of a team. That means sitting back sometimes when other people are explaining their ideas, or trying to help someone who's diffident have her voice heard, because perhaps she's got the best ideas of all.

*George*: You mean the effective team player isn't always effective in the most in-your-face kind of way?

*Chris*: I suppose I do. And that seems to mean that I'm agreeing with your point.

*George*: Or take the baby of the human species. It's dependent for longer than the young of any other species. It can't manage on its own for over a year, years maybe if you imagine an infant trying to fend for itself in the wild. Yet the reindeer calf, if that's what you call their young, can follow the herd and keep up within hours of being born. How does the human baby survive? In what sense does it survive because it is the 'fittest'?

*Katie*: Ah, we did that in Psychology. There's something about the curve of the baby's head going down into the neck. When we see that we go all gooey and we want to pick it up and cuddle it.

*Matthew*: Ugh. Some of us more than others.

*Katie*: Those of use who're *normal*, Matthew. Anyway, that's how babies survive. They make us want to protect them – we're hard-wired to do so. Apart from Matthew.

*Hinna*: To protect them: they appeal to us because they are so vulnerable?
*Matthew*: I see what's coming. The survival of the fittest for babies means being best at being vulnerable! The most helpless and ineffectual baby wins the prize!

(*General mayhem, babble of voices, something of a sense among some of the students that they've been sold dodgy goods.*)
*George*: We might come back to that later. Maybe this is the point where we should turn to that newspaper article. Where shall we start? Why have they drawn this picture of a man with a peacock's tail?
*Tom*: Because the peacock is a bit of puzzle for Darwinists. The flashy tail is a dead liability. It's not going to do much for your camouflage, it's hardly going to help you run away from predators faster.
*Anthea* (*diving into her bag*): Look what I found in the shop this morning! (*Displays greetings card. It shows one deer looking mournfully at another, who has what seems to be a classic target, comprising concentric rings, painted on his chest.*) He's saying: 'That's one hell of a birth-mark, Hal!'

(*General laughter*)
*Anthea*: I bought it for my cousin, it's her birthday next week. I hadn't seen the connection!
*George*: So how do we explain the peacock's tail – or the occasional deer that enjoys dangerous pursuits?
*Chris*: The theory is that the peacock has this tail to say to the female of the species, 'I've got talent to burn, baby. I can go about looking like this and still run rings around foxes and human beings with guns. Impressed, huh?'
*Alice*: The peacock is the George Best of the animal kingdom.

(*Baffled silence*)
*Alice* (*She is a mature student. She explains slowly, as if speaking to the exceptionally dim*): George Best was a footballer –
*Several*: Oh, another 1960s footnote!

(*Laughter. Most sessions of this class contain at least one such footnote. It is something of a puzzle, for Alice's references are hardly obscure: most of the other students are well aware who George Best is. It seems to be a way of acknowledging that Alice is at least twice the age of the other students, of deferring to her without really deferring. She appears to enjoy the role.*)
*Alice*: – a footballer who became the first real popular idol. He dressed really fashionably, if any of you know what Carnaby Street was –

(*Cries of 'footnote, footnote'*)
*Alice*: – and the girls used to go wild over him.
*Jane*: Did you dress like that in the 1960s, George?

(*Laughter*)
*George* (*primly*): Certainly not. I wore well-pressed trousers from Marks & Spencer, and concentrated on my Chemistry homework.

(*murmurs of 'Poor George'*)
*George*: Eventually someone is going to explain what this man-peacock is doing in that newspaper article.
*Vaz*: The writer says that creativity is a puzzle. What makes a Mozart or a Rembrandt? Especially given that most of these characters die in poverty, starving in a garret or whatever. Why did the caveman paint pictures of animals on the wall of the cave? He was impressing the female of the species with his creativity. He was saying 'Come in and see my etchings!' So that's what creativity really is: it's the man impressing the female with his creativity, showing her he has more talent than the other cavemen, to increase his chances of, er, spreading his genes.
*George*: Thank you for that neat and tactful summary. How impressed are we with this story about creativity? Do we think it's true?
*Matthew*: It certainly explains why most artists, novelists, poets and so on are male...

*Several* (*amid general uproar, in which the ownership of voices is unclear*):
   You mean the ones we've heard of because they had the money to promote their careers –
   You're completely ignoring all the social factors –
   Have you ever read Virginia Woolf, *A Room of One's Own*?
   There are *thousands* of women novelists, they just got excluded from the canon, yet look at Virago Press –

(*We rejoin the discussion after several minutes.*)
*Sam*: There's a small problem here. Those cave paintings are often deep, deep down narrow tunnels, you had to crawl sometimes for hundreds of metres to paint them or see them. It's hardly likely you'd paint them there if you wanted the woman you fancied to come and look at them.
*George*: Well, I don't know how we're supposed to have these discussions if people start bringing facts into them. But seriously, does

this story about peacocks and cave-paintings fit into anything else we know or think we know about what the opposite sexes find attractive in each other, remembering of course that the whole picture is complicated by the point that for many people it isn't the opposite sex but the same sex?

*Katie*: We did this in Psychology last year, with questionnaires and stuff. The general conclusion seemed pretty clear. Women go for alpha males, men who they think will be good providers, look after them and their children. Men go for women with obvious sexual characteristics, big bosoms and big hips, because these are the signs that they'll be able to bear them children. Which is what men want, even if not consciously: to spread their genes.

*Penny*: That's right. I certainly want an alpha male. Nobody wants a loser.

*Sally*: So why do I keep falling for totally unsuitable men?

*Katie*: There you are, you've said it yourself, you know they're unsuitable because you're programmed to be averse to them. I don't know why you keep falling for them – loose connection or something.

*Sally*: Oh, *thanks*. But on your theory I shouldn't be attracted to them in the first place.

*George*: Leaving aside the issue of possible problems in Sally's wiring, I wonder if we might try a little experiment. Would you all take a couple of minutes to write a lonely hearts ad. Thirty words to spell out what you're looking for in a partner. You personally. No questions. Just do it.

(*Two minutes of concentrated and silent activity*)
*George*: So what have we got? Let's go round the room and see what your top two qualities were, the two things you most wanted in a partner...

(*Collation on the blackboard reveals a largely uniform picture*)
*George*: Right, then. Nearly all of you want slim partners with a good sense of humour. GSOH! If you look at the lonely hearts ads in the newspaper or *Time Out* or wherever you'll find that you're the same as the rest of humanity. Good sense of humour seems to win every time, generally followed by a predilection for log fires and anything that makes you sound sensitive and soulful. Where is the drive and energy of Penny's alpha male, bringing home the mammoth steaks or the mammoth city bonuses to feed the hungry family? Where are those broad child-rearing hips all the men were supposed to want to spread their genes by way of?

*Matthew*: A good sense of humour has evolutionary value, though. If you've got a good sense of humour, then you'll...you'll be less likely to fall out with your partner, the marriage will be stronger.

*George*: Well, fine. I only want to say that we seem to be moving further and further away from the crude picture of the alpha caveman impressing the little lady with his surplus creativity. Always assuming, of course, that it was him rather than her that painted the pictures in the first place, which I don't think we have any evidence for whatsoever. Yes, I'll appeal to facts when it suits me. What's our verdict on this newspaper article, then? Are we convinced that, little known to them, Mozart and Van Gogh and the rest were really trying to impress the women? So that the whole of aesthetics, and the notes on the backs of records – sorry, CDs – and museum catalogues and so on are just a big mistake, since art is really about something else altogether?

*Vaz*: That's not fair to the writer. Something can have an origin in something, but still mean something else.

(*Cries of 'eh?'*)

*Vaz*: Like, the Bible may be a collection of Near-Eastern myths and legends, but it's come to signify something else to lots of people. Or a particular way of dressing comes about who knows how, but it comes to mean 'student'.

*George*: That's certainly helpful. So in the context here, as a matter of evolutionary psychology what we now call art may have started with young cavemen trying to impress potential mates with their paintings of bison, which is what Geoffrey Miller, the evolutionary psychologist quoted,[5] would have us believe. But that would be a long way from suggesting that art is nothing more than that.

*Matthew* (*reading from newspaper article*): 'Miller acknowledges that artists may not be conscious of what they're really doing'. *Really* doing. Either Miller, or the journalist who wrote the article, or both, do seem to think that art is nothing more than that. What Van Gogh is really doing is not creating art at all!

*Jane*: You're just trying to rubbish the article on the grounds of a few careless ways of putting things. I thought it was really interesting, it made me think.

*Vaz*: You were impressed with the article, Jane, you thought this guy Miller had quite a creative idea there?

*Jane*: Yes, absolutely.

*Vaz*: So he's quite a creative thinker, in your view?

*Jane*: Yes, and I don't see why everybody has to...

*Matthew* (*interrupting*): Jane's walked straight into the trap! Nice one, Vaz!

*Jane*: Trap? What trap?

*Matthew*: Well, if Miller's a creative thinker with creative ideas, and if being creative is just an evolutionary throwback to trying to get a mate, then little does Miller know it but what he was trying to do here was pull the girls!

*Vaz*: And Jane's been pulled!

(*Assorted laughter and cheers*)

*Penny*: So if Miller's theory is right, then we can discount it because he isn't producing a theory at all, but getting Jane's juices going! If he's right, he's wrong!

*Jane*: You clever sods.

*George*: Very neat. What you've spotted is that if taken too far these evolutionary theories turn out to be what's called 'self-annulling'. They offer an explanation for things that is so powerful that they explain themselves away too. It's a bit like trying to say that everything's in the genes: that there are criminal genes, gay genes, aggressive genes. If there was a gene for coming up with genetic explanations then we wouldn't take such explanations seriously. They wouldn't be the rational, scientific processes they claim to be, but just the outcome of having a particular sequence of DNA. And the same would be true of my criticism, the one I've just made. So there would be no place for argument, discussion, persuasion – there would just be these animals we call humans barking at each other as a result of their genetic programmes. Yes, I can see it coming: 'a good description of this seminar'. Anyway, time to stop barking. This point about 'self-annulling theories' is the kind of thing you may find you grasp one moment and lose your bearings with the next, and sometimes, as Jane seemed to imply, you find yourself wondering if it's just a clever trick. So we'll start on Tuesday by going back over it.

## III

When these things go well, there is a sense of flow. Discussion goes where it goes – it evolves – not without some steering on the part of Socrates (or Plato, or whoever is pulling the strings or writing the words here) but the students too have a good eye for what is relevant and what is tangential. The badinage is not tangential or irrelevant. The humour, almost all of it affectionate, is a major part of what anchors the participants in the seminar as flesh and blood individuals – 'in particular places and times' (Fendt and Rozema, quoted above, p. 155) and not, as one said once, as note-takers, brains on trolleys or examination question-spotters. George senses that humour and irony are crucial here, but finds it hard to say quite why. It is the essence of irony that you move between different perspectives: perhaps this is connected with the 'examination of underlying assumptions' listed as one of the module's non-aims. The occasional use of language which might have struck an earlier generation as inappropriate is interesting. Its use is almost always ironic; and to receive it unjudgementally, George theorizes, reassures the students that they are accepted here as they are and do not have to wear a mask.

George also senses the importance of educational *space*. Some rooms lend themselves to this kind of seminar, and some do not. Students at his university complain about the seminars in other subjects that regularly descend into silence, which the tutor seems to feel obliged to fill by going over the last lecture again. Perhaps there is a connection with the fact that so many of these seminar rooms have desks in rows facing the front, where naturally the tutor stands or sits. None of the university's senior managers, as increasingly they are called, seems very interested in this problem; perhaps all this talk of the information age and the delivery of modules is having its effect, and the default conception of students as disembodied, passive consumers of knowledge – brains on trolleys – is being steadily reinforced. If George put potted plants and posters around the seminar room he regularly uses, most of his colleagues would probably think he was going soft in the head. Plato regularly sketches the setting of his dialogues with some care, often to the bewilderment of scholarly commentators who cannot see why he doesn't get on with the philosophical action straightaway.

The students are real as well as fictive. Katie, for instance, is disposed to be impressed by what goes on in that scientific department, Psychology, and her craving for certainty seems more than academic. Jane is often irked by what she sees as mere cleverness, an impatience which has more than once turned out to be valuable in a room of clever students. Chris seems to find contributing an embarrassment, which he sometimes tries to hide by affecting the tones of a particularly solemn American television documentary. If these seminars do their job, none of these people will be quite the same at the end of the year, and the change will be more than an intellectual one. Katie will need less certainty, Jane's impatience will be more forgiving, Chris will be more comfortable with the fact that he is a bright and articulate man.

It is part of the flow, or evolution, of the proceedings that there are no *techniques* being used here. That is to say, George thinks of himself as one who does not deploy an array of skills, as if they could be brought out again for the first-year seminar tomorrow. This is not altogether clear-headed of him, perhaps not wholly honest, because the knowledgeable onlooker could easily enough identify certain skills here, such as the use of eye-contact and the ability to re-phrase and reflect. George perhaps means that he has never acquired these *as* skills: that if he possesses them they are rather ways of being with people that he has grown into. Much may hang on that distinction. And he would certainly insist that nothing here is concealed: that is, nothing covert is being practised on these students, as it would be if he started seminars with a 'round' purely in order to get the students more relaxed and ready to talk. The notion of manipulation is worth exploring. We none of us like to think we are manipulative, but perhaps all teaching contains elements of manipulation or even arts of seduction – trying to put students at their ease, to get through to them on a personal level, and so on. George worries about this. He would say that he makes great efforts to help students understand what he calls the 'stage machinery', the talk of aims and outcomes and so on, that exercises a potentially bewitching power on the intellect. Something important is lost (perhaps more than something) if we expect our learning to be as tidy as Quality Assessment seems to require it to be. Student social scientists should surely bring their developing intellectual powers to bear on that familiar social science topic, education, including their own education. If performativity is one of the greatest challenges in our age to humane and imaginative education, to education that evolves – that has its own dynamic – rather than trundling mechanically from banal aims to pre-ordained outcomes, then students as well as their teachers need to grasp what is being done to them, often in their name, and to learn to criticize it. George's high, evangelical tone on such matters has the soothing effect of repressing another of his worries, which is that perhaps there is something a bit self-indulgent going on in his seminars.

Not everything goes smoothly here, though. Loose ends are often left hanging, unsatisfactory lines of argument are not always nailed down. 'The answer is never clearly given in the back of the book', to quote Fendt and Rozema (above) for the last time. Many an *aporia* is encountered, there are lacunae, marginal matters that push their way to the centre of things, the injustices that occur when something demands to be phrased, ought to be able to be phrased, but nevertheless cannot yet be phrased.[6] All of which takes us neatly into postmodern approaches to social science, but still... Then there are those students – some seven in this group – who never speak before the whole class, except maybe to utter some nervous platitude in the 'round', or to answer a direct question. They follow the discussion, quick-eyed and interested, and join in the laughter, and often achieve the highest marks. Something seems in need of being addressed here. In the absence of necessity perhaps it would be wrong, as well as pointless, to compel these students to speak. Reticence may be behovely. They are good stutterers, still heading towards what they want in order to say it.

On a bad day the loose ends are a concern. How much simpler it is to inculcate knowledge, and then check that the students have acquired it, train them in discrete skills and ensure that they know how to exercise them. Those academics who manage to find the whole business so straightforward can seem enviable: they have 'a corpus, a method, a bibliography, a strategy' (Lyotard, 1993, p. 73). At other times the very riskiness of education, its being a matter of chance rather than necessity, is exhilarating:

> You like what is unfinished. Nothing of what you write will be authoritative. You lend yourself willingly to this prescription: 'to go there, without knowing there'. You're certain that nobody can do it, least of all yourself. (*ibid.*, p. 74)

# Part III

# Redeeming Philosophy, Redeeming Therapy

# 11
## Beyond Cure

Sleep, my fancies and my wishes,
  Sleep a little and wake strong,
The same but different and take my blessing –
  A cradle-song.
And sleep, my various and conflicting
  Selves I have so long endured,
Sleep in Asclepius' temple
  And wake cured.

(Louis MacNeice, Autumn Journal XXIV)

Perhaps we need to be cured of the idea that, in the area of what is sometimes called mental health and illness, we need to be cured. That is to say: perhaps talk of illness here is misleading. And, more than this, if anything is sick here maybe it is not the self or selves – as if it were just as though a lung or lungs, kidney or kidneys, were diseased. *If* anything is sick: what a difference it makes if, like Hamlet, we think of the time as being out of joint, or our world as itself schizophrenic. It is our investment in, addiction to, the medical analogy that can seem wrong and, more than wrong, pathological – requiring more than correction as a matter of fact. Requiring the therapy not of being countered, opposed, but shown to be an idea we are often better off without. Of being, in the end, dissolved, drained of its power to haunt us.

To begin, then, there are many conditions, not all of them pleasant, to which human beings are susceptible. They fall in love, grow disenchanted with professional sport, experience depression, become fascinated with mathematics or skateboarding or wild birds. They believe they have been passed over for promotion, or abducted by aliens. They turn into grumpy middle-aged men who can find nothing to praise in the younger generation or become exasperated by the inanities of television. They hear voices that enjoin them to give away their worldly possessions, to commit murder or to eat more cheese. Perhaps they learn to see the world in a more charitable light, or they think, on the basis of what seems to others scanty evidence, that people are out to kill them.

Now some and only some of these conditions have acquired the status or reputation of mental illnesses, and as in need of cure. We are used to the idea that if you are depressed the appropriate person to go to see is your doctor. Yet this really might strike us as odder than it does. Why exactly are some states of being candidates for cure and thus the province of the medical profession while others are not? After all, a feeling that the government of your country is undermining its institutions and betraying its best traditions – for instance – can make you debilitatingly unhappy, but you are unlikely to seek treatment for it. The philosopher Ludwig Wittgenstein famously wondered if we might think of the kind of conditions listed above more like 'more or less sudden changes of character' and less like illnesses, less like measles or pneumonia. At least they may look, in a certain light, less like illnesses.

We start by attempting to undermine the idea that 'mental illness' exists in a straightforward and fairly uncomplicated way, as physical illness does. We emphasize the dissimilarity of 'mental illness' to physical illness, and following Bentall (2003) we use the word 'mad' to avoid connotations of sickness. If this word seems unfortunate then it can only be because we have forgotten what Freud taught us: that the mad are not a separate species but are remarkably like the rest of us – indeed they *are* us. We touch on the idea that the mad often turn out to have something perfectly real and tangible to be mad about, and we make some mention of the rise of the various self-confirming and sometimes pernicious therapies that claim to be able to help the mad. The therapy that they need, we argue, often looks more like a kind of education or clarification than any cure as usually understood.

This chapter is nevertheless not entirely an anti-psychiatry text of the kind associated with writers such as R.D. Laing and Thomas Szasz. There is a case for saying that they, and other leaders of the anti-psychiatry movement, fell into the same error as their biologically-minded opponents: that of setting up a dichotomy between mind and brain, psychology and pathology – and, in their case, focusing exclusively on the former category. We do not deny that things happen in the brain when people are mad, just as they do when people are ordinarily distressed, elated or when they experience the world in any other way (things are happening in your brain as you read these words). *Chemical imbalances may sometimes be helpfully addressed by drug regimes.* Alcohol, chocolate and caffeine all have their place, as may other drugs. Because a condition can be chemically alleviated, however, does not mean that it is essentially chemical in origin. Nor does it mean that the question of its origin can always be relegated in favour of selecting a cure that 'works'. Perhaps you do not need to worry excessively about the causes of mild indigestion if a proprietary remedy clears it up. It is less obvious that the question of what makes you stressed should be ignored just so long as the doctor can prescribe something to suppress the symptoms. If that does not seem obvious, should we worry less about child-abuse if its survivors could take a pill that did away with its effects?

## Unsettling confidence

Richard Bentall offers an excellent example of what we call 'undermining' in *Madness Explained: Psychosis and Human Nature* (Allen Lane, 2003). His strategy, reminiscent of Nietzsche and Foucault, is to show how our current categories such as 'the mentally ill' have come about, and by demonstrating that what we now tend to think of as the mind and its infirmities have been conceptualized very differently at other times and in other places to unsettle our confidence that our notions of mental illness have anything like the same solidity and reliability that our notions of physical illness do. Terms such as schizophrenia, manic depression and paranoia are far from hard and fast. Nineteenth century distinctions and classifications went through so many transformations in the course of a hundred years that 'we may be forgiven for wondering whether these explorers of the mind were writing about the same illness' (p. 37). Even now diagnoses are not particularly consistent among clinicians, and there have been considerable differences in diagnostic practices in practices around the world, even between the UK and the USA. Thus the reliability of the whole medico-scientific approach to 'mental health' is called into question. Kidney stones and their symptoms have been understood in much the same way for thousands of years; by contrast the state of a soldier unable to face another day of combat has been thought of variously as lack of moral fibre, shell-shock, and post-traumatic stress disorder. Melancholy or *Weldschmerz*, a general sense of malaise concerning the state of things, was actually prized in the late eighteenth century: it went along with an interesting pallor and a sense that its owner was a sophisticated person whose passions ran deep. Today young Werther is likely to be encouraged to go for counselling.

The process by which madness became the province of biologists, psychopharmacologists and medical practitioners in general is a fascinating and certainly a disturbing one. Freud, as is well known, was equivocal about whether the psychoanalyst should have had a medical training, and his inclination to conclude that 'lay analysis' should be the exception and not the rule appears to owe much to his canny sense that psychoanalysis would be more readily respected if people saw the psychiatrist as a kind of doctor. The psychiatrist's couch, often explained as necessary for the patient (significantly so called, of course) and analyst not to see each other – or the patient will read evidence of what he is meant to say and not to say from the analyst's expression – is a surrogate hospital bed for someone who is sick. A distinction made later by the philosopher and psychologist Karl Jaspers between understanding and explanation proved particularly unfortunate. Where symptoms could be understood as meaningful in the context of the individual's life history, Jaspers thought, an empathetic and non-technical understanding, of much the same sort that we use for ordinary human relations, could be brought to bear on them. Where they defied understanding they could only be explained as caused by the kind of endogenous factors familiar to medicine. The effect of Jasper's otherwise familiar and philosophically respectable distinction was accordingly that 'he gave madness to the biologists and inadvertently discouraged the psychological investigation of the psychoses' (*ibid.*, p. 29).

More recently, United States health insurers will only pay out if claimants meet the criteria of the *Diagnostic and Statistical Manual* (*DSM*). The impetus behind psychiatric diagnoses is thus as much economic as it is scientific. Academic journals are not innocent, often refusing to accept papers for publication unless the patients investigated have been diagnosed according to the *DSM* system, thus ensuring that these psychiatric criteria 'became a standard among researchers, not only in America but also elsewhere in the world' (*ibid.*, p. 62). Meanwhile, our own university students remind us that Boards of Examiners tend to expect medical evidence in the shape of a doctor's letter to support their claims that mitigating circumstances should be taken into account. In this way they are required to think of themselves as suffering from mental *illness* if they are anxious or depressed – or to adopt a profound cynicism that may extend *a fortiori* to all potential sources of support ('All the doctor could give me was a letter saying I was depressed').

A particularly striking example of a condition whose medical credentials can be unsettled without too much difficulty is Attention Deficit Hyperactivity Disorder (ADHD). This was barely heard of in the UK and USA before the late 1980s, and is yet to achieve a secure foothold in continental Europe. Around 2,000 prescriptions for the drugs (such as Ritalin) that suppress the kind of symptoms ('butterfly mind', hyperactivity and aggression) supposed to be typical of ADHD were issued in the early 1990s, mainly to children; this rose to over 271,300 in 2002–3 and over 329,300 in the following year (McKinstry, 2005). Has a kind of 'mental illness' been *discovered*, or in some way brought into existence? As McKinstry (*ibid.*) notes, the symptoms listed in *DSM-IV* are extremely vague. These include 'Loses materials needed for activities (assignments, books, pencils, tools, toys)', 'Easily distracted by extraneous stimuli', 'Doesn't appear to listen when told something', 'Talks excessively'. Some of the symptoms look very much like the behaviour typical of early adolescence. Others ('Appears driven or "on the go"', 'Answers questions before they have been completely asked') seem more characteristic of a high level of attention than its opposite.

McKinstry argues that there are at least three sets of factors working to promote the idea that ADHD is a distinct, quasi-medical illness. The first is a coalition including 'child psychiatrists, counsellors, special-needs advisers and pressure-group lobbyists whose work depends on the belief that large numbers of children are suffering from mental illness' (*ibid.*, p. 19). Drug companies have a clear interest here since it is their products that are prescribed as cures. The second is that parents are often desperate to be told that their child suffers from ADHD, since this appears to absolve them of being bad parents who have not taught their children to behave and cannot control them. They can also benefit financially since if the ADHD child is classified as 'disabled' by the condition the family is entitled to a range of social security allowances. The third concerns the mainstream education system. Teachers, like parents, may be relieved to learn that the pupil whom they cannot manage displays ADHD rather than ordinary naughtiness, and so can be handed over to the relevant expert.

Psychopharmacology has a normalising effect. If children are given Ritalin for the 'ADHD' that supposedly causes them to be disruptive in the classroom, the docile, passive child is implicitly elevated to the norm. There is then no motive for wondering whether it is the conditions of contemporary schooling – an overly academic curriculum that has changed little in fifty years, and obsessive regimes of testing and assessment not just for pupils but for their teachers – that are at fault. Perhaps it is the child who responds placidly to all this that should be seen as giving cause for concern. It may indeed be fresh thinking about education that is needed, rather than any kind of therapy.

The spectacular advances in neurological research over the last couple of decades (our rapidly increasing knowledge of DNA and the central nervous system, for instance, and ever more sophisticated brain-scanning techniques) have resulted in an increased willingness to believe that all questions about mental illness will be answered purely through these scientific advances. Bentall (2003, p. 178) notes that 'Biological findings about madness have often been greeted by a dramatic suspension of the critical faculties of both researchers and bystanders'. Steven Rose (2005) writes in similarly sceptical terms of neuroscience, making again the point that research in this field is often driven by the simple desire for financial profit (the market for Prozac, Ritalin and similar drugs is now worth nearly $50 billion per year). He also observes that researchers often work with a crude model of the brain, achieving such results as they do quite by accident: drugs developed for a particular purpose frequently turn out to be useful for something entirely different.

One reviewer of Rose's book writes:

> Of course, medical researchers will start with proposals to fix diseases, seeking to inject corrective genes into those at risk of Huntington's or Parkinson's, perhaps even schizophrenia and Alzheimer's. But what is stopping them once they feel they have identified genes responsible for intelligence, verbal ability, criminality or whatever? (McCrone, 2005)

This is an interesting question, to which the answer is partly a philosophical one. It is very common to assume that a whole range of attributes – perhaps sexual orientation, altruism, violence, autism, eating disorders, and self-esteem, in addition to those listed by the reviewer above – may turn out to be 'in the genes'. To see what is odd here it is perhaps helpful to list some other attributes or qualities and ask if they are susceptible to genetic explanation:

• A melancholic or a phlegmatic disposition
• Lack of moral fibre, as displayed by Great War soldiers who deserted their posts

- *Megalopsychia,* the 'greatness of spirit' of which Aristotle writes
- Neurasthenia
- Being a witch

It is immediately clear that these attributes are historical constructs that we now do not employ. There cannot be a gene for being a witch, one wants to say, not because we have not found the gene but because witches – in the sense that women were persecuted in past times for being witches – did not and do not exist. There is no such thing as a phlegmatic temperament of the sort that was distinguished in the medieval doctrine of the humours. What was once called lack of moral fibre and then 'shell-shock' is now post-traumatic stress disorder and attributed to the horrors of war rather than to any particular personal deficiencies the soldier brings with him. 'Neurasthenia' ('a malaise that exhibits lassitude, weakness, loss of will, with such symptoms as sensitivity to light or noise and headaches' – Smith, 1997, p. 709) was commonly diagnosed in the nineteenth century but is no longer thought to label a distinct medical condition.

Obvious enough in the case of these examples, perhaps. But in the matter of sexual orientation , which might seem a more plausible candidate for genetic explanation, Michel Foucault argues that the distinction between heterosexuals and homosexuals is a modern invention. It made little sense for the ancient Greeks: married men regularly enjoyed sexual relations with adolescent boys and with *hetairai*, sophisticated prostitutes who offered civilized conversation and music as well as the more obvious pleasures. Criminality, to take another example, can surely not be 'in the genes' since what counts as a crime changes as the law changes. Smoking cannabis is illegal in some countries but not others: we are not presumably supposed to imagine that the smoker's genes change as he flies by airplane from one country to the other. Or again, the notion of 'intelligence' is problematic since so many varied capacities, from picking out a football team mate with a perceptive pass to solving crosswords, are called 'intelligent' yet are not always found in the same individual.

This is to say that much more counts as socially constructed than we readily notice. And what is socially constructed *cannot* be in the genes, because what we construct socially in one way at one time we construct very differently at another time. There is no one thing called 'crime' in the same sense as there is one thing called Down's syndrome, or retinitis pigmentosa, or (probably) Alzheimer's. These latter are what are called 'natural kinds': they are characterized by unvarying

symptoms, and are identified uncontroversially by appropriate specialists in different countries at different times – specialists who are properly so called because there is something to be a specialist in, some
one thing for which a genetic explanation is plausible.

## The capture of madness

There is a problem here about language. There are ways of writing
about madness, and so of conceptualising madness and of dealing with
or responding to mad people, that have a seductive power. It is for
example instructive to read *DSM-IV* (a version is on the Web at
http://www.psychnet-uk.com/dsm_iv/_misc/complete_tables.htm).
Conditions are listed in decimal notation: *290.21 Dementia of the
Alzheimer's Type, With Late Onset, With Depressed Mood.* Links can be
followed: to symptoms, set out in an orderly way; to support organizations and relevant literature; to , in the above case, a picture of a CT
scan of the brain of an Alzheimer's patient 'showing widespread
destruction (purple) of brain tissue (green)'; to notes on cause, caregiv-
ing and treatment. A last link, to the psychopharmacology section,
takes you to details of various drugs and to information about drugs.
All this can seem so authoritative in its scientific way as to preclude
other ways of thinking about madness. The problem goes beyond
psychopharmacology. Even our remarks above about sociobiology,
with their talk of natural kinds and what can and cannot be explained
genetically, may help to make a certain kind of language seem natural
and at home. As we emphasize in many places in this book, a crucial
question in the areas under discussion concerns 'what it makes sense to
say', and it may seem to make sense to speak and write only in one
kind of way and one kind of language: one that over and again
excludes and marginalizes those who articulate their experience in very
different ways.

An instructive parallel can be drawn with Michel Foucault's attempt
to write his *History of Madness* in a way that did not subject the mad to
the very process of exclusion that had in his view historically been
their fate. According to Foucault, what is often called the 'Enlightenment project', consisting centrally of the elevation of universal Reason,
had its shadow side in the incarceration of the insane: in rendering the
irrational invisible in the asylums of the seventeenth and eighteenth
century. In a famous passage Foucault analyzed Descartes' conclusion
that whatever he can doubt he cannot doubt that he himself is there
doing the doubting and thinking (*cogito, ergo sum*). Foucault saw this as

'an allegory of modern thought in relation to madness as the feared and excluded "other" of rational discourse' (Norris, 1987, p. 215). That is to say, according to Foucault Descartes is to be understood as driven by the desire to demonstrate the impossibility of an uncertainty that is so extreme (a doubt that is so hyperbolic, as it is sometimes put) that it puts the entire Enlightenment project at risk. But what this in turn requires Foucault to undertake is a history of madness written from its own perspective and not from that of the philosophical or scientific reason which, effectively demanding to take centre stage, always threatens to cast madness as eccentric, as a property of those in the outer circle of humanity. Derrida criticizes the undertaking in his paper 'Cogito and the history of madness' in a passage that is worth citing at length:

> By letting madness speak for itself... Foucault wanted madness to be the *subject* of his book in every sense of the word... Foucault wanted to write a history of madness *itself,* that is madness speaking on the basis of its own experience and under its own authority, and not a history of madness described from within the language of reason, the language of psychiatry *on* madness... on madness already crushed beneath psychiatry, dominated, beaten to the ground, interned, that is to say, madness made into an object and exiled as the other of a language and a historical meaning which have been confused with logos itself. 'A history not of psychiatry', Foucault says, but of madness itself, in its most vibrant state, before being captured by knowledge'...It is a question, therefore, of escaping the trap or objectivist naiveté that would consist in writing a history of untamed madness, of madness as it carries itself and breathes before being caught and paralysed in the nets of classical reason, from within the very language of classical reason itself, utilizing the concepts that were the historical instruments of the capture of madness – the restrained and restraining language of reason. (Derrida, 2002)

How are we to write about madness without capturing it in our knowledge and language, rendering it immobile in linguistic straitjackets like those used to restrain the insane? The immobilizing – paralysing, one might put it – language is, despite what Derrida sometimes seems to say, not so much the language of reason but that of a particular *kind* of reason, the scientific reason that elevates the language of medicine and its cures. It is the kind of reason that makes it natural to think of offering psychiatric treatment to people as if their minds or selves were organs that could be diseased like a kidney or pancreas. This is the reason and the language that we need to move beyond.

Wittgenstein, as we have mentioned above (p. 172) suggested that we need not regard madness as an illness: it could be seen for example as more like a change of character. When someone develops eccentricities (perhaps they dress all in black, believe they have been abducted by aliens, or pray to a god for whose existence there is no evidence whatsoever) it is not obvious that they ought to see a psychiatrist. Homosexuality appears as a disease in *Diagnostic and Statistical Manual II* but not in subsequent editions. What other conditions might follow it out into the light? Yet talk of a 'change of character' here seems odd, and too close to positing some mysterious inner, personal entity. Bentall's own preferred approach is to 'abandon psychiatric diagnoses altogether and instead try to explain and understand the actual experiences and behaviours of psychotic people' (2003, p. 141, italics removed). We should think of them as having *complaints* rather than as suffering from symptoms, so that when we have understood their complaints (eg their delusions) there is no 'ghostly disease' requiring further explanation. 'Complaints are all there is' (*ibid.*). And, though Bentall does not emphasize the point, sometimes there may be something to complain about. It is this last point that is worth developing.

## A short stroll in the fresh air

Deleuze and Guattari open their book *Anti-Oedipus: Capitalism and Schizophrenia* by asking us to think of our bodies as machines (though they do not use the word 'bodies' here, since this would reinstate the body-self binary that they wish to dissolve). '*It* is at work everywhere', they begin (our emphasis). Sometimes it works wells, sometimes fitfully. It breathes, eats, shits. This is a materialist language, but not the language of medicine. Does this mean, though, that *it* can be fixed, mended in ways analogous to curing it? Deleuze and Guattari ask us to think of a schizophrenic: 'A schizophrenic out for a walk is a better model than a neurotic lying on the analyst's couch. A breath of fresh air, a relationship with the outside world' (p. 1). The schizophrenic imagines the life of rocks, water and plants flowing into and out of him, and him into them. There is no dichotomy here between humankind and nature.

> There is no such thing as either man or nature now, only a process that produces the one within the other and couples the machines

together. Producing-machines, desiring-machines everywhere, schiz-ophrenic machines, all of species life: the self and the non-self, outside and inside, no longer have any meaning whatsoever.

The schizophrenic is released from the Oedipal triangle of me-mummy-daddy. It is not that the family does not matter: rather that instead of thinking of it and its complexes as timelessly inscribed within the psyche we do better to conceive me, mummy-daddy and the wider world that they call the *socius* as different levels between which there is flow of energy and interconnection, or as machines that plug into each other and couple with each other.

Parts of these machines however only work when, in conventional terms, they are not working properly. There are echoes of the classic Marxist critique of alienated labour. In the factories of the industrial revolution, the production line of the twentieth-century factory or the call-centre in Mumbai where a western corporation has outsourced its services we are in one sense working but our machines are operating in fits and starts. If we had a dishwasher or a car in this condition we would say 'It's not working right at all'. Marx's collaborator, Friedrich Engels, in *The Condition of the Working Class in England* (1845), describes factory 'work' as 'no activity which claims the operative's thinking powers, yet it is of a sort which prevents him from occupying his mind with other things. We have seen... that this work affords the muscles no oppor-tunity for physical activity. Thus it is, properly speaking, not work, but tedium'. The machine is trying to do work for which it was not meant.

Conversely, we may find that when the machine is broken it really works at last. A child is ill and this requires us to take 'time off work', or we succumb to stress ourselves. 'I can't do this', we think. 'There are these important reports to write, these classes to teach, these meetings to attend. How can things possibly run smoothly if I am not there?' Yet on the second day of sitting with the sick child, reading her stories and changing her sweat-soaked pyjamas, perhaps, a new perspective and an older rhythm assert themselves. We see our paid work for the torture (from the Latin *torquere,* to twist and distort) that it is. Engels writes (*ibid.*) that 'This condemnation to be buried alive in the mill, to give constant attention to the tireless machine is felt as the keenest torture by the operatives, and its action upon mind and body is in the long run stunting in the highest degree'. At the child's bedside, at the funeral ('How like him to die now, just the busiest time for me' had been our first thought) we bring our attention back from the machine. Now at last we are working properly again.

Madness, or what Deleuze and Guattari call schizophrenia, is according to them one way of escaping from the deadening, alienating routines of the work-machines our machines are coupled to – routines made worse and more inescapable since Marx's and Engels's time by the ubiquity of global capitalism. Our world, the world of late- or post-modernity, is the time of what Frederic Jameson memorably calls the 'waning of affect', loss of depth, meaning and intensity. Older forms of association (trades unions, for instance) decline and leave the individual socially and politically disengaged. The intense subjectivity and absorption with self of the schizophrenic or psychotic, the flight into 'a world of his own', opens space for desire – desire that is not captured by the economy of capitalism and is thus persuaded to desire its own oppression (p. 131: Deleuze and Guattari write of fascism, but we might equally think of the facility with which we are persuaded that satisfaction lies in meeting the demands of performativity, of 'maximising the input-output ratio' in our own line of work – cp. Lyotard, 1984). Thus the politics of schizophrenia is a journey from the suppression to the intensification of feeling. In this sense Deleuze and Guattari ask us to consider the possibility that 'schizophrenia is the product of the capitalist machine, as manic-depression and paranoia are the product of the despotic machine, and hysteria the product of the territorial machine' (p. 33). In perhaps their most powerful formulation of their thesis, they write (p. 131):

> Schizophrenia is our very own 'malady', modern man's sickness... [The schizophrenic] does not speak of another world, he is not from another world: even when he is displacing himself in space, his is a journey in intensity. These men of desire are like Zarathustra... They know incredible sufferings, vertigos, and sicknesses. They have their spectres. They must reinvent each gesture. But such a man produces himself as a free man, irresponsible, solitary, and joyous, finally able to say and do something simply in his own name, without asking permission, a desire lacking nothing, a flux that overcomes barriers and codes, a name that no longer designates any ego whatever. He has simply ceased being afraid of becoming mad. He experiences and lives himself as the sublime sickness that will no longer affect him. Here, what is, what would a psychiatrist be worth?

The therapy, then, is to know that the late modern world in which we live is itself sick, and produces sickness. Replace the idea of the self as disembodied, confident that its Cartesian cogitation guarantees that it exists; think rather in terms of a flowing in of the social world, out of which what we call the self emerges. 'The self and the non-self, outside and inside, no longer have any meaning whatsoever' (above). What we have thought of as inside and outside are transformed as they inter-penetrate and flow into each other. 'Man and nature are not like two opposite terms confronting each other... [they] are one and the same essential reality' (p. 36).

Think of this text that Deleuze and Guattari have written, then, as a kind of poetry. No doubt not every schizophrenic (whatever this term is taken to mean) is joyous and has ceased to be afraid of becoming mad. But to read *Anti-Oedipus* is to enter a language and a perspective from which, briefly and tantalisingly perhaps, other languages and per-spectives show their limitations. This is a medicine that liberates us if only for a while – sends us out for a stroll in the fresh air – from our craving for medicine and medical cure.

## Back to work

However, we shall be readmitted to the ward and the analyst's couch soon enough. 'Whatever is this nonsense you have been dreaming up?' the doctor asks, and 'Engages in writing behaviour' is written in our case-notes, together with remarks concerning our paranoia about machines and interpenetrating flows. After all, if these drugs do not work research is being done on others that will. It is only a matter of time. And as for the self, it is now officially multiple. The UNESCO Universal Declaration on Cultural Diversity declares, universally:

> Each individual must acknowledge not only otherness in all its forms but also the plurality of his or her own identity, within societies that are themselves plural. Only in this way can cultural diversity be preserved as an adaptive process and as a capacity for expression, creation and innovation.[1]

Acknowledge otherness and confess that you are plural. Otherwise there will be no cultural diversity (except, oddly, that this seems to lead to the cultural uniformity of universal plurality), the Darwinian or neo-Darwinian process of adaption and evolution will grind to a halt and creation and innovation will cease. We seem, finally, to have come back to the idea of work and the haunting thought that the reason that we need to be cured, and that we need unified identities at one point in history and plural ones at another – when we are forever being told that nothing is certain but change, and that we shall all have 'portfolio careers' in the future' – is that we need to be put back on our feet to service the economy: to engage in productive work.

There was an extensive debate on the nature of work in the middle of the nineteenth century, contributed to by Marx and Engels, of course, but also Dickens (eg in *Hard Times*), Ruskin (*The Stones of Venice*, 'The veins of wealth'), Carlyle and others. These writers were aware that the nature of work was changing under the impact of the Industrial Revolution. Here is Carlyle writing optimistically and resonantly in *Past and Present* (1843):

> The latest Gospel in this world is, Know thy work and do it. 'Know thyself': long enough has that poor 'self' of thine tormented thee; thou wilt never get to 'know' it, I believe! Think it not thy business, this of knowing thyself; thou art an unknowable individual: know what thou canst work at; and work at it, like a Hercules! That will be thy better plan... Consider how, even in the meanest sorts of Labour, the whole soul of a man is composed into a kind of real harmony, the instant he sets himself to work! Doubt, Desire, Sorrow, Remorse, Indignation, Despair itself, all these like helldogs lie beleaguering the soul of the poor dayworker, as of every man: but he bends himself with free valour against his task, and all these are stilled, all these shrink murmuring far off into their caves. The man is now a man. The blessed glow of Labour is in him, is it not as purifying fire, wherein all poison is burnt up, and of sour smoke itself there is made bright blessed flame!

Work has changed again in our own time. The clinical psychologist David Smail writes (1993) that many therapists like himself noticed in the 1980s that they were encountering a new kind of 'client' from the professional classes – doctors, accountants, lawyers and academics – whose working lives had been changed drastically under the influence of managerialism, the market and performativity. The anxiety and neurosis that these people experienced as something wrong with them and that was in need of curing is better understood as the changing nature of the institutional, public and professional world that damages people's sense of self-respect and self-worth. What Smail calls 'distal power', the operation of political, economic, global and other forces remote from us 'becomes mediated proximally as psychological or emotional distress' (*ibid.*, p. 99). Perhaps it is above all a greater understanding of work and its effects that we need. It is the idea of work that we need to work on.[2]

# 12
# Narrative and Number: What Really Counts

According to an American television station, it is expected that approximately 160,000 people will suffer from the consequences of the event of 9/11. Nervous breakdowns are predicted to increase, and so are the divorce rate, alcohol abuse and the number of suicides. How do they know that? Well, there is scientific evidence that natural disasters, wars and other calamities have these kinds of effects. And even if some people do not exhibit these 'normal reactions', that is react to extreme circumstances in the way that human beings usually do, this would in itself not be strong enough to overthrow the insights that sophisticated research has achieved. Their reactions would rather be seen as anomalies: one would speak of 'strong individuals' for instance who can cope with everything or, even more likely, who would be expected to suffer in the more distant future from what has happened. Clearly, we do not need scientific research to come to these conclusions; more precisely, science does not add in this sense to our general knowledge of human beings. We already think we 'know' that people are very likely to be deeply damaged if such kinds of events take place. Not only do we not need, we tend to feel, any kind of research to enlighten us on this sort of matter, but specifically quantitative research poses its own problems. Particularly in an educational context, where the focus is often on the individual, probability and causality seem not to be appropriate to explain what is at stake, and to tell us how to act in the future. At first sight a move to a narrative approach to the phenomena looks promising, but we shall argue that this too leads to problems.

The nuanced insights of writers such as Hans-Georg Gadamer, Ludwig Wittgenstein, Paul Ricoeur, Alasdair MacIntyre, Charles Taylor and others to the effect that human lives are necessarily to be understood in interpretive (*Verstehen*) and sometimes narrative terms, have been distorted into a *credo* amongst many researchers in education, as well as in a range of other disciplines. Narrative research promises to correct – through its reference to lived experience, through its emphasis on gaining a better understanding of ourselves – the positivistic research still dominant in many educational and other professional contexts. It aspires to provide findings that are in one sense or another useful for practitioners – in other words, to improve practice. Research of this kind not only sets out the different factors that are significant in any particular situation, but seeks to do this in such a way that the reader might herself benefit. This chapter questions the presuppositions of this kind of research. It suggests that it thrives on an overly self-conscious, if not somewhat precious, theorization of its own approach. Moreover, it can encourage a degree of narcissism in both its practitioners and its research subjects. This is not to say that it is entirely without merit. But a proper conception of the nature of these merits may lead us to direct our energies elsewhere. In short it should lead to the recognition of the need for a different language of education. There is indeed a need to respond to the multi-layeredness of what we say and do, to the world of human beings that is the concern of education and therapy. There is a need to challenge and thus perhaps change the way we make sense of the world. But the presumption that these needs warrant the adoption of narrative research involves a false constriction of these very ideas, risking the creation of what can become a refuge from the engagement that these matters require.

Thus we will argue here that what we need is not so much 'knowledge', echoing the refrain that 'more research is needed', but a certain kind of thoughtfulness in the search for what can be of any help at all either for the practitioner or the theoretician. This requires a preparedness to take into account the particular situation of the individual person one is entrusted with. In various chapters in this book we draw attention not only to the significance of language but also to the specific importance of narrative. We think partly of the kinds of account that we naturally give of ourselves in our daily lives. On the face of it these appear secondary to – that is to say, they are reflections or reports of – the way we in fact are, but closer consideration reveals that they also have a determining effect on our self-conception and on the very shaping of our lives. We think also of the special importance that literature has in helping us to recognize and to take forward the ways of thinking that are involved in this process: it can extend the possibilities of our self-understanding or self-conception.

Here, we will start with an example from the educational context which deals with research concerning the experiences of primary school teachers during their first year in the classroom. It is, incidentally, an example of what we take to be excellent qualitative, narrative biographical research. We will then go on to a more theoretical level and will offer an elaboration of the presuppositions and problems of quantitative research. Following this, we will again focus on qualitative and more particularly on narrative research, where looking for causes or distributions of variables is replaced by looking for understanding. We argue that, given the characteristics of educational research generally, for a large class of cases it cannot, as it is normally conceived, deliver what is generally expected from it. It is in need of therapy, and has to be cured of the tendency to scientism, of fantasies about science. Finally, we dwell on the situation each and every individual finds herself in and how she makes sense of the world. We conclude with a plea for the adoption of a richer language to do research, and refer to examples given in this book of such a language, thus indicating some ways in which this might be realized.

## Qualitative educational research: some problems

The educational example that drew our attention concerns an investigation of the professional development of primary school teachers (Mahieu and Vanderlinde, 2002). Recently qualified, they have for the first time their own class. It is an important year for their professional development conceived as lifelong and complex processes of learning. They still have to learn a lot, particularly matters which could not be taught during their college training. The leading research question is: how does the personal frame of reference and their micro-political learning evolve and change during the first year of their career? The research method employed was qualitative, in this case specifically biographical. After a questionnaire in which some background information had to be filled in, there was an initial interview and then three more interviews with in total eight primary school teachers. The interviews were recorded and typed up, subdivided in fragments which were then coded (to facilitate a content analysis) and a text was written by way of synthesis of each interview which was then presented to the teacher for final approval. All the time two researchers were involved who checked each other's interpretations concerning codes and syntheses. Then a so-called vertical (or in-depth) analysis was made for each teacher and a horizontal analysis for the different aspects across the groups. Again checks were made between the researchers who also kept a log of everything that they did or that happened within the context of this one and a half year period in which the data were gathered. The researchers were conscious of the part they themselves played in conducting this research and the way in which it could influence their findings. They tried to be as honest as they could and worked as methodologically as possible.

This research is detailed, sophisticated, aware of what could go wrong and it attempts to anticipate future problems. It used the lived experience of the teachers as related in the interviews (their own words reflecting their experiences) and thus it necessarily has a high degree of what is technically termed as validity. It goes without saying that the researchers were also anxious to have reliable data and constantly monitored the quality of what they were doing. After having indicated the research question, the design and the method that was followed, we will now briefly deal with the results. Clearly a selection has to be made in which we focus on the elements that were used in the comparative analysis of the syntheses:

- The first year is a year of intense learning, particularly relational. Being responsible for their own class, the teacher needs to develop relationships with other personnel in the school. This has its own problems, is a big challenge and an important task. They say they know too little about this from what they have been taught in college.
- When they applied for a job they really felt the micro-politics of reality, the power of the local school governors.
- They all speak of the importance of the teacher who teaches a parallel class (as someone they can or would like to rely on) and of the crucial importance of their dealings with parents.
- The relation with the headteacher too was felt very important, and so was the experience of functioning in a team.
- On the material level they were all concerned with having to secure a job the following year, and furthermore they all experienced the importance of material resources in the context of the day-to-day functioning of the school.

There are a few more points of this sort, but let us end with a final and interesting conclusion: all teachers experienced themselves as insecure, badly prepared, inexperienced and not fully-qualified.

We have deliberately gone into some detail about this research and have tried not to caricature it. Moreover, we want to acknowledge that in our opinion this research has been carried out according to the highest standards. Yet, one cannot but wonder whether the findings, i.e. what we know now, after so much work and such deployment of expertise, is really something that we did not 'know' beforehand. To put this more precisely, when we say 'we know now' there is a kind of circularity at stake that is reminiscent of Meno's discussion of virtue in the Platonic dialogue that bears his name: what we now understand is recognizable because we had already accepted its importance. But even if there is something we would not have come up with in our arm-chair thinking, is this kind of knowledge useful, and for whom, in what circumstances, and to what extent? Certainly, if you know nothing at all of teaching and teachers all of this will be very informative about the primary school teacher's first-year experiences. But would not you and we, and of course experienced schoolteachers, be able to tell a very similar story? And in as far as details are concerned, naturally they will be different from case to case, so there is not very much point in trying to be too specific here. We do not disagree that the insights and the well-written research report might be interesting for headteachers, and even for lecturers teaching in Teacher Training Colleges, but the question is whether this is really more than a collection of truisms, more than 'common sense' that draws on a particular context.

These general conclusions are very similar to the relationship between speeding and accidents, drinking and driving, being depressive and suicidal, and so on. Of course, sometimes people need to be reminded of these general facts of human nature, but is that proper research? It comes as no surprise that critics of such qualitative research turn to its quantitative counterpart. As most of us are very familiar with it, there is no need for an example, so we will move on immediately to the presuppositions and problems that quantitative research confronts us with at a more theoretical level.

## Presuppositions and general problems of quantitative research

The debate concerning the way the social sciences should proceed has not reached unambiguous conclusions. In summary, this debate has been in part between those who argue that the so-called 'scientific method' of the 'empirical' natural sciences (mainly quantitative approaches) should be mimicked, and those who emphasize the role of interpretation in all understanding and enquiry (mainly qualitative approaches). This is not to say that no creativity is involved in natural sciences, nor is it to ignore the ineliminable ethical dimension in the social sciences, but what we want to draw attention to is something different. It is the technical discussion which is interesting for us in seeking a genuine research stance, a stance that has examined the status of its own presuppositions and assumptions in relation to the nature of what it is studying. An astronomer recently interviewed about the 'storms' on the sun said without hesitation: 'We don't understand what is happening there in the sense that we can't predict it'. It is indeed the notion of prediction that is critical to the debate. So let us go a little deeper into the characteristics of empirical, or quantitative, research. And here, though what we will draw attention to is generally very well known, we fear that the relevance of it is often not fully realized.

In quantitative research, the search for causes can either assume a kind of determinism, or the distribution of particular variables and their relations can be situated within the indeterminism of so-called probabilistic causality. In the former case, a scientific explanation consists for instance in a deductive subsumption of that which is to be explained under one or more laws of nature. In other words, according to causal conceptions of empirical science, we thus explain facts (general or particular) by exhibiting the physical processes and interactions that bring them about. Incidentally, that we are unable to make perfect predictions in all cases is for the determinist no counterargument but simply the result of human ignorance and other limitations. The mechanisms we refer to, however, need not be deterministic to have explanatory force: they may be irreducibly statistical. In an indeterministic framework necessary causes have at least some degree of explanatory force, but sufficient causes do not. A scientific explanation of a particular event is therefore not necessarily rigidly determined by general laws and antecedent conditions. To offer an explanation then comes down to the assembling of a total set of relevant conditions for the event to be explained, and the citing of the probability of that event in the presence of these conditions. The explanation is in this case not an argument (a logical structure with premises and conclusions governed by some rule of acceptance), but rather *a presentation of the conditions relevant to the occurrence of the event, and a statement of the degree of probability of the event given these conditions.* Doubts about the possibility of finding causes for everything (either on the basis of logical or empirical considerations) or on the basis of a theory such as that of relativity, suggest indeterminism as the more rational choice for the overarching framework.

But both the determinist and indeterminist approaches are beset by similar difficulties. Neither causal explanation nor statistical-probabilistic causality can come to terms with the fact that we can never be sure that a new condition might not turn up. Moreover, scientific explanation requires a sufficient condition that is based on empirical evidence that something actually happened; inference on the other hand refers to something in the future, sometimes also called the *temporal asymmetry*. If the determinist persists, she assumes what she has to prove and ends up in logical circularity. Indeed, nothing whatsoever could ultimately falsify her claims. Hers, then, is essentially a structure imposed on reality. An indeterminism (say the kind inherent in statistical causality) already accepts an adherence to the idea that one cannot be sure of what will happen in the future. And that means for a particular circumstance that there will remain a 50% chance that something will happen or not and this cannot be made more precise. The only thing one can do is therefore to try to explain or describe what happened in the past – and even that only for as long as the explanatory theory in use, and its concepts, are generally accepted.

There are other ways to come to the same conclusion. One can point for instance to the presupposed invariance of perception, of meaning and of methodology; to the fact that there are no *really* fundamental laws (not even in physics or chemistry), no natural sorts or essences; and to the necessity always to apply laws 'when the *same* circumstances apply'. The latter condition, the so-called *ceteris paribus*, is even more problematical in the indeterministic stance than in its determinist counterpart as the following example may illustrate. If a particular phenomenon (a stroke for instance) is the result of 31 causal factors and we want to study the probabilistic effect of those factors in any possible causal homogeneous set, we need $2^{31}$ sets (which is more than 2 billion), many of which will be empty.

What follows from this is that within the context of science itself there can be no scientific ruling whether determinism or indeterminism is the correct paradigm for doing research – which is why determinism is sometimes called a 'metaphysical' hypothesis. But there is more. In its approach to the stance that *should* be taken, quantitative empirical research necessarily goes in circles. As it is based on 'output', that is, prediction, whether it 'works' is logically ultimately irrelevant in the case of determinism and is simply 'empty' in the case of indeterminism. This logical reconstruction of how science proceeds is to be

observed not only in its use in the natural sciences, but also applies to
the social sciences. In our argument we have not permitted notions
such as 'interpretation' to cloud the conclusion. Evidently, there are
reasons why human behaviour should not be studied along these lines,
but these will not convince for instance neuroscientists who are eager
to revive hard core behaviourism.

All of this raises serious doubts about the paradigm to be used for
educational research and the kind of theory one should be looking for.
If quantitative empirical research necessarily suffers from the *logical*
problems reviewed above, it is by no means clear that this should be
*the* way to be followed to study the educational process. That is not
to say that proceeding in this manner may not generate interesting
results. We know more in some sense (for instance about the degree of
probability of a particular event), but it may be the case that other
relevant aspects of what is to be understood will have been left out,
because they do not fit within the scope of the quantitative design or
paradigm. As we have argued, it is indeed the notion of prediction
which is the Achilles' heel in this debate.

## Pre-understandings, objectivity and research

In trying to be objective, and in identifying 'objective' with 'free of
bias', the fact is concealed that we always and inevitably bring our
pre-understandings with us into any situation. In this sense understanding, as the German philosopher Hans-Georg Gadamer insists,
*requires* 'prejudices' in the sense in which he uses that term, as equivalent to 'pre-understandings'. This is no more than to make the familiar distinction between *verstehen* and *erklärung*. *Verstehende* social
science concerns itself with interpretation and meaning: it asks for
instance what drug-taking among young people means – is it to be
seen as a rite of passage, a means of social bonding, a way of marking
out a dissident identity? The kind of social science that fits the *erklärung* model seeks explanation (the literal meaning of the German
term): it asks for example what causes young people to drop out of university, just as the physical scientist investigates the causes of chemical
changes. Neglect of the distinction between *verstehen* and *erklärung*
creates a world of confusion and often leads us to forget that social
science does not always work like physical science.

An example may help here. The researcher seeking to understand
why teenage pregnancy rates are much higher in one part of the
country than another may come to the tentative conclusion that for

low-achieving youngsters in marginalized communities giving birth to and looking after a baby gives them status among their peers, and confers a sense of purpose on their lives. Perhaps it is the most meaningful thing they will ever do. Statistics have an important place here in marking out coherent categories of 'low-achieving youngsters' and 'marginalized communities'. At the same time the researcher could not formulate her hypothesis unless she understood what it is like to find life meaningful or meaningless. Thus her pre-understandings are a precondition of her work. A second example: a researcher may hypothesize that the under-age consumption of alcohol in many western societies is to be understood as a kind of rite of passage between different phases of adolescence, or between adolescence and adulthood. It is hard to see how he could think thus unless he brought to the phenomenon he is investigating some pre-understanding, perhaps felt and personal, of the struggle to attain a sense of being an adult.

By contrast there is a standing temptation to embrace the notion of objectivity that consists in imagining that the explanations of phenomena are waiting 'out there' for us to discover with our instruments and techniques. When we declare, for instance, that '42% of the sample had experienced significant periods of separation from one parent or from both' we may forget that such separation cannot be unproblematically identified. This is not to embrace the claims of a crude constructivism to the effect that all meaning is created *ex nihilo*, but only to argue that whenever we conceptualize a particular part of reality, this necessarily occurs within the boundaries of what already makes sense for us. Ideas about what is worthwhile, about the nature of a human being, necessarily enter into the picture. That is why we cannot without further qualification make statements such as that 'European explorers brought civilization to primitive people'. Unlike earlier generations we are aware that what is civilized and what is primitive can be contested. Similarly, the common claim that a particular approach to a problem 'works', or that research should endeavour to discover 'what works', must not be allowed to conceal how much is dependent on just how 'what works' is defined. Unacknowledged metaphysical and ethical assumptions are usually lurking here: for instance to the effect that this or that is an acceptable way of achieving results.

At the heart of things here there is a kind of unacceptable reductionism. It is only in as much as we can define particular things, expressions or activities in terms of necessary and sufficient conditions, so that they can be referred to unambiguously, that we can compare them or talk about them sensibly at all. But, as many epistemologists have argued, this cannot be done from 'the view from nowhere'. We are always embedded in a particular (cultural, historical, social) world, a position that constitutes our viewpoint, where some things count and others do not. Sexual harassment for instance does not mean the same thing in Nicaragua as compared to Norway, nor does it mean the same thing over time. It is only by bracketing off and ignoring numerous aspects of a phenomenon that it is possible to make such comparisons. This always raises the issue whether the result is still worth looking at. We risk falling into the well-known artichoke trap: if you continue to peel off the leaves in search of the essence you discover that there is nothing left. Along rather similar lines Stephen Toulmin (in Kayzer, 1993) makes an instructive comparison between Shakespearean theatre and its modern counterpart. Where in Shakespeare's day the audience was not physically separated from the actors, in later centuries it became placed opposite to and distinct from the stage. Toulmin uses this as a metaphor of how knowledge has fared since Descartes. We have become objective spectators and through that acquired one kind of knowledge but lost touch with another. We are no longer aware of things in terms of their multifarious meanings and interconnections, but isolate them in order to study their 'reality' and then worry about how they are linked and connected to each other.

We do this because we are unwilling to live with complexity. We crave for the general in the particular in order to cope with the dazzling differences we are confronted with, we cherish the illusion that this will save us from getting lost amid the contingency of the world. We like to fantasize that issues of power can be ignored, that knowledge can be made safe from factors that distort it. Worst of all, we behave as though even if we cannot fully meet the requirements implied by these demands, we should nevertheless try to get as far down this road as we can. To insist or imply that this is the best option is to make a metaphysical claim for which it is impossible to show empirical evidence: empiricism cannot be justified empirically, and the empiricist tends to fall back on the assertion of 'it works' that we have discussed above. Part of the problem here is that the very ideal of crystalline purity may obscure our sight.

To replace scientism and doctrinaire empiricism with a more modest view of science is perhaps the first step towards wisdom. Of course we do not say that scientific method has no role at all to play within social science, but that it must make out the case for its relevance in each particular instance against other approaches that also offer insight and understanding, whether in conjunction with measurement and statistics or apart from them. Let us now return to the qualitative approach, where understanding, *verstehen*, is involved, and see whether it fares any better.

## Making sense of the world

In the field of 'narrative inquiry' the distinction made by Polkinghorne (1995) between an 'analysis of narratives' and 'narrative analysis' is of relevance. In an 'analysis of narratives' one looks for common features in different cases in order to define them within a broader category. For instance, the result could be a typology of teachers (authoritarian, progressive) based on interviews. The purpose is not only to discover and to describe categories, but also to indicate the relationships between categories. In 'narrative analysis', the data are mostly not in a narrative form. To give an account of what happened in a school, information is gathered for instance from records, reports of incidents, besides from interviews, thus from different sources. Here the researcher arranges events and actions by showing how they contribute to the evolution of a plot. The plot is the thematic line of the narrative: the structure that shows how different events contribute to a narrative. The writing of it involves an analytical development, a dialectic between the data and the plot. The resulting narrative must not only fit the data but also bring out an order and a significance that were not apparent in the 'raw' data. The result is not so much an account of the actual happening of events from an *objective* point of view as the result of a series of constructions. Such a kind of research, as for instance ethnography, realizes objectivity in a different way as compared to how it operates within the natural sciences. The researcher is right from the very beginning embedded in a particular system of values and beliefs. In this sense she cannot be 'objective'. But she can be so in the sense that she avoids distorting her conclusions as a consequence of preconceived notions that, unlike Gadamerian 'prejudices', she had never subjected to critical examination, or by just not being truthful in her report concerning the facts. In a 'narrative analysis' the construction itself is of course always her own, to be judged on its merits (by others) on the basis of the justifications that the researcher gives for a particular interpretation. Where in the 'analysis of narratives' the narratives are the source of knowledge, the narrative in 'narrative analysis' is the result of the research. This echoes the idea of some authors that the understanding that is offered has to be of the same kind as the understanding involved in the practice in question, involving the descriptions of everyday language and offering a particular reconstruction: resembling, so one could say, a philosophical interpretation (Winch, 1958).

How does this 'narrative' position deal with the problems that explanation in quantitative research is confronted with (namely 'temporal asymmetry' and *'ceteris paribus'*)? In as far as it accepts that no nomological theories are possible and that we can only offer description, it has no difficulties; neither with new facts nor with temporal order. The point surely is that it does not attempt to predict the future. When understanding of any kind takes place the representation we offer starts necessarily in terms of the concepts we already have, and what the researcher does is put these in a particular order, for which he or she tries to give convincing arguments. In some sense this understanding either sees what is already known or gives the label 'understanding' to the contingent order that is found. And this understanding of why things are so, it seems, helps us to decide what to do. Such appears to be the moral of qualitative research, at least in as far as its results are used in an output-directed context, say in as far as we are interested in prediction or manipulation; for instance interested in changing the world of education. In summary, both qualitative and quantitative research, when conceived in such causal-empirical terms, go in circles in a way that is not always recognized. Neither of them can convincingly argue that the method they use is to be preferred above another one in order to determine what to do. And yet, they give the impression that research itself, in order to be valid, has to proceed along one of these lines or follow a combination of both. It is in this sense that some kinds of research are in need of therapy and have to be cured of fantasies about science.

But there is another way that 'description' might be interesting. Wittgenstein advises us *to refrain from formulating theories*, because they are not capable of doing justice to the heterogeneity of cases and always presuppose more homogeneity than in fact can be found. Moreover, he suggests that not everything is explainable and draws our attention revealingly to different kinds of understanding. It becomes important then to ask such questions as 'What is important for a human being?' and 'What is there that may be relevant without necessarily being useful for something else?' The important difference between understanding and explaining, according to Wittgenstein, can be indicated by the difference in the effects they have upon those involved:

Compared with the impression that the description makes on us, the explanation is too uncertain. Every explanation is an hypothesis. But an hypothetical explanation will be of little help to someone, say, who is upset because of love. It will not calm him. (Wittgenstein, 1979, p. 63)

For instance in the case of research about adoption, it is important to be clear for whom the research is done, who is supposed to learn from it and what the researcher is interested in.

Wittgenstein strongly opposes the view that the understanding to which the *Geisteswissenschaften*, the human sciences (but without Anglophone associations of empiricism and laboratories), should adhere must be that of the natural sciences. In these 'human sciences' the task is to try to understand human conduct, to try to comprehend the reason or reasons for our actions. In order to talk about the same issues as those who are involved one has initially to describe the situation in such a way that they are able to recognize it for themselves. Some insightful remarks can be found in his *Remarks on Frazer's Golden Bough* (1979) and secondly in his *Lectures and Conversations on Aesthetics, Psychology and Religious Belief* (1966). Concerning Frazer's 'assembling of facts' Wittgenstein recommends:

> ... the arrangement of its factual content alone, in a *'perspicuous'* representation. ... This perspicuous representation brings about the understanding which consists precisely in the fact that we 'see the connections'. Hence the importance of finding *connecting links.* (Wittgenstein, 1979, p. 69)

To look for a further explanation is in his view wrong. When we come to a perspicuous representation, it becomes clear that there is no further job to be done. The tasks of research in the human sciences are therefore to be found in interpretation, which according to Wittgenstein means one must 'place things side by side' (cf. Moore, 1955, p. 19). Wittgenstein often uses similes in his work. Here one may refer to what we often say to someone, namely 'What was it like?' Philosophy is poetic, it helps lay bare what otherwise remains an obscure intuitive sense. We argue to this effect in Chapter 13 where, using the Hansel and Gretel example, we say that myth supplies a new language, and may offer the patient and analyst a new framework for looking at the world. There we recount how this apparently gives the young woman a metaphor she finds helpful: a way of acknowledging that home is both sweet and threatening, potentially fateful. There are many other examples from the context of feminist and multicultural research that tell us similar things, where metaphors, descriptions and 'new languages' help us to see with greater clarity situation in which we have found ourselves.

Now so far we have argued that causal explanation does not help us to decide what to do. Neither from the deterministic nor the indeterministic perspective can we be sure what will happen if we do A instead of B. There is just not enough information available (and there never will be). And we have seen that turning to qualitative research, and thus to 'understanding', is no way out of this deadlock, as that too involves causal connections to the past. It can make the problem or confusion we experience disappear but it does not help us to decide what to do, if by that we mean doing something in order to achieve particular results. Evidently, statisticians too tell a story, as do accountants. But this kind of research ends the discussion, where narrative on the other hand goes on. Then accountability is replaced by giving an account, by using various kinds of language where no limit is placed upon what counts as a story.

Of course it cannot be doubted that, by the means of research as it is usually conceived, our knowledge has grown. Medicine is a good example of that. So in many important ways it would be absurd to deny that science is helpful. We build better bridges and buildings, and because we understand at a biochemical level how the body functions, we have better treatments of illnesses. But matters of what to do in an educational context are of a different kind. If I have to cross a bridge, it is indeed relevant to know that there is only a chance of one in a million (or billion) that it might collapse, never mind the point that in the end they will all fall apart, that no bridge will last forever. But if empirical research in the educational sciences were to use the same criteria as those applied by the engineer, the consequences would be self-defeating. Indeed, that 'bridge' to reality would fall to pieces. Social scientists content themselves usually with the fact that there are many variables in play and that 'more research needs to be done'. It is touching to witness their perseverance, as it is overwhelmingly the case that their paradigmatic model does not achieve its aims. All of this does not mean that the social scientist, as a rational human being, has nothing to offer for educational practice, but that her insights are conducive to understanding in the sense of bringing clarity rather than leading directly to prescriptive conclusions. And where we have clarity we are less inclined to intervene in the wrong ways. For example, when it seems clear to us that girls go through with their unplanned pregnancies because their babies confer meaning on their lives, we are less inclined to suppose that the solution lies in contraception.

There are, of course, other reasons as well why we cannot simply base what we are going to do exclusively on a consideration of outcomes. These are reasons of an ethical kind. Moreover, education necessarily refers to a person making sense for herself of the world (and of herself in that world), and that is something she has to do and which no one else can do in her place, at least not in those things she cares most about. She is learning something, an active process, as distinct from something that merely happens to her. The concepts 'to care for something' or 'to make sense of something' would not be meaningful otherwise. This entails that too exclusive a 'skills approach' in educational contexts is wrongheaded, because making sense of something cannot properly be conceived as a skill. And this also means that a practice such as teaching cannot be held to consist entirely of skills. Making sense of something can only be offered to someone else in the hope that it is helpful for her to do just that for herself.

Causality, deterministic or probabilistic, cannot be reconciled with this. Neither can qualitative research whose presuppositions still remain within the domain of the causal and descriptive. The use of a research paradigm that relies in a crucial (dependent) sense on the past is not very helpful in terms of ascertaining how someone will make sense for herself in the future. The theories that are the result of all such approaches seem unfit for understanding what is really at stake in educational practice. They embrace the idea of an applied science in which educational activities are a consequence of a form of understanding that is essentially empirical and they ignore the importance of what is happening in an intervention oriented toward action for the future. As in a good detective story, where the detective chief inspector reconstructs what happened on the basis of forensic material, interviews with witnesses, intuition and a good deal of luck, a problem is solved. But is this enough to draw insights for the method to be followed for next day's problems, or for the choices to be made today? Of course it might. But it can also prevent us from seeing clues in the new situation because we cannot distance ourselves from what impressed us so much in the past. And if we do not need research that basically is aimed at controlling a particular output, what do we need? Or are we really arguing that it is all the same whatever we do? Of course we are not. But we think we should give up the voyeurism and the illusion of power that goes with this 'empirical' kind of theory. Because education is about persons (the teacher, the student, the parent, the child) in particular cases, what educational understanding asks from us is a preparedness to answer to humans' need to make sense of the world. Thus what is called for is a kind of theory that seeks to do justice to this demand: one that does not put education itself at risk. We might here recall Aristotle's perceptive point that one should not demand more exactitude than the nature of the matter permits.

In such a case the best thing one can do is to undertake exploration by making explicit how one makes sense of the world oneself. Some general knowledge of how things are is of course relevant for that. Let us call this 'local common sense' about how events which happen beyond our control have disposed our world and ourselves: how cell phones and chat-rooms have changed our world, as have refrigerators, television sets, means of transportation, talk of animal rights, and of course 'nine eleven'. To that extent descriptions help us to cope with the future, as does, in particular areas, a grasp of causality. But if there is no certainty, no particular steps to be followed which can ensure results in education, how could it be decided which method is to be followed when engaging in educational research? To dwell thoughtfully upon what is implied in a particular ethical situation or predicament, to decide what to do from the right kind of receptivity and trust, to do justice to the persons involved, one can use poems, art or calculative reasoning. This, in some sense, terminates the discussion about method. In the end it is because of what we understand by *education* that this must be the conclusion. Thus methods have to be found, not *the* or *a* method. Just as there are different therapies, as Wittgenstein claims, there are different methods (Wittgenstein, 1953, # 133).

Researchers in the human sciences may find themselves bewildered by this. The tasks of research are to be found in enquiry-as-interpretation. This means, as we have said, that one must 'place things side by side'. It goes without saying that academic psychology nowadays, still very much operating along Popperian lines, will find it hard to come to terms with such a programme. But even among educational researchers who have come to accept the legitimacy of both quantitative and qualitative research designs, enquiry-as-interpretation will be found to be problematical. What is the point of these designs, it will be asked, if not to generate a theoretical approach that is useful for the examination of future cases? Are we to take it that all theory is superfluous then? No. Quite the contrary. As we have already hinted above, there may be an important aspect that we seem to have forgotten in thinking about the kind of educational theory we need. It was alluded to in the characterization of education as 'making sense for oneself'. The perspicuous representation that was spoken of earlier is ethically rich, and looking at particular cases may indeed change our behaviour. It not only exemplifies through the variety of contexts the shades of meaning we have not yet fully realized – something one might want to call the result of an empirical investigation; it also reveals itself as ethically charged. By unravelling the different aspects of a particular situation one realizes how much the future is at the same time related to the past and yet can be seen as something to work towards, for instance for greater justice. It provides us with the elements necessary to be able to go on. Thus it becomes clear that the question what to do next is not simply a matter of 'what works', as one cannot judge 'what works' without a full sense of what one is trying to achieve. What to do next ought not to be limited to previous experience, but indeed should go beyond it by conceiving possible and not yet existent social forms. There is a place for utopian writing, as can be found in Plato's *Republic* and Rousseau's *Emile*: it has the capacity to release us from rigid and unimaginative ways of thinking.

One of the roots of our current educational crisis or impasse is to be found in the fantasy that it is the chief or only function of language to represent the world of reality. It may be very interesting to know a lot about current educational constraints and practices, about regularities and highly probable outcomes, but it is never enough. Or more precisely, it is only *a* starting-point, not even necessarily *the* starting-point, as the ethical nature of an educational situation requires us to go beyond mere application or mere logical deduction. Once important details of our life are reduced to numbers, a sense of alienation is difficult to avoid. Against this and against the overwhelming insistence on accountability, a different narrative for education is required. The reflection one needs here is philosophically engaged and will necessarily go beyond the empirical. It will go beyond means-end, instrumental reasoning and is thus unsettling in contrast to the kind of empirical research which draws on and reinforces the pull of precisely that kind of reasoning. This kind of reflective research does not sacrifice itself on the altar of prediction. And though it may want to start from the wisdom to be found in common sense, it will go beyond that in realizing a person's own values, in coming across new possibilities for education. Looking for causes, for distributions of variables, for 'understanding' as in qualitative research, all of this leads to different kinds of malaises. We have argued that such kinds of research are in need of therapy, as decisions in the sense of conclusions do not simply follow from the shallowness of the data. Sometimes they offer us only truisms; in other cases they ignore the nature of education and frame it in an output-oriented, performative straitjacket. Finally it may thus have become clear why it is that the paradigm of science does not yield the envisaged results for the context of education and how initiation into a particular research community and the ways it operates – the way it justifies its research findings, the allocation of research money, the ranking of journals, and more generally what is publishable – will always fall short of what is really at stake and what, in education, we need.[1]

# 13
## Learning from Psychoanalysis

'Freud thinks that psychoanalysis is something scientific; he
does not see that it is before everything a moral question.'
(Simone Weil, *Lectures on Philosophy* (1978), p. 98)

## Introduction

Education is always vulnerable to being assimilated to a medical
model. Just as the doctor cures your disease, so the teacher will
improve your educational health, by equipping you with the appropriate knowledge and skills. Just as medical research seeks to discover
which drugs and regimes are effective in combating infection or
obesity, so educational research sets itself to discover which ways of
teaching children how to read or calculate long division really work,
no doubt with double-blind testing to establish what works and what
does not. The medical model now threatens to reach its apogee in
neuroscientific approaches that talk of 'brain learning', seeing no
problem in the idea that debate about education can be replaced by
scientific research into synapses, receptors and peptides. This looks like
progress in the age of the twenty-first century, still wedded to the idea
that science is the way to solve all our problems.

This is not the place to enter into discussion about the complex
relation between the mind and the brain. Nor do we want to deny
that properly scientific research can sometimes yield benefits for education, for instance in demonstrating the propensity of convenience
food to engender the kind of hyperactivity incompatible with classroom concentration. What we want to explore here is the way that
the concept of intervention, as a matter of doing something to
someone, as making a kind of diagnosis followed by a prescription,

gets something fundamentally wrong about education. We consider how some writers have turned to the idea of psychoanalysis for an alternative model of education. We suggest that psychoanalysis is unhelpful if it is understood as offering a cure after the medical model: as if it could be used like a cold cure, indifferent to the particular patient; as if it deployed techniques *as* neutral, decontextualized techniques. While it is not a cure – a talking cure or any other kind – nevertheless there are ways of thinking of psychoanalysis, foregrounding language and interpretation, that are valuable here. There are insights from Freud and his work that should not be neglected simply because Freud and psychoanalysis are now generally out of favour. As Bentall makes clear in his groundbreaking book *Madness Explained* (2003), the disenchantment with psychoanalysis is partly due to the hopes that have been placed in biological and specifically neuroscientific approaches: to psychosis in the context of his work, and to education in the context of ours.

## Analysis

We need the idea of psychoanalysis, some would say, because education in our time has come to name a process that is relentlessly instrumental. It is always a matter of doing things to people, however benignly and humanely. In the light of our knowledge of those whom we teach (this Key Stage or that developmental phase, this child here or these adolescents with their distinctive popular culture, with which we try to become reasonably familiar) we design programmes of study (or have them designed for us) with various aims and outcomes predetermined and set out in advance. Teachers at all levels busily move between the pupil or student and the curriculum – effecting literal interventions indeed – to make the former receptive to the latter and the latter accessible to the former.

This is so much our everyday experience of education that we find it much less remarkable than perhaps we should. In fact some of our best efforts as educationalists go into 'knowing the learner' for the purposes of helping him or her to learn better. Whole degree programmes in Early Years Education are largely devoted to investigating how small children think and behave, as if we were anthropologists encountering that strange tribe, the Infants. The kind of developmental psychology associated with Jean Piaget and Laurence Kohlberg is still a mainstay of teacher training courses across the western world. A current fashion is for those working with young adults to try to establish their students' preferred 'learning style', which might, it is supposed, be for example predominantly verbal, iconic or kinaesthetic. While engaged in these essentially instrumental endeavours – for really we are only attempting to move our students up the ladder of educational achievement, however worthy that aim may be – perhaps we pride ourselves that we are not simply in the business of filling empty pitchers. So much more progressive than those whom we repudiate for (or fantasize as) teaching the subject and not the child.

Even when, conscious that the whole enterprise of education has become coloured by means-end rationality, we try to recover its distinctively ethical dimension, instrumentality re-emerges. As Zygmunt Bauman in particular has convincingly demonstrated, most classic conceptions of ethics are bound to cast education in the role of handmaiden. If ethics is understood as a system of principles or moral laws – or perhaps as a matter of the Kantian Moral Law – education's part is to teach what needs to be learned. Once again, and this time in the ethical context, the learner, the other with whom the teacher is confronted, is treated first and foremost as a recipient for knowledge or training whose content has already been set out in advance.

It is for reasons such as these that some have turned to psychoanalysis as a model for a very different way of relating to the learner: one in which we do not neglect learning *from* our pupils and students in our earnest desire to learn *about* them; where we can conceive of *attending to* them in ways that are not at root ways of *knowing* them. (It is customary in this context to note that the origin of the word 'therapist' is the Greek *therapeutes*, which meant 'attendant'). The nature of the 'psychoanalytic turn' is clearly put by Sharon Todd in a passage that is worth quoting at length:

> Psychoanalysis has taught us that what transpires in the everyday practices of education between teachers and students, and students and curriculum, involves complex layers of affect and conflict that specifically emerge out of an encounter with otherness. Feelings of guilt, love, and empathy, to name but a few, powerfully work their way in and through pedagogical encounters, and they do so not via conscious intent or purpose but in startling and unsettling ways that, in turn, fashion one's engagement with the Other. Thus one's capacity for response is shaped by factors that often lie outside one's control. It is in the *relating* to an unknowable Other through the adventure of learning (and teaching), that students and teachers become *psychically* implicated in the very possibilities for ethical interaction. (Todd, 2003, p. 4)

Thus the educational and the ethical no longer go separate ways. Here the encounter with the other precedes understanding. At its heart are susceptibility, vulnerability and openness rather than any kind of knowledge as conventionally conceived. Just as the clinical psychoanalyst can only work with her patient by pondering on issues such as transference and counter-transference ('Am I being manoeuvered into becoming this person's father?' 'Am I beginning to think of this patient as the sister I never had?') so the teacher who is sensitive to the psychodynamic dimension of teaching and learning (which is how 'psychoanalytic' is perhaps helpfully to be glossed here) is continually learning about herself and from the learner (less from the learner's opinions, of course, than from his or her condition of being in the world), whatever more conventional forms of teaching and learning are taking place.

An example: Alice is a primary school teacher in the fifth year of her career (this is a real example and one of a widespread problem: see also Chapter 1. Of course 'Alice' is not her real name.). Despite being a successful teacher by all available criteria, including popularity with children and their parents, Alice is almost incapacitated by the prospect of the start of each new term, and especially by the start of the school year. The last week of every school holiday is ruined by agonies of self-doubt and despair. She cannot believe that past success will turn into future success. Specifically she seems to worry that this time the children will not like her, will not do as they are told and will prove uncontrollable. In-service courses on 'How to get the year off to a good start' and 'Effective opening strategies' prove no help at all. Eventually, under the guidance of an experienced colleague, Alice finds the courage to begin by asking the children about their feelings at the start of the term and the year. They talk, and write and draw, about bullies, school lunch, lavatories; about rowdy playgrounds, and PE lessons, and maths. Quite a lot of this rings uneasy bells for Alice. Somehow knowing that the children come with these fears seems to help her with her own.

A second example: George (also a real example, name changed; George also appeared in Chapter 9) teaches a third-year undergraduate class that he tends to describe as consisting of bright, articulate and assertive students. The subject of the course is postmodern social thought. The ideas here and the reading – by for instance Foucault, Derrida, Lacan – are difficult and dense. Every evening that precedes the regular Friday class George is conscious of feelings that range from mild anxiety to panic. Surely this week the students will complain about the difficulties and obscurities; they will rise in revolt, declare the course impossible, pretentious; they will discover that George often grasps Derrida little better than they do; they will demand a paraphrase that he cannot supply; they will decamp to a module of renowned clarity and straightforwardness where the lecturer provides the proverbial good set of notes and regular risqué jokes; they will march George out to the car park and hang him from a lamppost. Such are George's Thursday evening nightmares, and their effect, if he is not properly reflective, is to impel him in the direction of the photocopier (supplying photocopied articles and chapters makes him feel he is at least giving the students something), or towards preparing a lecture consisting of a dozen bullet-pointed paragraphs – this too will surely make the students feel they are getting something solid, and besides its delivery will take the full hour and leave no space for the complaining and lynching.

George succumbs to these devices from time to time. Sometimes however he is able to reflect: that perhaps it is his perception of these students as bright, articulate and cheeringly assertive that makes him feel excessively and unnecessarily responsible for what transpires in the classes. Perhaps his very perception is at fault here: it is not that they are instead dull and ordinary students, but that he has possibly invested them with particular hopes of his own. They are, in their otherness, less knowable than he imagined. Perhaps it is not the students who cannot bear the difficulties of the material and will revolt, but George who has problems in not being in easy command in the way he is with other courses and other classes. These and other such reflections enable him on a good day to meet his students in a tentative and explorative spirit that allows all participants to acknowledge the imperfections of their understanding and work with the difficulties together, with no great sense of despair or inadequacy if everything has not been clarified at the end of the hour. In fact it is this, the students often say, that they value in this course and that makes it different from the others that they take.

## Resistances

Heady stuff: too much of this kind of thinking and one begins to long for the clean simplicity of old-fashioned didactic teaching: where, for instance, the teacher shows the student or pupil how to solve the mathematical problem or translate the foreign language text, and then later the learner comes back and shows she can now do it on her own. It is a comfort, when we have such longing, that the climate of opinion has moved fairly conclusively against psychoanalysis: that there are major criticisms especially concerning its scientific standing. Our purpose in considering some of these criticisms is not to conclude that if the criticisms can be in some ways rebutted then we have rescued psycho-analysis. It is rather to suggest that what is still worth taking seriously in psychoanalysis is not very different from what is worth taking seriously about some aspects of education.

We start with the issue of refutability. A scientific theory – that is one that makes a claim to respectability – is one that can in principle be refuted (the classic Popperian position). A theory where by contrast every counter-example is turned into a confirming instance is not a scientific theory at all. (At the extreme, recall the sort of *X-Files* conspiracy theory that maintains government is complicit in concealing visits of aliens to our planet. To the objection that there is no evidence at all of such visits, the response may be that this shows precisely how thorough govern-ment has been in its concealment.) And it seems a problem of Freudian analysis that disconfirming instances are prone to being turned into confirming ones. We are invited to imagine such cases where the analyst's proferred interpretation is rejected suspiciously vigorously. 'Is it possible that in being a "tennis father" you are trying to realize your own thwarted ambitions via your daughter?' – 'My daughter has real poten-tial, I'm simply trying to help her realize it. My own history has nothing to do with this'. The hostile critic sketches the knowing smile, the rather smug satisfaction with which the analyst sits back in his chair, perhaps, in this fictitious scenario, saying 'Aha … ' slowly, or words to the effect that 'This idea seems to upset you quite a lot, I think'.

Part of the problem here is that sometimes people *do* disavow our interpretations in a way that encourages us to suppose that they are in denial. A fictional example will help to make the point. In Garry Trudeau's *Doonesbury* cartoon Honey, helpmate to the appalling Duke, currently corrupt and self-serving stand-in governor of some war-torn Iraqi city, and whose disregard for Honey is clear throughout the narra-tive, tells the boss for whom she secretly yearns that two Iraqis are seeking her hand in marriage (*The Guardian* 5.1.2005).

- '*Two* ardent suitors! Can you believe it, sir? I don't know how I got in such a pickle!'
- 'Honey, I explained this to you: you're a US citizen. Whoever marries you gets a ticket out of this sorry-ass country!'
- Sir, sir, sir. How much pain must you be in to lash out at my suitors that way?'

The story continues with Duke's dismissive 'So marry whoever ... although I have to admit that in some small, meaningless way I'll miss having you around' and Honey's self-deceiving interpretation of this as sufficient reason to send her suitors away. This part of the story concludes as Honey 'refines her memory' in rapt contemplation under the starry sky: 'In some small way, I'd miss you, Honey' becomes 'In some way, I'd miss you, Honey', and then 'You complete me, Honey'. 'There we go', she concludes in thought, the job of self-deception well done (*ibid*. 8.1.2005). That we can enjoy the humour of this shows how familiar we are with the possibility of denial, self-deception and wishful thinking.

Then how are we to distinguish such cases from those where the diagnosis of denial is, we want to say, simply part of the psycho-analyst's self-confirming mechanism? Alasdair MacIntyre touches on this in his book *The Unconscious* (1958, pp. 56–9):

Of course, it is a feature of the psychoneuroses that the patient will in the short run deny, and deny vehemently, the analyst's interpretations of his conduct ... [if the denial] was especially vehement we should perhaps treat this as almost as conclusive as an avowal. Incidentally, in ordinary attributions of motive and intention we find exactly the same tendency to treat avowals as confirming but denials as not necessarily overthrowing our interpretations that we find in the psychoanalyst's treatment of the patient's response to his interpretations. Those who have criticized Freud and his followers for acting thus have missed this link between the treatment of unconscious motives in ordinary speech and their treatment by Freud.

There is, that is to say, nothing *technical* here about psychoanalysis such that it is the proper deployment of a technique (in a scientific kind of way) that guarantees the soundness of the interpretation or the failure to deploy it in the right way that causes the attempt to go awry. MacIntyre, again, notes that 'psychoanalysts, like personnel officers, clergymen and doctors, learn empirically what a convincing tale sounds like and come to have a good ear for deception and self-deception' (p. 81). This is hardly likely to reassure the sceptic (properly so called, we shall shortly suggest). You mean, he may ask, that whether disavowal is to be taken at face value or as *denial*, in the sense used above, comes down to something like the ordinary common sense of the analyst? It is precisely the force of what MacIntyre writes about 'ordinary attributions of motive and intention' (above) that something like common sense (refined in the case of the analyst by experience of difficult cases and subjected to deeper reflection than most of us undertake for our attributions) will have to do here, in that there is nothing more precise, sure or reliable that we can turn to instead.

Behind one standard criticism of psychoanalysis, then, there appears to lie a craving for a greater degree of certainty than the matter allows. The sceptic is not satisfied with what might be called ordinary knowledge as the answer to his doubting but requires something more solid. This is the essence of philosophical scepticism: like Descartes in the quest for ideas so clear and distinct that they could not possibly be implanted in his head by a mischievous demon, the sceptic sets his criteria for plausibility higher than ordinary life can accommodate, and may justify his demand by insisting that higher than ordinary criteria are called for if psychoanalysis is to make any claims to being a science. Before turning to this broad issue it is worth noting that in the case of the particular scenario pictured above, in which the psychoanalyst glibly interprets disavowal as denial, psycho-analysis is taken to do exactly what it takes pains to avoid: to imagine that it grasps, sums up a person, readily comprehends him, perhaps on the basis of some theory or generalization ('all tennis fathers are projecting their own unfulfilled ambitions'). A major task for the therapist is to see through, and help patients to see through, the fantasy that he has 'the answer' (Collier, 1977, p. 109); the analyst is not concerned to hand over solutions, ready-made or otherwise, but to help the patient learn to find his or her own way to solutions, and this not as a matter of acquiring techniques but of the reorientation of self to the world (cp. Lear, 2003, p. 155).

## Science and myth

Freud often laid claim to being a scientist. It is familiar for instance that he is inclined to see the mind in terms of fluid mechanics, as if psychic energy swirls around the system, gaining in pressure the more it is repressed and sublimated, and emerges in dreams, slips of the tongue and so on like puffs of steam; or, to take another example, that the meaning of dream symbols is fixed as if they were mathematical constants. Freud's followers and translators generally perpetuated this picture. Adam Phillips shows convincingly in *Darwin's Worms* how Freud's biographers were concerned to show the great man as heroic scientist in his last days, refusing morphine in order to preserve the clarity of his mind. Bruno Bettelheim in *Freud and Man's Soul* (1983) has reminded us that Freud wrote not about the mind but the soul, *die Seele*, and that Latinate terms such as ego, super-ego, id and cathexis sound considerably less scientific if they are translated from the German as 'the "I"', 'the "over-I"', and so on.

Of course given the prestige of science in Freud's time, as well as in ours, this is unsurprising (we might compare the way some thinkers today are happy to be called 'social scientists' even when they believe the methodology of their subject bears little resemblance to that of the physical sciences). But how are we to understand Freudian psycho-analysis, if not as some kind of science?

The philosopher Ludwig Wittgenstein is illuminating on this ques-tion. He disparages Freud for 'constantly claiming to be scientific' (1966, p. 44) yet is reported (p. 41) as saying: 'I happened to read some-thing by Freud, and I sat up in surprise. Here was someone who had something to say'. The mistake, according to Wittgenstein, is to take physics as our 'ideal science' when studying psychology (p. 42): 'we think of formulating laws as in physics' (*ibid*.). We should rather think of Freud as offering us a new mythology to live by:

> Freud refers to various ancient myths ... and claims that his researches have now explained how it came about that anybody should think or propound a myth of that sort ... Whereas in fact Freud has done something different. He has not given a scientific explanation of the ancient myth. What he has done is to propound a new myth. The attractiveness of the suggestion, for instance, that all anxiety is a repetition of the anxiety of the birth trauma, is just the attractiveness of a mythology. (*ibid*.)

In giving us a story about the unconscious, repression and so on, Freud is doing the same kind of thing as when he reminds us of the story of Oedipus. In both cases he tells us 'life's like this'. Wittgenstein declared approvingly of Freud's work that 'It's all excellent similes' (Monk, 1990, p. 357). On this account, the value of the myth of Oedipus is not that it prefigures or dramatizes the Oedipus complex, the latter being seen as a piece of psychopathology, independently and scientifically knowable, which bears the Greek name for the sake of vividness. To make the acquaintance of the myth is rather itself to learn some-thing helpful, in that the myth shows a pattern in which aspects of our lives fit and make sense. It is, Wittgenstein says, *speculation* rather than 'insight' (eg into the timeless human condition). 'It is something

which people are inclined to accept and which makes it easier for them
to go certain ways: it makes certain ways of behaving and thinking
natural for them. They have given up one way of thinking and adopted
another' (1966, pp. 44–5). Mythological explanations have the attraction that they say 'this is all a repetition of something that has happened before. And when people do accept or adopt this, then certain
things seem much clearer and easier for them. So it is with the notion
of the unconscious also' (p. 43).

Myth supplies a new language, a new framework for looking at the
world. It offers the patient and analyst an alternative to languages
and frameworks which seem necessary, 'written in the stars', even
obsessive; meanings that appear fixed and determinate. An example
may help here. A young woman found it difficult to resist her
parents' blandishments to return to the family home which she
alleged had been a place of abuse during her childhood, and visits
back to which correlated accurately with what her psychiatrist diagnosed as subsequent 'psychotic episodes'. She was on one level well
aware of the damage these visits did her, but repeated that 'mum
was only trying to be kind', that it was nice to be in a house that was
well-decorated (compared to her student accommodation), even if
rather fussy, with everything colour-coordinated and ubiquitous pot
pourri ; that 'there was always food available' and that mother constantly joked about 'fattening her up'. At one point the young
woman's counsellor commented that home sounded like the ginger-
bread house (from the fairy-tale of Hansel and Gretel: the children
are lured there by a witch who only wants to fatten them up to eat
them). This apparently gave the young woman a metaphor she
found helpful: a way of acknowledging that home was both sweet
and threatening, potentially fatal. It seems it released her from the
fantasy that 'home is home after all' (this one is indeed home, sweet
home) and from the difficulty of acknowledging its threats.
Wittgenstein says that 'it may then be an immense relief if it can be
shown that one's life has the pattern rather of a tragedy – the tragic
working out and repetition of a pattern ... ' (p. 51): or, we might say,
the pattern here of a fairy story.

To summarize: in its focus on language psychoanalysis reminds us
that we live in and through language: language is not a neutral
instrument. It offers us a new myth in the form of its own characteristic frameworks of understanding (the anal stage, the oral stage and
so on). The technical jargon that it generates is both liberating *and*
dangerous.

## A philosophy of mothering

We offer an extended example of what we mean by the use of a new and richer language through one writer's examination of what it means to be a mother. Naomi Stadlen argues persuasively in *What Mothers Do: especially when it looks like nothing* (2004) that motherhood has fallen victim to the language and dominant ideas of our time. When confronted with new challenges we expect to be trained and equipped with skills to deal with them. As one of her interviewees notes, 'the dominant culture ... is all about planning and controlling' (p. 48). We are used to jumping through hoops and over hurdles – examinations, Duke of Edinburgh's awards, applications for jobs and for promotion – and so childbirth too comes to seem another hurdle, after which life will surely go back to normal (p. 34). When it turns out, by contrast, that life will never be the same again we naturally look to the appropriate experts to tell us how to manage, and the book-shops are of course full of guides to the appropriate techniques. But what Stadlen calls 'the intimacy of mothering' cannot be reduced to a series of practical techniques and the books that offer these are being less than honest (p. 251).

Being a mother to a small child, however, 'is all about feeling your way', as the same interviewee puts it. According to Stadlen it is less a matter of techniques than of something like responsiveness, a constant alertness and attuning of oneself to the needs and nature of this part-icular child now, to whom no-one else is responsible in the same way. And this is all the more difficult for us to understand because we do not have the words for it: which is why what mothers do can look like nothing from the outside and often feels like not very much from the inside either. At the heart of being a mother is the state which can only be described as 'Being instantly interruptible' (the title of Chapter Four): the condition in which she is endlessly there for her child to the point that she may feel she has no life of her own. We have many words for being a bad mother – Stadlen gives a list of over thirty words and phrases – but the list for being a good mother is much shorter and the words (eg caring, nurturing, patient) do not so much describe what mothers do as what they are like as persons (pp. 18–19).

Part of what is at issue here is that our world recognizes and values busyness and activity: as Stadlen notes, a 'busy mother' is a cliché of our time. Mothering however requires a kind of passivity, being there for the baby rather than exercising techniques on her. It requires the mother almost 'to loosen her active conscious mode and sink into something older and simpler in order to get close to the world of her baby' (p. 89). This may sound fuzzy and unfocused but it is not. It means the kind of awareness of the baby that shows the child her mother takes the moral dimension seriously. Babies are less concerned about anything particular we do around them than 'about the sense that they matter profoundly to us, and that we have given some thought to their interests as well as our own' (p. 132). They are observing us with the closest attention, the same quality we must bring to them. A story makes the point vividly. A mother was impatient to get home with her two year-old because she (the mother) wanted to try something out on the piano. Usually her daughter, always copying mother, would sit beside her on the piano stool; on this occasion she disappeared and reemerged with an old hat: wearing this, she sat down next to mother and 'played' the keys. 'There doesn't seem to be a word for what the mother is doing. It means: being available for her baby to observe' (p. 136). Cultivating the faculty of attention brings sometimes unexpected, almost Zen-like, rewards: 'A mother trying to understand her child may suddenly notice the astonishing beauty of an ordinary gravel path. From this perspective, it can seem amazing to see everyone else in time-conscious haste. Whatever is all the hurry for?' (pp. 190–1).

We generally expect people to become more focused and confident as they begin to get the measure of new demands made on them, but this may not be the mother's experience, and she may be right not to experience things like this:

> If she feels disorientated, this is not a problem requiring book-shelves of literature to put right. No, it is exactly the *right* state of mind for the teach-yourself process that lies ahead of her ... If she really considered herself an expert, or if her ideas were set, she would find it very hard to adapt to her individual baby ... Each child will be a little different and teach her something new. She needs to feel uncertain in order to be flexible. So, although it can feel so alarming, the 'all-at-sea' feeling is appropriate. Uncertainty is a *good* starting point for a mother. Through uncertainty, she can begin to learn. (p. 45)

The new mother has no map, and the available maps that display the techniques of motherhood cannot be trusted. In offering help Stadlen too acknowledges that the map is under construction. And although she does not say so, the problem is essentially a philosophical one, and her efforts are philosophical in the way that Ludwig Wittgenstein conceived of philosophy as non-dogmatic and therapeutic. He writes that 'a philosophical problem has the form: "I don't know my way about"'(Wittgenstein, 1953, 1.123). Stadlen sets about the difficult task of assembling the reminders that help us to achieve a new map, a new way of looking at things. Thus too Wittgenstein writes (1. 127) that 'The work of the philosopher consists in assembling reminders for a particular purpose', and of the philosopher who makes progress (1. 401), 'What you have primarily discovered is a new way of looking at things. As if you had invented a new way of painting; or, again, a new metre, or a new kind of song'.

This 'new way of looking at things' requires finding the right language. Stadlen's book is full of examples where mothers struggle to find the right words for their experience. Stadlen herself challenges the widespread and somewhat *a priori* assumption that motherhood is fundamentally a period of 'ambivalence' (pp. 162 ff). She has a quick ear for when her interviewees find words that catch something important. There is an unbridgeable gap between mothering and what one mother calls 'the jagged and sharp world of work' (p. 206). Another speaks of the rhythmical nature of life with a baby:

> I'm hoping to have another baby in a few years. But another baby will be a different baby... Life with a baby goes in waves like the sea. [She gestured in a slow, wavy motion with her hand.] And work is all... [She briskly gestured slicing bits of something.] (p. 207)

This is the philosophical business of exploring 'what it makes sense to say', as Peter Winch put it (*The Idea of a Social Science*, p. 72). It makes sense to Stadlen to write of motherhood in terms of alertness and attunement, flexibility and the qualities of the mother's character rather than the skills she has acquired. In this her description comes very close to the Aristotelian picture of *phronesis* or practical wisdom. Wittgenstein writes that 'Philosophy simply puts everything before us, and neither explains nor deduces anything. – Since everything lies open to view there is nothing to explain' (*Philosophical Investigations* 1.126); Stadlen writes that although 'the right words' are continually elusive 'Whenever I'm sitting with a group of mothers, everything seems so obvious that there doesn't seem anything to explain' (p. 210). Indeed there *is* nothing to explain, but the problem is solved, the 'mother knot' is untangled, in Suissa's (2005) words, through the discovery of a rich and responsive language that does justice to the phenomena.

## Conclusion: language and meaning

Much of what we have written here is reminiscent of Peter Winch's position in *The Idea of a Social Science* (1958). There he argues against the idea that new knowledge is only or even primarily acquired by scientists by experimental and observational methods, leaving philosophy merely the role of underlabourer in clearing away conceptual confusion. A proper focus on meaning, according to Winch, is also knowledge-productive. To ask 'What is real?' involves 'the problem of man's relation to reality, which takes us beyond pure science' (*ibid.* p. 9): in discussing language philosophically we are discussing *what counts as belonging to the world* (p. 15). Winch writes:

> The question of what constitutes social behaviour is a demand for an elucidation of the *concept* of social behaviour. In dealing with questions of this sort there should be no question of 'waiting to see' what empirical research will show us; it is a matter of tracing the implications of the concepts we use. (p. 18)

Since our relations with others are permeated with our ideas about reality, an enquiry into the nature of our knowledge of reality and into the difference which the possibility of such knowledge makes to human life always presupposes taking into account the ideas around which our lives revolve. An excellent example would be whether mental illness is 'real' or, as some would have it, a myth of a particularly unhelpful kind. Social relations, Winch writes, are an 'unsuitable subject' for the formulation of 'generalizations and theories of the scientific sort' (*ibid.*, p. 133).

It is one of the best insights we own to Freudian psychoanalysis that language is not an indifferent medium through which we conduct our value-neutral scientific interventions. Lear notes that 'Every analyst knows that in addition to the truth of what one says to an analysand, it is crucial how one says it' (Lear, 2003, p. 11). What may be in a sense true enough ('You have problems with authority figures because of your relationship with your father') is of no use to the client without a whole framework of language, a kind of mythology, in terms of which he can reconstruct his life to incorporate this truth. We might reflect that the development of a richer and more responsive framework of language to replace the prison-house of 'fixed concepts with absolutely determinate meanings' (p. 52) is clearly as much a task for the teacher, at every level, as it is for the psychoanalyst.

How different things would be if we could tear ourselves away from the physical sciences as our model for knowledge, taking for instance literary criticism as the model instead. No-one supposes that there is one correct interpretation of *Bleak House* which we will one day reach, after which literary discussion of this particular novel can stop; at the same time no sophisticated reader is inclined to imagine that any interpretation of *Bleak House* is as good as any other. We do not bring neutral techniques to bear on a novel, poem or play and come away, the interpretative work done, unchanged by the experience. Rather we find that Dickens, or Shakespeare, or E. Annie Proulx, has so to speak entered our bloodstream. So too the analyst is enriched by discussion with the analysand, the social worker with the client, and the teacher with the pupil or student, as long as they enter into the relationship in the spirit of openness and susceptibility that lie at the heart of the idea of psychoanalysis. And might it be that this gives us some insight into what is sometimes expressed as the intrinsic value of education: that there simply are no human interactions better than those entered into in this spirit; and that life offers fewer better possibilities than to talk with each other in this way?[1]

# 14
## Enlarging the Enigma

'I think I summed up my attitude to philosophy when I said philosophy ought really to be written only as a *poetic composition*.'
(Wittgenstein, 1980, 24e)

We closed the preceding chapter with the thought that in order to tear ourselves away from physical sciences as our model for knowledge, we might turn to literature and to literary criticism. We open this chapter with the thought that in order even to understand a characteristically modern form of alienation – with its loss of the better possibilities of life we have just considered – we need to turn our attention again to the mainstream of philosophy itself. Driven by the pressure towards ever greater specialization, much philosophical work has become a matter of the elaboration of concepts and abstractions that are of questionable relevance to daily life. Philosophy is seen as divorced from the practicalities of our daily lives and as having only an indirect potential to change the world; sometimes it appears an abstract, intellectualized game, offering little more than idle commentary on the world beyond. This was the suspicion of Wittgenstein already in the first half of the twentieth century. In this chapter we draw upon his reaction to that mainstream, which led him at times to speak of the philosophy that was needed in resistance to these trends, as we saw, precisely as a kind of therapy. As social science generally as well as aspects of philosophy of education specifically suffer from the same illness (recall the forms of apoplexy we considered in Chapter 5), we shall endeavour to show the kind – or kinds – of educational theory and philosophy that Wittgenstein might inspire. The major part of the chapter examines the connection between the idea of philosophy as therapy and the achieving of a 'perspicuous representation'. In the remainder of the chapter we focus more directly on Stanley Cavell's Wittgensteinian elaboration of the themes of scepticism and acknowledgement, which have surfaced recurrently in this book.

## Wittgenstein: philosophy as therapy

Wittgenstein understands the aim of philosophy in its most general form in terms of the offering of an *Übersicht* – a *surview* or *perspicuous representation*. This can be achieved only by a patient investigation of the way that sentences and expressions are 'applied' and of their rule-governed connections. He uses many examples: of language-games that are imaginary or exaggerated or impossible; of cases that juxtapose our ordinary experience with the limits of intelligibility; of segments of 'grammar'. Philosophy should not preoccupy itself with metaphysical propositions that purport to express the essence of things; and there are no new facts to be discovered, only new insights into old facts. Theorization always tempts because it carries the allure of an expertise that transcends the boundaries of context, bringing with it a vocabulary of 'super-concepts'. Thus in education, 'motivation', 'play', 'development', 'creativity', 'imagination', 'learning', 'aim', 'objective', 'competence' and 'skill' all acquire a bogus aura of significance. Wittgenstein would bring these words back to the ordinary circumstances of their use (Wittgenstein, 1953, I, # 116). Theorization can take root where what is really an unclarity about the meaning of words is missed through the formulation of the problem as a *scientific* question; but what purports to be scientific in this way characteristically turns out to harbour a metaphysical question (Wittgenstein, 1969, p. 35). The urge to theorize is telling, however, in that it is symptomatic of a reaching after significance; the sense of lack that has been brought about by the decline of religious belief and observance may exacerbate this. Thus, to recall the particular – to find a new way of looking at things (cf. Wittgenstein, 1953, I, # 401) – is to be taken as *the* method for every philosophical investigation. Philosophy, for Wittgenstein, is like therapy, for when we see how language actually works philosophical problems disappear and philosophical questions come to an end:

> The real discovery is the one that makes me capable of stopping doing philosophy when I want to. – The one that gives philosophy peace, so that it is no longer tormented by questions which bring *itself* in question. – Instead, we now demonstrate a method, by

examples; and the series of examples can be broken off. – Problems are solved (difficulties eliminated), not a *single* problem.

There is not *a* philosophical method, though there are indeed methods, like different therapies. (*ibid*. I, # 133)

The aim is to teach someone to pass from a piece of disguised nonsense to something that is patent nonsense (cf. *ibid*. I, # 464), as the 'repressed nonsense' is made explicit. In the face of the question why, one sometimes has to say simply that this is what we do: 'What people accept as a justification – is shown by how they think and live' (*ibid*. I, # 325). The aim of philosophy can be said to be 'To shew the fly the way out of the fly-bottle' (*ibid*. I, # 309). Elsewhere he describes the result of a philosophical investigation as follows: 'I wanted to put that picture before him, and his *acceptance* of the picture consists in his now being inclined to regard a given case differently: that is, to compare it with *this* rather than *that* set of pictures. I have changed his *way of looking at things*' (*ibid*. I, # 144). It is 'as if you had invented a new way of painting; or, again, a new metre, or a new kind of song' (*ibid*. I, # 401). Wittgenstein lays the way for our turn to literary criticism by suggesting that giving reasons in philosophy can be compared with giving reasons in aesthetics. One may speak of a debate, but this does not lead to conclusions; rather, the purpose is to sensitize those involved to the way something can be appreciated (cf. Moore, 1955). Philosophy of this kind, he says, may be written as a poetic composition (cf. Wittgenstein, 1980, p. 24e, quoted above).

The 'craving for generality' (Wittgenstein, 1969, p. 18), with its contemptuous attitude towards the particular case and its ideal of over-arching theory, is to be resisted. The perspicuous representation, by contrast, is manifestly not an exhaustive explanation: it is necessarily partial, covering a limited domain of our experience or a limited segment of grammar. It is also closely linked with the idea of 'seeing aspects'. Wittgenstein deals with this extensively in Part II, xi, of the *Philosophical Investigations*. In the puzzle picture of the duck-rabbit (Wittgenstein, 1953, II, p. 194), it is not the addition of a datum that allows the alternative picture to be seen but the dawning of an aspect such that the structural role of each part of the picture is quite different. A key point here is the primacy of (non-deliberative) interpretation. What is first seen is a duck or a rabbit. It is not the case that we first 'see' the visual data and then construct from these one or the other meaningful image. It would be closer to the truth to say that it is through abstracting from the picture of the duck or the rabbit that we can identify the lines that make it up, and this move would be a privative one along the lines of the procedures of science. But even through this abstraction we do not arrive at an atomism of visual data. For what is to count in our observation will itself be determined by further interpretations, as, for example, to do with the idea of a drawn line. The duck-rabbit image is, of course, unusual since a reading of the drawing can go either way: normally an interpretation forces itself on us. Even a proof in mathematics is not a logical deduction from a series of propositions but rather is something that we *see*. Not seeing a pattern will mean that we do not know where we are or how to go on; seeing it will be the result of a training, not in generic skills but in correct judgements.

In a paper called 'The *Investigations*: Everyday Aesthetics of Itself' Stanley Cavell (2004a) argues that Wittgenstein claims for the ordinary its own possibility of perspicuity. He sees Wittgenstein as pointing to resemblances between mathematical proof and perspicuity. Understanding a proof requires seeing connections, but so does understanding a unity among sentences. Thus, one discovers a new manifestation of the concept in seeing something new about the ordinary. 'Seeing connections' is understood as supplying the substance of language-games and as the basis for showing grammatical derivations or differences. Wittgenstein is not interested in the formal ideal of logic, not in logic as the ultimate formal systematization of the unity of knowledge, but in the sense in which logic is something sublime. Yet it is philosophy's 'fantasy of logic', Cavell claims, that remains the mark of its intellectual seriousness. Philosophy demands an extraordinary understanding, but this is not of something new; it is not in competition with science. The experience – perhaps therapeutic – of initially destroying everything great and important is seen by Cavell in terms of a movement from being lost to finding oneself: 'Perspicuous representation is accordingly the end of a philosophical problem that has *this* form of beginning' (*ibid.*, p. 23). He recalls that the philosopher's treatment of a question is said by Wittgenstein to be like the treatment of an illness, a sickness of the understanding as well as a sickness of the will. In order to give itself peace, philosophy must break itself off from asking the wrong questions; it must surrender, entrusting itself to the ordinary. This 'eventual ordinary' does not refer merely to the everyday, the 'actual ordinary': it is rather a matter of passing through but giving up the disappointment with criteria from which philosophy too readily suffers. The shedding of the demand for something more, the sceptic's insistent dissatisfaction, is the therapy that Wittgenstein speaks of. Consider, for example, the demand for authenticity that looks without respite for 'the real self' or perhaps the more characteristically philosophical disappointment with the limits of natural language.

What is said about philosophy holds as well for the philosopher in each of us. Following the *Investigations*, Cavell suggests,

> requires a willingness to recognize in oneself the moments of strangeness, sickness, disappointment, self-destructiveness, perversity, suffocation, torment, lostness that are articulated in the language of the *Investigations*, and to recognize in its philosophizing that its pleasures (they will have to reach to instances of the ecstatic) will lie in the specific forms and moments of self-recovery it proposes – of familiarity (hence uncanniness, since the words of recovery were already familiar; too familiar), of soundness, of finitude, of the usefulness of friction, of acknowledgement, of peace. (*ibid.*, p. 27)

The importance of the literary lies particularly in the way that it directs attention to the workings of language. Moreover, in their telling of stories novels can achieve a new perspective on everyday situations, themselves exploring not only the grammar of our language but also the limits of our form of life. The short, carefully crafted poetic text invites detailed, critical analysis with attention given to nuances realized in the minutiae of expression. The finding of a new image moves beyond the fixity of meaning to realize through that expression new responses and new possibilities. The poetic, exploiting the connotative and figurative power of words and the rhythmic and sonic quality of phrases and sentences, brings something new into the world. That philosophy may be written as poetic composition reflects Wittgenstein's openness to such invention and his realization of this as a condition of language. In this sense philosophy does not leave everything as it is.

Language, according to Wittgenstein, requires neither reform nor theory: it needs to be described in all its dense, intractable, living hurly-burly (Cf. Wittgenstein, 1967, # 567). We lack a clear view of the use of our words and our grammar. Given that a perspicuous representation produces just that understanding that consists in 'seeing connections', the philosopher is to be seen less as a systematic cartographer than as an itinerant sketcher. The bewilderment – say, the lack of connections – that arises from finding oneself lost in a wilderness rather than at home in a domestic garden arises from the 'inexpressible'. But unlike the sense of what cannot be said with which the *Tractatus* famously concludes, the sense here is of the immense complexity of a background that escapes even the most exhaustive attempts at synthesis. As David Schalkwyk puts this,

> The desire for the elevated overview stems from a wish both to see the nature of the background and its relation to any particular concept clearly, and also to map completely the relationships among all concepts in the language and the totality of background against which they 'have their meaning'. While there is no logical prohibition against this, Wittgenstein is forced to acknowledge that one can sketch such relationships only from a situated position. (Schalkwyk, 2004, p. 71)

In this way Wittgenstein registers a personal sense of bewilderment and limitation. His task is to be carried out in the vast network of the literary in which the situatedness of human life is registered and imaginatively renewed and tested. What is crucial is alert thinking, sensitive use of words, with the imaginative use of language creating new possibilities of being. Literature stages and embodies our alternating perceptions of where we find ourselves, now as in a wilderness, now as in a well laid-out garden. There is a strong case for saying that a work of art enlightens the human condition not by explaining it but by making us feel in an intensified form its unnameable enigma. If language and reality neatly coincided, there would be no enigma. Without coincidence, it is only art that can do justice to the way things are, sustaining the enigma, making it vivid by enlarging it. Philosophy as poetic composition offers the best grammatical investigation of our concepts: this is what perspicuous representation implies. In the *Tractatus* Wittgenstein says that anyone who understands him – that is, anyone who recognizes Wittgenstein's propositions as nonsensical once he has used them – must climb beyond them: 'He must, so to speak, throw away the ladder after he has climbed up it' (Wittgenstein, 1992, # 6.54). So too, once we have reached a perspicuous representation and seen the world aright, that representation can be abandoned. It must not become a new metaphysical idea, so that the perspective is no perspective but rather a view from nowhere; nothing should be taken from the flux of meaning-and-world. Philosophy's therapy is not then the elimination of what is impossible: it involves breaking the grip of what seems all too necessary in order the better to accept what may otherwise seem merely – say, accidentally – to be the case.

In offering new criteria in this way for the use of certain concepts philosophy, by way of aesthetics, comes close to religion. This position explains why a philosopher who has ostensibly been concerned with grammatical investigations does not necessarily turn away from the religious life. The fly cannot simply be *shown* the way out of the fly-bottle because it is its prison only at a superficial level: at a deeper level it is the home the fly, at least to a certain extent, has built for itself. The perplexity is part of that home. The grammatical investigation helps to reveal what could not be seen before; or, in Heidegger's terms, the true is brought into the openness of what could not be seen before. But the offering of new criteria for the use of certain concepts demands particular attention as it is sometimes not completely clear what *kinds* of problems philosophy is dealing with. A conceptual problem does not usually arise from a disagreement with someone else's ideas but rather from a discomfort with their way of expressing them. Wittgenstein often refers to the way of *solving* a problem, but he rarely says much about how it is *detected* – hence he does not provide a characterization for what a philosophical problem consists in. In connecting the manifestation of a problem with expressions such as 'confusion', 'bewilderment, 'puzzlement', or 'perplexity', he offers little more than a clue: such problems are conceptual problems; we fail fully to understand the different uses of some expressions in our language-games. Conceptual discomfort arises because an expression, a gesture, an action, appears out of place in a particular language-game.

Joseph Margolis (2004), however, puts forward the view that Wittgenstein's procedure is far from clear. In terms of method he cannot rightly be said to bring words back from their metaphysical to their everyday use, because 'everyday use' is often deeply affected by one or another form of the mind/body dualism that Wittgenstein rightly opposes. Furthermore, because the seeming correction of such a 'mistake' is itself 'metaphysical', and thus exceeds whatever counts as 'everyday use', we can no longer supply a rule for determining what the right scope of a pertinent generalization should be – a matter that follows directly from Wittgenstein's position concerning rule-following. In other words, trying to do something against one form of 'bewitchment' seems necessarily to invoke another. In the light of this Margolis argues that departure from prevailing usage in order to secure a possible philosophical gain cannot be disallowed on the grounds of past or prevailing linguistic usage alone and that this is not as such incompatible with Wittgenstein's therapeutic intuition. What Wittgenstein proposes does not in Margolis's view, therefore, constitute a determinate method but is rather a way of following a particular intuition – in this case Wittgenstein's 'feeling' of what is minimally required in order to avoid philosophical nonsense. Once again this strengthens the idea of philosophy as poetic composition.

Insofar as philosophy is therapy, it is about undoing knots in our thinking and understanding. Varying the metaphor, Wittgenstein speaks of a cloud of metaphysics condensed in a drop of grammar (Wittgenstein, 1953, II, p. 222e); what one is attacking are castles of air or houses of cards (I, # 118); it is a matter of going back to the rough ground (I, # 107). The therapy philosophy offers can be a reminder for human kind and its so-called civilization: his several references to Spengler in *Culture and Value* alert us to what he saw as a contemporary cultural malaise. Elsewhere the therapy that philosophy offers is said to relate more to the overcoming of a crisis in his life – as, for example, in the *Lecture on Ethics* (Wittgenstein, 1965); elsewhere again, and perhaps more pervasively, to the need to live with scepticism, to withstand our longing simply to overcome it. This is to see scepticism in existential rather than purely epistemological terms. It is to recognize, with Cavell, the existential truth in scepticism, which is to be respected as saying something deep about the human condition, about the human need to run up against the limits of language and to be disappointed in criteria. The eventual ordinary then, the ordinary achieved in acknowledgement of this, should not disappoint us but rather give us peace to the extent that we can give up our craving for criteria, for the general, and no longer succumb to idle, metaphysical talk.

We shall shortly have more to say about the relation between these thoughts and Cavell's reading of ordinary language philosophy, but first let us recall, as we argued in Chapter 12, the way that the descriptive method and the understanding Wittgenstein attributes to philosophy can also be applied to the human sciences. In place of the advancement of hypotheses that purport to explain behaviour in general terms, attention can be turned to the characterization of a particular practice, its perspicuous description. Wittgenstein sometimes speaks of this as a matter of 'seeing connections', at other times as a matter of 'putting things side by side'. The task of the social sciences as conceived by Charles Taylor is analogous to Wittgenstein's aim in this respect. 'Naturalistic' interpretation is, in Taylor's view, necessarily limited, as it has no eye for the interpretation of the interpreter. Because of its supposition of a neutral scientific language, it fails to place human beings, the object of study, against the background of the values and ways of thought that are constitutive of the

social practices under observation. Taylor speaks of 'practice' precisely to draw attention to the way that meaning permeates human
behaviour: the agent is in a relationship towards others in society,
governed by implicit as well perhaps as explicit norms. The task of
social science is to bring clarity to the understanding of these
practices.

In some circumstances a successful interpretation will bring clarity to
an area of practice that is confused, fragmented, strange, puzzling or
contradictory, and it may help to improve that practice. A strong
motive for the construction of theories but also for their adoption is
the fact that our implicit understanding is in one way or another inadequate or mistaken. Theories enlarge, criticize and challenge our understanding. In educational contexts, however, what is sometimes most
needed is not the analysis of a situation in terms of a broader catego-
rization, or in the light of generalization, so much as better attention
to its particularity. This is likely to involve listening to what people
say. Let us recall that for Wittgenstein meanings are not 'in the head'
but in words anchored in social practice and physical environments.
The data in empirical social science research will take multiple
forms: transcriptions of interviews, diaries, policy documents, reports
of observations, notes of fieldwork... In preparing the report the
researcher may relate the events and activities in terms of the development of some kind of narrative plot. The resulting story needs not only
to reflect the data but also to attempt to provide a particular account
and, through this, a meaningfulness that was not evident before. It will
then be not simply a representation of what has been observed but also
a kind of construction. This gives the lie to any expectation of a
definitive account, and hence it may be that multiple accounts will
better do justice to the multifarious nature of reality. But it also makes
more apparent the proactive – as opposed to representational – nature
of such research.

Taylor's stance is similar to Wittgenstein's, but Wittgenstein's aversion to theorization and generalization is much stronger. This gives a
particular character to the implications of his thought regarding the
ethical demands of education. Putting an end to all the idle talk in
ethics does not prevent us from getting things done; indeed it may be a
condition for authentic engagement. The irrelevance of theory must be
recognized and paradox confronted, yet our urge to say something true
in ethics seems to involve running up against the limits of language, a
tendency that Wittgenstein deeply respects (Wittgenstein, 1965, p. 12).
This acknowledgement points towards the thinness of the conceptions

of certainty and of truth that drive science, something recognized by Wittgenstein already in the *Tractatus*. At the end of the *Lecture on Ethics* Wittgenstein comments on the special importance of speaking in the first person in such matters. There is in ethics no counterpart to the disinterested relation to truth that characterizes scientific knowledge. Neither can one's relation to ethical truth be one of indifference, as it might be in the case of other matters of fact. Something is at stake. To speak the truth in such matters one must be at home with it. The voice of the first person has a peculiar weight in this.

The philosophy Wittgenstein advocates starts from a real problem that someone is facing. Doing philosophy is therapeutic for that person in the sense that it changes *her*, undoing the knots in her understanding. This conception of philosophy foregrounds the idea of a working on the self, in which understanding is achieved not so much through explanation but rather through faithful description and proper attention to particulars. Wittgenstein sometimes spoke, as we saw, of the release that such clarity brought as a kind of peace. We see the implications of these thoughts as extending well beyond any specifically philosophical context to the manifold ways in which thinking holds us captive. Recognizing the constraints of particular formulations of our difficulties and the ways in which we might be released from these is not only the business of good philosophers, of novelists, playwrights and other artists: it is rightfully also the work of therapists, of parents, managers, colleagues and friends. Hence there are ideas here that are of rich significance for the advancement of learning, in education and therapy alike.

There is for Wittgenstein no single method in philosophy, and neither is there in the study of education. But there are methods and these may work as a kind of therapy. It is difficult to see how anything so pervasive but diverse as education could warrant something other than this piecemeal and flexible approach. Sometimes these methods will involve changes of aspect: to enable us to gain a clear view of a facet of learning; to enable us to understand the circumstances of an individual or of a social group; to enable us to see other possible ways of doing things, perhaps altering the horizons of our understanding of what education can be. Such dissolutions and resolutions do not settle things finally but recurrently, clearing the way for engagement. For education is always something that is to be struggled with, never comfortably to be settled. The picture here is, therefore, at odds with anything that could be called science.

In the following and final chapter, we shall extend our comments on the ways that the threat of scepticism has been countered by various configurations of the idea of return and on the burden of expectation that is, therefore, placed on return. To lay the way for this and to make clearer the modulations of the idea of the ordinary sketched here, we turn in the remainder of the present chapter to Cavell's reception of ordinary language philosophy and to its connections with themes of scepticism and acknowledgement threaded through the pages above.

## Cavell, ordinary language philosophy, scepticism and acknowledgement

Scepticism is to be understood first and foremost in philosophy, and specifically in Anglophone philosophy, in terms of the concern to find a secure basis for knowledge claims. Indeed this is what has character-ized epistemology over the past four centuries, especially, that is, since Descartes. Cavell's interest was shaped particularly by his encounter, in the 1950s, with the ordinary language philosophy of J.L. Austin and, as is evident above, with the writings of the later Wittgenstein. The *Philosophical Investigations* has been widely read, within Anglo-phone philosophy, as an attempt to refute the sceptic – that is, to show that the sceptic's questions (Is this a table in front of me? Are there other minds? How do I know that I exist?) always presuppose a background in which, in effect, these items of doubt are taken for granted. In epistemological terms, then, these sceptical questions involve a kind of circularity, with the conclusions of enquiry embed-ded in the premises. Cavell's reading of the *Investigations*, however, finds rather more to be at stake here, and in the process it exposes the inadequacy of the idea that scepticism is *refuted* in this way. It is not so much that scepticism is wrong as that it misses the point, and this lapse is at the heart of the sense of strangeness that we have tried earlier in this chapter to evoke. A key point of emphasis is that the sceptic's questions can only be raised where there is a suppression or repression or denial of the background, and, as these terms indicate, and as Cavell's subsequent writings richly show, this resonates with forms of denial to which human beings are peculiarly prone. Cavell develops the theme of denial in terms of the failure not so much of knowledge as of *acknowledgement*, the burden of which is examined especially in his writings on literature, particularly Shakespeare, and on the Hollywood film of the 1930s and 1940s, where the principal focus of his attention is on genres that he identifies as the 'Hollywood comedy of remarriage' and the 'melodrama of the unknown woman' (Cavell 1981, 1996, 2004b).[1]

That the *Investigations* is something other than an epistemological refutation can be seen in the way that Wittgenstein 'dissolves' the problem only to allow it to start up again – and this he does repeatedly. The itch returns. The question will not go away. This is tantamount to an acceptance not of the truth of scepticism but, as we saw, of the truth *in* scepticism; this is not an epistemological but an existential truth. It testifies to something deep in the human condition: our compulsion to doubt; our inclination to demand a greater reassurance than the circumstances allow or a more robust verification than they could reasonably bear. Cavell attends to the mild deflation of the Wittgensteinian claim that explanation must come to an end somewhere, that there must be an end to justification in acknowledgement of our 'form of life', and hence in acceptance that ultimately 'This is what I do'. Cavell speaks of the disappointment in criteria that we discussed above. It is a denial redolent of this aspect of scepticism that he finds also at the heart of Shakespearean tragedy, as well as in the stuff of our more everyday meanness of spirit.

A part of Wittgenstein's purpose is, as we saw, to undo the knots that develop in our thinking, and these are knots for which philosophy has often been responsible. The untying of these knots, sometimes requiring movements more elaborate and more difficult than those that created them, is part of the 'therapy' of philosophy that Wittgenstein seeks to provide. In doing this he repeatedly returns philosophy to the ordinary. In the flights of philosophy to which the sceptic is drawn, language goes 'on holiday', suggesting, at a different level, the kind of ineffectuality that, as we saw in Chapter 8, Thoreau sees in the lives of his neighbours, for all their ostensible busyness: language spins on ice and can make no progress; it needs to be returned to the rough ground, against which it can gain purchase. In the successful return to the ordinary, we do not achieve a resolution of our doubts; it is rather that we are, for a time, relieved of the compulsion to raise them, and hence it is that we 'know how to go on'.

Cavell's assessment of Wittgenstein's position is qualified heavily, however, by the claim that the emphasis on the therapeutic can be overplayed or misconstrued. That Wittgenstein speaks of finding peace yet worries away at these doubts again and again not only testifies to but dramatizes this. To return to the ordinary, to find the eventual ordinary, is to realize an economy of living that incorporates and acknowledges this fragility and disturbance in the human condition.

This economy of living will involve a proper appreciation of the various things we do with language. In Austin's work, as we saw, this is elaborated in terms, for example, of the distinction between the constative and performative functions of language, where the latter statement does not describe the promise but is itself the act. In spite of Austin's largely dismissive attitude to Wittgenstein, his procedures and purposes are not so far removed, priority being given to the piecemeal study of particular examples of usage or segments of experience, a procedure that is itself a principled defiance of the pressure in philosophy towards larger metaphysical claims. Like Wittgenstein, Austin returns words from their metaphysical to their everyday use, a return demonstrated in various ways in *Walden*, as we tried to show in Chapter 8.

Cavell is struck especially by the way that the characteristic procedure of ordinary language philosophy, its characteristic mode of appeal, takes the form of 'When we say ..., we mean...'. This is an appeal to ordinary use but not to some kind of empirical generalization about the behaviour of a particular people; a survey of usage would be beside the point. This procedural form, it should be noted, is first person plural. That it is first person shows the significance of voice; the authentication of the statement has to do with the speaker's sincere assent, with how things seem to her, and with her desire or responsibility to express this. That it is plural testifies to her desire or responsibility to speak *for* others, to find community of some kind with them. This is by no means to impose on their views, nor is it simply to align herself with them in terms, say, of shared characteristics (a community of the same); it is rather to offer her own assertion as exemplary in some way, testing this against the responses of others, and testing her responses against what those others themselves say. That this relation to others does not spring from a fully-fledged personal autonomy is evident in the importance attached to reading, the theme we have accentuated throughout this text: reading is a metonym for the ways in which our responses are drawn out and tested in the words of others – hence the salience of receptiveness. This then is to see the individual's autonomy as inevitably implicated in the political (the creation of the *polis*) – as two sides, so it might be said, of the same coin – and to see it as inextricably tied to the conditions of response within which she finds herself. The political is to this extent internal, and the language we find conditions political participation. This helps to show that the enigma is not only in the ordinary but at the heart of our political lives.

In the course of this book we have shown ways in which scepticism extends from some of the most well-known passages of philosophy to aspects of our personal and professional lives: How do I know that I am not dreaming? How do I know that I exist? How do I know that you are telling the truth? How do I know that learning is taking place? How, as a researcher, that I have taken fully into account the circumstances of my positionality? How, as a historian, that I have avoided the dangers of 'presentism'?[2] The sceptic, preoccupied by doubt, is always orientated by the quest for certainty. Thus, the typical concern of epistemology has been with the grounding or securing of knowledge claims, where knowledge is understood in terms of *an axis extending from certainty to doubt*. But, as Wittgenstein shows – for example, repeatedly in *On Certainty* – there are pathologies attached to thinking this way. Thus, in response to the question, 'How do I know that the world exists (that there are other minds/that I exist/etc.)?', his strategy will as we have indicated be not to provide evidence but to show the ways in which the existence of the thing in question is presupposed by, or built into the very terms of, or necessarily constitutive of the background to the question that is asked. That he shows this successfully is abundantly clear, but, as we have already shown, it is necessary to move beyond the terms of epistemology.

Let us pause here over a reformulation of the sceptic's question that points towards the various ways in which Cavell has pursued these matters in many aspects of his work. Imagine, for example, the following. Being consumed by doubt, I ask you: 'How do I know that you love me?' When I am not satisfied with your ready reassurance, you point, of course, to the wonderful times we have, the candle-lit dinners, the way you always call me, the flowers you send... But how do I really know? There is, it seems, something elusive about your love, something I cannot get hold of, and I can never quite rest content with this. We shall shortly see something of the way things are going wrong here, but first let us turn back to the nature of knowledge and the axis of scepticism. What of expressions of knowledge where the point does not seem to be a matter of *claiming* to know something? Consider, for example, the following cases. I arrive late for our appointment, fully aware both that this is the case and that you must know this too, and I say: 'I'm sorry. I know that I am late.' Excessively anxious about arriving at the airport in good time, I make my family, much to their irritation, take me there three hours in advance, and yet again I say: 'I know that I am a nuisance.' Or, to take a less negative case, feeling honoured to be giving the keynote address, you begin: 'I should like to express my thanks for the invitation. I realize that this is an important occasion.' It is not that a claim is being made in these cases, for it is clear that those involved are already party to the knowledge in question: the point of the remarks is *acknowledgement.*

An expression of acknowledgement is unlike a claim of knowledge in that it does not relate to any question of doubt; hence, it cannot be positioned on an axis extending from certainty to doubt. Failures of acknowledgement are manifested not in ignorance or doubt but in various kinds of denial. Consider the following cases. Passing you in the street and for some reason not wanting to see you, I wilfully avoid greeting you: this is a kind of denial. Deep down I know I am a coward, but I cover this over in various forms of bluster: denial once again. Or perhaps, knowing I have cancer, I refuse to face up to my condition... And finally, seeking proof that the world exists, I pare down my thoughts to what I cannot doubt, I make my exacting demands in rigorous observance of an axis stretching from certainty to doubt... And yet my question presupposes language, and language presupposes other beings and social practices: I pare down my thoughts, but the world sneaks back in. This then is the epistemologist's denial. We deny facts, people, aspects of ourselves, the world itself – here, in the anxious grasping for security or grounding, with its complementary suppressions and repressions, is an amplification of scepticism's existential truth. These cases fall then on *an axis extending from acknowledgement to denial.*

Shakespeare knew this well. Cordelia, in *King Lear*, finds herself faced with her father's variation on the question 'How do I know that you love me?'[3] The declaration of love made by one sister, Goneril, is assured in its response to these demands of accountability, but this is at once emulated and exceeded by the still more inflated declaration of the other sister, Regan. Cordelia refuses to play the performance game, to subject her love to her father's measures. Unable to get hold of this word 'Nothing' that is her response, her genuine love that is no *thing*, he condemns her to receiving nothing in return. Indicators of performance and economies of exchange in Shakespeare take a still more excessive, exorbitant form where the exaction of evidence or proof inflames close scrutiny into a kind of voyeurism. Othello, crazed by doubt, and clutching at a handkerchief, demands evidence of his wife's unfaithfulness: 'Give me,' he says, 'the ocular proof.' Othello ends up suffocating Desdemona with a pillow, taking away her breath, and closing off the possibility of further words, further action, further uncertainty. For Lear and Othello, the love they receive is a love they are inclined to deny, for all the evidence they have that the love is real. The possessiveness and voraciousness of their own conceptions of love, revealed in an imagery of material acquisition and exchange, on the one hand, and of fixation and containment, on the other, is shown to lead in the end to a kind of self-consumption or consumptiveness ('Humanity must perforce prey on itself, / Like monsters of the deep.' *King Lear*, IV, ii, ll. 49–50).[4]

Cavell speaks of a 'stratum of symmetry in which what corresponds to *acknowledgement* in relation to others is *acceptance* in relation to objects', suggesting that failure in these respects has to do with an 'inability to acknowledge, I mean accept, the human condition' (Cavell, 1979, p. 454). Failure to accept the conditions of knowledge – or, more broadly, the conditions of our relation to objects – is manifested in a grasping or clutching relationship to those things, as if we were never satisfied with the kind of security that these relations ordinarily afford. A further symmetry here would be with a failure to accept the ordinary conditions of learning, and the substitution for these of various systems of 'quality control' with its inflated demands for accountability and its voyeuristic scrutiny of performance indicators.

The grasping relation to objects of knowledge and understanding, the acquisitive and accumulative, perhaps totalizing assumptions of empiricism, tend also towards a kind of reification of those objects. Cavell's exploration of these matters shows the closeness of these tendencies of thought and practice to two myths. The prospect of gaining knowledge without reserve – that is, ideally of gaining unlimited knowledge – is tantamount to a pact with the Devil, the damnation of Faust. And the fact that knowledge, in the 'knowledge economy', is commodified invites the thought that everything that one comes to know may somehow turn to gold, that learning becomes tainted, as it were, with the Midas touch. Corollaries of this would be that commodification – with its visibility and commensurability – becomes the gold standard for what is studied, and that learning itself is fetishized.

We shall have cause in the final chapter to consider once again the ways that the world can go dead at our hands, just as the abstractions of a certain kind of thinking – in philosophy itself, in social science, as we have seen – can drain the world of its life. Sometimes this seems like an avarice for knowledge, a fingering of its web, imposing pressures the ordinary cannot bear and excessive expectations of return.

# 15
## Expectation of Return

> 'You only need sit still long enough in some attractive spot in
> the woods that all its inhabitants may exhibit them to you by
> turns.'
>
> (Thoreau, 1986, p. 275)

In Part III of this book, we have tried to show that the alienation that
characterizes much human distress consists partly in disenchantment
with the world. The forms of scepticism we have begun to chart are
perhaps less the cause than the symptom of this. We stand in need of
redemption of a kind, and each of our three themes – therapy, education, philosophy – has its stakes in this; yet we are wary of redemption
stories, burdened as they can become with a drama of eschatology,
perhaps the promise of salvation, just as we are wary of the sentimental
idealization of the ordinary. How then shall we proceed? What we
intend in this final chapter is to retrace some of the threads that we have
woven into this text as a whole, a weaving that has profited from some
unravelling too. The questions that are opened as these themes inter-
twine might marry easily with a number of ready-made responses, which
present themselves with the insistence of confident suitors. Our investment in these questions has caused us, chapter by chapter, to extend our
refusal of such solutions, in continuing expectation of a better return.

When Wittgenstein makes the mild, deflating remark that philosophy
'leaves everything as it is' (1953, # 124), the point is not to accept Marx's
rebuke (that philosophers have sought to understand the world when
the need is to change it): it is to recognize something like therapy in philosophy's power to overcome a recurrent inflation or inflammation in
our thinking – especially, as we have tried to show, in certain kinds of
education or therapy or philosophy itself. Scepticism, the doubt inspired

by the desire to know what things are *really like*, is one facet of this inflation. The anxiety of this desire to know puffs up the fantasies of narrative and number that we have diagnosed, just as it swells the illusions of self-knowledge and wholeness to which therapy, so it is often imagined, should lead. We have seen philosophy's inflation in a number of ways: in excessive preoccupation with lofty questions about the sublime and the beautiful – to the neglect of 'the dainty and the dumpy' (Austin's ordinary language philosophy, introduced in Chapter 2); in epistemological anxiety over the grounds for knowledge – so unlike the holism of building-dwelling-thinking (Chapter 7), or the physics of walking (Chapter 8), or the autonomy of grammar in the practices of language-games (Chapter 14 and elsewhere); in the state of abstraction that denies contingency and trust (Chapter 13); and in the wonder that, refusing to be dissipated in the course of ordinary life, turns into benumbment (Rosenzweig in Chapter 5).

But if Wittgenstein's deflating remark signals the way that these problems are to be therapeutically dissolved, if philosophy brings peace, this is a peace, as we have emphasized (Chapter 14), that is recurrently to be disturbed. The way that this is, as it were, staged in the *Philosophical Investigations* expresses the sense that this metaphysical craving is not something simply to be cured. A mature philosophy would then be one that avoided the various forms of inflation into which we are habitually drawn but at the same time recognized and found a way of living with our inclination to go beyond the ordinary: it would recognize that inclination as itself part of the ordinary. Such a philosophy would not, of course, be the preserve of a professionalized discipline – a professionalization that is itself part of the problem – but something closer, as Cavell puts this, to the 'education of grownups' (see Chapter 8, n. 6). Our account of the qualities of such an education has involved modulations of the theme of return – of turning away from the extravagances of wonder, or the false securities of metaphysics, or fake identities or phony happiness, and, by a number of routes, towards the ordinary. This is a recovery of the human that does not deny but somehow acknowledges that human tendency to dehumanize itself.

At one point, when Wittgenstein sets out the terms of his method, saying 'What *we* do is to bring words back from their metaphysical to their everyday use', this is juxtaposed against a kind of metaphysical avarice: 'When philosophers use a word – "knowledge", "being", "object", "I", "proposition", "name" – and try to grasp the *essence* of the thing, one must always ask oneself: is the word ever actually used

in this way in the language-game which is its original home?'
(Wittgenstein, 1953, # 116) The fact that Wittgenstein's word for home
is *Heimat* presses the question: What is the force of this return to
origins? The home of the language-game turns out not simply to be a
place of rest, for that would imply the perpetual peace that the
*Investigations* repeatedly offers then frustrates, just as home may be
sweet but threatening too, even potentially fatal (Chapter 13).
The economy this gestures is a politics, no less: Heidegger, intent on
belonging and authenticity, may insist on a homeland for thought –
the world made intelligible in terms of houses, temples and bridges;
but there is a Judaism that imagines itself at home in society before
being in a house (Chapter 5); and Thoreau's sojourn in the hut that he
builds is temporary and provisional (Chapter 8).

To disturb home is to unsettle the ordinary. Cavell's phrasing of
this, as we saw most fully in the preceding chapter, is that we are to
pass from the actual to the eventual ordinary, the ordinary to which
we return. That this return may require us to pass through the experience of scepticism – where we run up against, and try to exceed, the
limits of language – is powerfully suggested by the voyage out and
return depicted in Coleridge's *The Rime of the Ancient Mariner* (see
Cavell, 1988). The Mariner crosses such a limit – figured here as the
line of the equator – and travels to a 'cold country' where, perversely,
in a kind of recoil, he kills the magnificent albatross. The world, like
Desdemona, goes dead at his hands. Killing his connections with
others, whose otherness he cannot accept, he denies the humanity in
himself. The world he confronts is full of the animated bodies of a
kind of life-in-death (perhaps Santner's 'undead', Chapter 5).
Redemption, if it is possible, requires a reanimation, but this must
not come (through inflation) from outside, through a fabrication
within ourselves that would turn us into replicants (Chapter 10).
Reanimation *from outside*, we can imagine, may take a number of
contemporary forms – involving drugs, or makeovers and facelifts, or
theme-parks, or marketing and spin; or, let's add, the box of tricks,
the *Novum Organum* for our education and therapy, that is sometimes
presented in the name of neuroscience (see Chapter 11); or, for that
matter, the new 'science of happiness', which is promised by Richard
Layard to provide the 'single over-arching principle' for social policy
(Layard, 2005). Reanimation *from within*, we imagine, will require a
closer reconciliation with the ordinary human unhappiness that
Freud, foregoing any fantasies of personal beatitude, took to be the
real advance on neurotic misery (see Chapter 1). It is to be achieved,

the poem seems to say, in some kind of new connection with marriage – not exactly that of the wedding party to which the Mariner strangely returns but in something closer to a remarriage, with its sense of intimacy lost but (provisionally, perhaps comedically) regained (Chapter 14).

Alternatives to what we shall take to be this metonym of marriage – understood, with John Milton, as the 'meet and happy conversation' – seem to be something like a rejection of that intimacy, a denial of one's connection with others, in favour of what might be various kinds of contract. This might be to find in scepticism's denial of connection the smarting resentful silence left by a quarrel that prevents return. That it is language, as Aristotle claims, that makes human beings 'fit for, and fated for, political association' leads Cavell to propose 'confrontation and conversation as the means of determining whether we can live together, accept one another into the aspirations of our lives', where the 'conversation of justice' conveys not only a way of talking but a way of life together (Cavell, 2004b, p. 24). How unlike the life imagined here to that familiar political scientist's vision of us as preference-expressing monads conforming to the rules of rational-choice theory (Chapter 10)! And unlike also the more subtle, more robust, more sophisticated democracy of John Rawls. When Rawls (1971) emphasizes co-operation, this invokes 'the idea of a society as a whole either as having a project or, at the other extreme, as being a neutral field in which each can pursue his or her own projects' (Cavell, 2004b, p. 173). The virtues most needed in cooperation, as, for that matter, in game-playing, are 'participation and forbearance, in which the limitation of mutual involvement is paramount and well defined' (*ibid.*). Conversation, in contrast, emphasizes neither any given social end nor a field of fairness for individual projects. It draws attention to the opacity of our interactions, which are seen as the outcome of a history of attempts to reform ourselves in the direction of justice. Its democracy is not orientated towards any particular condition – say, of freedom or happiness – but 'havers at the crossroads' to wonder over which of its youthful aspirations it wishes to realize (Chapter 13), its adolescence a perpetual becoming-adult. The virtues it requires are listening, responsiveness to difference and willingness to change. It is not that we must choose between cooperation and conversation and their respective virtues; the issue is what their relation is, and whether one discourages the other (pp. 173–4). It is the 'banal fact of conversation', Levinas claims, that 'exits from the circle of violence. This banal fact is the marvel of marvels' (Levinas, 1976, p. 22, our translation).

There is, as we have tried to show, a rich tradition that sees philosophy and literature as *the* disciplines that transfigure the ordinary, and our engagements with the texts that we have emphasized have been explorations in what we take to be rich passages in that conversation. The images of return that recur in these texts include, almost as an archetype, the story we casually consider as something that might be told to children starved of myth: of what happened to Odysseus on his long way home from Troy (Chapter 13). And we find the elements of this story reassembling when we remember the copy of *The Iliad* open on Thoreau's table, and Michael Berg's thoughts as he rereads *The Odyssey* (Chapters 8, 4). The return, it turns out, is a return to a place different from the one you started from; this is an eventual ordinary, a place to sojourn, not the easing of nostalgia for home. 'How could the Greeks,' as Michael asks, 'who knew that one never enters the same river twice, believe in homecoming? Odysseus does not return home to stay, but to set off again.'

But does this acknowledgement of departure amount to a sufficient disturbance of that idea of return, or does it too settle down too well? Is this a way of maintaining the myth and, in the end, simply making it more serviceable, perhaps better accepting its therapy? We find ourselves recurrently drawn in our writing, however nuanced we fancy this to be, towards a Nietzschean yea-saying to life, and this voice can assert itself with too masculine a force. Recognizing that this is indeed one of our voices, we make our efforts to contain it: the tide of the heroic is something we try to stem (Chapter 6). Yet it will, will it not, reassert itself, as here in this hero of heroes, in *The Odyssey* itself, and in the monumentalizing of this classic, Greek inheritance? Greek porticos on Las Vegas hotels release, at some subterranean level, a current of thought that issues in the question: Is it not a troubled relationship to the culture and the continent that this text supremely represents that has occasioned America's characteristic (self-)repression, globalized at the end of history in neoliberalism (Chapter 8)?

There is, however, no necessary reason for the gendering of this affirmation and myth in this way. At the end of Joyce's *Ulysses* it is Molly Bloom who says 'yes'. And in Wallace Stevens's extraordinary depiction of this anticipation of return (Stevens, 1954), it is through the eyes of Penelope that we are to imagine the scene. There is a refraction through Penelope's vision that is more than doubled in the reader's imagining of the American poet Stevens imagining her expectation of Ulysses' return, echoed in the poet's partial adoption of her voice. Can one find here also then a feminized America, anxiety of influence overcome, that wants no extravagant 'fetchings' but accepts its inheritance, always approaching from the East,[1] joyously and in right measure?

The epigraph to the poem, from the great musician Georges Enesco, speaks of a relation between 'working one's cloth' (his violin, Penelope's yarn) and meditation or reverie, a kind of instilling essential to the work of composition. In this last attempt to evoke the return that is not a return, let us attend to these words.

### The World as Meditation

> *J'ai passé trop de temps à travailler mon violon, à voyager. Mais*
> *l'exercice essentiel du compositeur – la méditation – rien ne l'a jamais*
> *suspendu en moi… Je vis un rêve permanent, qui ne s'arrête ni nuit*
> *ni jour.*[2]
> Georges Enesco

Is it Ulysses that approaches from the east,
The interminable adventurer? The trees are mended.
That winter is washed away. Someone is moving

On the horizon and lifting himself up above it.
A form of fire approaches the cretonnes of Penelope,
Whose mere savage presence awakens the world in which
she dwells.

She has composed, so long, a self with which to welcome him,
Companion to his self for her, which she imagined,
Two in a deep-founded sheltering, friend and dear friend.

The trees had been mended, as an essential exercise
In an inhuman meditation, larger than her own.
No winds like dogs watched over her at night.

She wanted nothing he could not bring her by coming alone.
She wanted no fetchings. His arms would be her necklace
And her belt, the final fortune of their desire.

But was it Ulysses? Or was it only the warmth of the sun
On her pillow? The thought kept beating in her like her heart.
The two kept beating together. It was only day.

> It was Ulysses and it was not. Yet they had met,
> Friend and dear friend and a planet's encouragement.
> The barbarous strength within her would never fail.
>
> She would talk a little to herself as she combed her hair,
> Repeating his name with its patient syllables,
> Never forgetting him that kept coming constantly so near.

The repeated questions ('Is it Ulysses ... ?', 'Was it Ulysses ... ?') and the contradiction of 'It was Ulysses and it was not' express the return that is not a return. Penelope composes herself in expectation of welcoming the other, in a 'deep-founded sheltering'. The promise of friendship is attuned to the 'mending' of the trees, and this is part of an 'inhuman meditation', the 'planet's encouragement' – a conjugation of world and imagination that is a mutual realization. The good measure of her expectation enables her conditionally to imagine the 'final fortune' of the encirclings of necklace and belt. The equivocation between Ulysses and the sun is a thought that beats like her heart erotically in Penelope: the 'barbarous strength' of her readiness for arrival is met by his 'coming constantly so near'. Does this not suggest a right relation to return, where meditative anticipation is continually met by a new dawn?

So let us extend the feminization of vision that conditions Stevens's text. 'We lie in the lap of an immense intelligence,' writes Emerson, 'which makes us organs of its activity and receivers of its truth.' (Emerson, 'Self-Reliance', 1990, p. 140) The lap of that intelligence is there too in the water of Walden to which Thoreau descends each day to bathe, a place for the instilling of thought. The surface of the pond receives the sky in a remarriage that occurs daily. And of the sun, whose warmth Penelope feels on her pillow, Thoreau writes, in the closing words of his book: 'such is the character of that morrow which mere lapse of time can never make to dawn. The light which puts out our eyes is darkness to us. Only that day dawns to which we are awake. There is more day to dawn. The sun is but a morning star' (Thoreau, 1986, p. 223).

We need not worry about being replicants, and we can forgive ourselves for not being perfect. If we can learn, so to speak, to sit like Thoreau in the woods and wait for the dawn, ruefully aware of our vulnerability to these anxieties but no longer haunted, obsessed by them, what solace may not be possible? If we can but listen responsively enough, perhaps the animals that are the ordinary creatures of this beloved world will diffidently show themselves to us; which is all the comfort, all the therapy that we shall find, or need.

# Notes

## Chapter 1    Self-Esteem: The Inward Turn

1 Therapy is of course not always couched in terms of *cure*. It can be thought of in terms of, for instance, enlightenment or the growth of autonomy – conceptions which, whatever their drawbacks, have at least the merits of moving away from the idea that therapy is always a response to some kind of dysfunction or *illness*.
2 David Smail (*The Origins of Unhappiness*, p. 82) similarly notes that the unreflective notion of 'inner resources' serves to 'lay the foundation for a moralistic calculus of "personal worth"'.
3 In an insightful column in *The Guardian* (16.6.2001) the journalist Julie Burchill notes that 'Counselling is the exact opposite of socialism; no wonder it started to be so eagerly preferred....at the same time as union rights were being destroyed'.

## Chapter 2    Diffidence, Confidence and Self-belief

1 On the other hand, John Bunyan, cultivating a more muscular version of Christianity, has Diffidence as the wife of Giant Despair.
2 The character of Fanny Price has been the subject of much debate. Those who find her priggish have perhaps never quite seen the force of such as the following conversation with Edmund, from chapter 21:

> 'Your uncle is disposed to be pleased with you in every respect; and I only wish you would talk with him more. – You are one of those who are too silent in the evening circle'.
> 'But I do talk to him more than I used. I am sure I do. Did not you hear me ask him about the slave trade last night?'
> 'I did – and it was in hopes the question would be followed up farther by others. It would have pleased your uncle to be enquired of farther'.
> 'And I longed to do it – but there was such a dead silence!'

It is of course slave labour on the sugar plantations of Antigua that provides the wealth on which Mansfield Park is built.

3 As Adam Phillips notes in *Terrors and Experts* (1996, p. xi), 'there is something unmanageable about being a person'. He connects this with the 'too-muchness', the 'excess of feeling' (p. xiii) that the notion of the unconscious brings with it.
4 It was the runaway winner of a BBC poll to find Britain's best loved poem in 1995.
5 The idea that the poem bears some direct relationship to the character of Leander Starr Jameson, of the eponymous 'Jameson Raid' in South Africa in 1896, is not we believe a helpful one, even though Kipling himself on occasion encouraged it.

## Chapter 3    What Can be Said, What Can be Shown

1  See Karibuni online at: http://www.karibuni.co.uk/. (Accessed 22 April 2006.)
2  The screenplay for *Fight Club* was written by Jim Uhls, based on Chuck Palahniuk's novel of the same name.
3  The in-your-face violence has prompted one critic, of such an aversive sensibility, to say that the fights themselves disgust and deafen eye and ear, that they are grotesquely explicit and pornographically amplified, and that they exceed the limits of screen violence seen in recent years (Alexander Walker in the *Evening Standard*, November 11 1999).

## Chapter 5    Learning to Change

1  'Just as each blossom fades and all youth gives way to age, so every life's design, each flower of wisdom, attains its prime, and cannot last forever. With each call of life, the heart must be prepared, courageously, without a hint of grief, to forge new ties. A magic dwells in each beginning, protecting us, helping us to live'.
2  Doses of Kant and Hegel, Rosenzweig mischievously implies (that is, of Criticcin and Mysticol respectively), are unlikely to be of much help.
3  Santner explains in a footnote that he is borrowing the title of G.W. Bowersock's review of Anthongy Grafton's *The Footnote: A Curious History* (Cambridge: Harvard University Press, 1998), published in the *New Republic*, 19 January 1998.
4  Rosenzweig makes reference to these remarks from a letter of Cohen, who was his mentor (see Santer, 2001, p. 144).
5  In a letter to his cousin Rudolf Ehrenberg in 1917, Rosenzweig set out what he took to be the contrast between his understanding of being-in-the-midst-of-life and the concept of the human subject, its life and world found in philosophy. The letter has come to be regarded as the 'germ cell' of *The Star of Redemption*.
6  For an elaboration of this idea of the raising of standards, see our book with Nigel Blake, *Education in an Age of Nihilism* (Blake *et al.*, 2000).

## Chapter 6    Practising Dying

1  The occasion was Stephen Fry's installation for a second term as the Rector of Students at the University of Dundee in 1995.
2  See http://www.winstonswish.org.uk (Accessed 7 May 2006).
3  For an extended discussion, which draws on Derrida's essay 'Plato's Pharmacy', see Chapter 11 of our book with Nigel Blake *Thinking Again: Education after Postmodernism* (Blake *et al.*, 1998).
4  The term *Dasein*, which is usually left untranslated, is used by Heidegger in order to avoid the burden of association that the idea of human being has accrued, specifically with the rise of humanism in the modern world.
5  Of course, there are museums of natural history, and techniques of carbon-dating provide a chronology of natural change that extends beyond the existence of human beings. But the point is that this conception of time, this synchrony, is derivative of the richer and more complex time that is described here. For an expansion of these ideas, see Standish, 2007a.

6 The translation of *Eigentlich* as 'authentic' tends to emphasize associations with 'realness' at the expense of connotations of the proper or one's ownmost (*eigen* – own).

# Chapter 7    Room for Thought

1 See http://www.chifengshui.co.uk/about.htm (Accessed on 16 February 2005).
2 For a vivid cinematic realization of this, consider Peter Weir's popular film *Witness* (1985), where the hardened city cop, himself the victim of police corruption, escapes with a mother and her son to the Amish community that is their home, following the son's witnessing of a brutal murder in a railway station toilet. In the community the cop is sheltered and nursed, and during the time of his recovery he becomes partially absorbed into the Amish way of life: he acquires the carpentry skills on which they depend and enters into the daily round of the community's life and work. Just as the opening of the film cross-cuts the peace of the Amish farm-lands with the sordid and frenetic life of the big city, so now the community's building of the new barn, its mainframe hoisted magnificently against the sky, stands as an expression of the good in stark contrast to the predatory corruption of the police department.
3 For a more developed critique of Dreyfus in this respect, see Paul Standish, 'Profession and Practice: The Higher Education of Nursing' (Standish, 2007b).

# Chapter 8    The Thoreau Strategy

1 'Happily, we must traverse realm on realm, cleaving to none as to a home, the spirit of the world won't fetter us, but raise us higher, further, step by step. Just as one circle of our life presents itself as 'home', we grow weary – only she who is ready to journey forth will escape habit's paralysis.
   Maybe even death's hour too will send us out new-born towards undreamed-lands, maybe life's call to us will never find an end… Courage my heart, take leave and fare thee well'.
2 For an example of the take-up of Thoreau in existential therapy, see Solitary Purdah's article 'The Henry David Thoreau of Philosophy' (Online at: http://batr.org/solitary/112805.html. Accessed 13 May 2006). For Thoreau's connections with harp therapy, see 'The Art and Science of Therapeutic Harp Music: Its History, Technology, Influence, and Potential from Ancient to Current Times', by Sarajane Williams, a Licensed Psychologist and professional harpist, Kenneth Turkington, a musician, woodworker and conservationist, and Michael Sperber, psychiatric consultant, former professor at Harvard Medical School and author of *Henry David Thoreau: Cycles and Psyche*.
3 As a topical footnote to this repression, we note that The Thoreau Society advertises itself as the oldest and largest organization devoted to an American author and as being dedicated to promoting Thoreau's life and works through education, outreach and advocacy. (See: http://www.thoreausociety.org/ Accessed 15 May 2006) Its shop At Walden Pond stocks a wealth of books about Thoreau as well as souvenirs, bumper-stickers, T-shirts, etc. On our visit, Cavell's book was not available, and the sales assistant, who sounded fascinated, had evidently not heard of it.

4   Literally the ordering (*nomos*) of the home (*oikos*).

5   That is, a scimitar – the oriental flat sword that curves towards the point.

6   Philosophers have typically been preoccupied with the kind of argumenta-
    tion that leads to conviction; the rigour of this other writing – of which
    *Walden* is exemplary – is that it leads the reader to feel convicted, 'convic-
    tion' carrying the sense of both being convinced and being a convict. And it
    does this in such a way that the full resonance of this word, beyond its
    somewhat anodyne significance in terms of the logical force of argument,
    impacts on the reader: the reader is tested, tried, put on trial; and conviction
    by the truth is not a matter of logic alone. So too, while philosophers have
    typically been concerned with necessary and sufficient conditions, the corre-
    sponding rigour here involves seeing, with Emerson and Thoreau, the ways
    in which our saying (-*dit*-) of things together (*con*-) is embedded in 'con-
    dition', a recognition that foreshadows the insights of ordinary language
    philosophy drawn upon in various chapters of this book.

7   'What I require is a convening of my culture's criteria, in order to confront
    them with my words and life as I pursue them and as I may imagine them;
    and at the same time to confront my words and life as I pursue them with
    the life my culture's words may imagine for me: to confront the culture with
    itself along the lines in which it meets in me.
    'This seems to me a task that warrants the name of philosophy. It is also the
    description of something we might call education. In the face of the ques-
    tions posed in Augustine, Luther, Rousseau, Thoreau ..., we are children; we
    do not know how to go on with them, what ground we may occupy. In this
    light philosophy becomes the education of grownups. It is as though it must
    seek perspective upon a natural fact which is all but inevitably misinter-
    preted – that at an early point in a life a normal body reaches its full strength
    and height. Why do we take it that because we must then put away childish
    things, we must put away the prospect of growth and the memory of child-
    hood? The anxiety in teaching, in serious communication, is that I myself
    require education. And for grownups this is not natural growth but change.
    Conversion is a turning of our natural reactions; so it is symbolized as
    rebirth' (Cavell, 1979, p. 125). We return to this passage in Chapter 14.

8   Perhaps Heideggerian being-with-others would seem sufficient to provide the
    mother tongue, our initiation into the language of our community; but it
    could not account for the father tongue. The father tongue is associated by
    Thoreau crucially with the written word. But in the end, for Thoreau, as we
    saw, it is not merely secondary: it conditions the mother tongue, providing
    its full-blown context. Crucial to present purposes is the fact that it is real-
    ized in an encounter with the stranger, an encounter beyond the natural. For
    a fuller discussion, see Standish, 2006.

9   An earlier version of sections of this chapter was presented by Paul Standish
    at the International Network of Philosophers of Education meeting in
    Madrid, in August 2004. We are grateful to those present for their comments.
    Michael Bonnett and Naoko Saito are also thanked for helpful suggestions. A
    version of the Madrid paper has been published, under the title 'Uncommon
    Schools: Stanley Cavell and the Teaching of *Walden*', in *Studies in Philosophy
    and Education* (25.1–2), and we are grateful to the Editor and to Kluwer
    Publishers for permission to reproduce sections of that text here.

# Chapter 9   A State of Abstraction: Knowledge and Contingency

1  An email recently issued an invitation to a seminar in the 'Knowledge and Skills for Learning to Learn Series'. It is 'about Effective Educational Interventions ... There will be an emphasis on learning-to-learn interventions which involve feedback and self-awareness'. The main speaker is 'a world expert on meta-analysis and the synthesis of evidence about "what works" in education'. One of his presentations will be about 'Factors that influence student learning: the results from a study involving meta-analyses and 100 million students'.

2  This is the *Interim Report of the Working Group on 14–19 Reform* (DfES, February 2004), on the web at http://www.14–19reform.gov.uk/index.cfm

3  This is the title of a South Australia programme to evaluate literacy and numeracy in high-achieving disadvantaged schools: see http://www.thenetwork.sa.edu.au/nltc/

4  The title of a UK Government Green Paper, 2003.

5  US Act of Congress, 2002. See http://www.ed.gov/nclb/landing.jhtml?src=pb Needless to say, of the four 'ideals' that the Act is said to be based on, 'stronger accountability' is listed first.

6  After we had written the text of this chapter we found that Alan Ryan had commented on Rimer's article: 'there is ... something worrying about the amount of unnecessary psychological distress that students seem to suffer...Many young people find it hard to believe that they can cope rather easily with failure and setbacks, and they fail to see how far failures and setbacks are the common destiny of humanity. They believe, unreasonably, that life should go seamlessly well, and that something is amiss if it doesn't...and so ordinary unhappiness comes to feel like failure' (Ryan, 2004). Of course we are also stopping children playing traditional street and playground games in case they get hurt (or perhaps more to the point in case their parents sue). No wonder they have difficulty coping with risk.

7  In a letter from Darwin to his friend Joseph Hooker in 1856: quoted in Dawkins (2003).

8  Williams (1998, p. 32) writes that there is 'really no such thing' as the theory of the Forms.

9  Rozema (1998, p. 210) writes: 'Socrates' examination is for something both specific – Theaetetus' soul ... his *moral* character; and *particular – Theaetetus'* soul, *his* moral character. Socrates' concern is *personal...*'

10  Newman writes of the university as 'an *Alma Mater*, knowing her children one by one, not a foundry, or a mint, or a treadmill'.

11  What Rorty describes in terms of 'sparks' is sometimes expressed in terms of the 'erotic' dimension of pedagogy.

12  Much of the last two paragraphs is adapted from Richard Smith, 'Dancing on the feet of chance: the uncertain university' (Smith, 2005).

13  Lear is not released from this fantasy until he comes up against the power of nature in the storm on the heath. Eagleton writes that 'Nature terrorizes him into finally embracing his own finitude' (2003, p. 182).

## Chapter 10   Unfinished Business: Education Without Necessity

1  Tom has not got this quite right: see the quotation at the end of the chapter.
2  The correct title of Gauguin's 1898 picture is 'Where do we come from? What are we? Where are we going?'
3  Mestel (1996).
4  Jones (1999).
5  See for example Miller (1996).
6  As Lyotard (1988) puts it.

## Chapter 11   Beyond Cure

1  See  http://unesdoc.unesco.org/images/0012/001271/127160m.pdf,  and thanks to Haley Dekorne for drawing our attention to this.
2  We have benefited greatly in the preparation of this chapter from conversations with Jenny Laws and from her unpublished dissertation, *Border People*. Elements of this chapter draw on Booknotes, *Journal of Philosophy of Education* 39.1, 2005.

## Chapter 12   Narrative and Number: What Really Counts

1  The argument on pp. 192–4 can be found in on earlier collaboration, Smeyers and Smith, 2003.

## Chapter 13   Learning from Psychoanalysis

1  Elements of this chapter draw on Booknotes, *Journal of Philosophy of Education* 39.1, 2005.

## Chapter 14   Enlarging the Enigma

1  Cavell identifies the genre of the 'Hollywood comedy of remarriage' as including: *It Happened One Night* (1934), *The Awful Truth* (1937), *Bringing Up Baby* (1938), *His Girl Friday* (1940), *The Philadelphia Story* (1940), *The Lady Eve* (1941) and *Adam's Rib* (1941) (Cavell, 1981, 2004). The genre of the 'melodrama of the unknown woman' is taken to include *Stella Dallas* (1936), *Gaslight* (1944), *Letters from an Unknown Woman* (1946) and *Now, Voyager* (1942) (Cavell, 1996, 2004).
2  The idea that both the anxiety over presentism amongst historians and the quasi-confessional commitment to acknowledging one's positionality amongst social science researchers may themselves be manifestations of scepticism is advanced in Paul Standish's 'Chroniclers and Critics' (Standish, 2007a, forthcoming).
3  *King Lear:* Tell me, my daughters
   Since now we will divest us both of rule,

Interest of territory, cares of state),
Which of you shall we say doth love us most,
That we our largest bounty may extend
Where nature doth with merit challenge.
(I, i, ll. 50–5)

4  The Hollywood melodramas Cavell examines are strewn with examples of the desire of the man to contain the woman, typically by in one way or another denying her voice, and motivated characteristically by various anxieties over control or security or possession. The man is drawn or provoked by the otherness of the woman but with a view to converting it into a further means of his own recognition (Cavell, 1996, pp. 13–14). Cavell ponders the question that these films seem to prompt of how far these pathological forms of doubt, or anxieties for security, may in fact be a 'man thing'. This is a question whose edge acquires a particular keenness in his reading of *The Winter's Tale* (Cavell, 1988). When Leontes says to his young son 'Art thou my boy?' – a remark that under other circumstances might have passed as affectionate and playful but that is burdened here with Leontes' doubts about his paternity – the thought arises that this is not a doubt that a woman could entertain, at least not in the same way. A woman may, under certain circumstances, wonder as to who is the father of the child she is carrying, but she cannot doubt that it is her child. Is it easier for a man to imagine himself as a disembodied mind, harder for him to accept the physical terms of existence?

## Chapter 15   Expectation of Return

1  And from a still further, earlier East. The writings of Emerson and Thoreau, in the light of whose inheritance the contours of Stevens's words gain sharper relief, are threaded with the acknowledgement of Asian thought. It is an irony of America's self-repression that Emerson and Thoreau are still to be received. It is an irony in a different register that America's (therapeutic) East is its West (see Deleuze and Guattari, 1999).

2  'I've spent too much time working my violin, traveling. But the essential exercise of the composer – meditation – nothing has ever suspended this in me... I live a permanent reverie, which stops neither in the night nor in the day.' (Our translation.)

# References

Aboriginal Health Council, 'Reclaiming Our Stories, Reclaiming Our Lives', The Aboriginal Health Council newsletter. Obtained by David M. Boje from David Epston, Restorying Institute in New Zealand.

A. Adams, letter to John Quincy Adams, June ?10 1778: http://www.masshist.org/ JQA/05-mother_advises_son/aa17780610p1.html (accessed 23 May 2006).

M. Allen and D.M. Edwards, 'Wilderness treatment: a journey of discovery', online at: http://home.earthlink.net/~durangodave/html/writing/Wilderness.htm (accessed 13 May 2006).

Althea, *When Uncle Bob Died* (Cambridge: Dinosaur Publications, 1988).

J.L. Austin, *How To Do Things With Words* (Cambridge, MA: Harvard University Press, 1975).

J.L. Austin, 'A plea for excuses', *Proceedings of the Aristotelian Society*, 57 (1957) 1–30.

R. Barnett, *Beyond All Reason: living with ideology in the university* (Buckingham: Open University Press, 2003).

Z. Bauman, *Postmodern Ethics* (Oxford: Blackwell, 1998).

R. Bellah, R. Madsen, W. Sullivan, A. Swidler and S. Tipton, *Habits of the Heart: individualism and commitment in American life* (Berkeley, CA: University of California Press, 1985).

M. Benedikt, *For an Architecture of Reality* (New York: Lumen, 1987).

R. Bentall, *Madness Explained: psychosis and human nature* (London: Allen Lane, 2003).

B. Bettelheim, *Freud and Man's Soul* (New York: Knopf, 1983).

N. Blake, P. Smeyers, R. Smith and P. Standish, *Thinking Again: education after postmodernism* (Westport, CT: Bergin & Garvey, 1998).

N. Blake, P. Smeyers, R. Smith and P. Standish, *Education in an Age of Nihilism* (London: RoutledgeFalmer, 2000).

D.M. Boje, *Story Deconstruction Guidelines*, online at: http://cbae.nmsu.edu/ ~dboje/deconstruct.html (2005a, accessed 15 May 2006).

D.M. Boje, *Narrative Therapy*, online at: http://cbae.nmsu.edu/~dboje/ narrativetherapy.html (2005b, accessed 15 May 2006).

P. Bourdieu, *Language and Symbolic Power* (G. Raymond and M. Adamson, trans) (Cambridge, MA, and London: Harvard University Press, 1991).

L. Canter and M. Canter, *Assertive Discipline* (Santa Monica, CA: Lee Canter & Associates, 1992).

J.D. Caputo, *Deconstruction in a Nutshell* (New York: Fordham University Press, 1997).

T. Carlyle, *Sartor Resartus; Lectures on Heroes; Chartism; Past and Present* (London: Chapman and Hall, 1894).

D. Carr, 'Reason, fantasy and moral responsibility: a psycho-philosophical motif in the work of John Wilson', *Journal of Moral Education*, 29.3 (2000).

S. Cavell, 'Aesthetic problems of modern philosophy' in *Must We Mean What We Say?* (Cambridge: Cambridge University Press, 1976, 91–2).

S. Cavell, *The Claim of Reason: Wittgenstein, skepticism, morality, and tragedy* (Oxford: Clarendon Press, 1979).

S. Cavell, *Pursuits of Happiness: the hollywood comedy of remarriage* (Cambridge, MA: Harvard University Press, 1981).

S. Cavell, *The Senses of Walden: an expanded edition* (Chicago and London: University of Chicago Press, 1982).

S. Cavell, *In Quest of the Ordinary* (Chicago: University of Chicago Press, 1988).

S. Cavell, *This New Yet Unapproachable America: lectures after Emerson after Wittgenstein* (Albuquerque, NM: Living Batch Press, 1989).

S. Cavell, *Conditions Handsome and Unhandsome: the constitution of Emersonian perfectionism* (Chicago and London: University of Chicago Press, 1990).

S. Cavell, *Contesting Tears: the Hollywood melodrama of the unknown woman* (Chicago: University of Chicago Press, 1996).

S. Cavell, 'The *Investigations*: everyday aesthetics of itself', in *The Literary Wittgenstein* (Gibson and Huemer, eds) (London: Routledge, 2004a, 21–33).

S. Cavell, *Cities of Words: pedagogical letters on a register of the moral life* (Cambridge, MA: The Belknap Press of Harvard University Press, 2004b).

S. Cavell, 'Thoreau thinks of ponds, Heidegger of rivers' in *Philosophy the Day after Tomorrow* (Cambridge, MA: The Belknap Press of Harvard University Press, 2005a), 213–35.

S. Cavell, 'Responses', in: R. Goodman (ed.) *Contending with Cavell* (Oxford: Oxford University Press, 2005b).

V.L. Chapman, 'A woman's life remembered: autoethnographic reflections of an adult/educator', *SCUTREA Conference Proceedings*, online at: http://www.leeds.ac.uk/educol/documents/000000980.htm (1999, accessed 15 April 2006).

R. Cigman, 'Self-esteem and the confidence to fail', *Journal of Philosophy of Education*, 35.4 (2001) 561–76.

R. Cigman, 'Situated self-esteem', *Journal of Philosophy of Education* 38.1 (2004) 91–105.

A. Cline, *A Hut of One's Own: life outside the circle of architecture* (Cambridge, MA: MIT Press, 1998).

A. Collier, *R.D. Laing: the philosophy and politics of psychotherapy* (Hassocks, Sussex: Harvester Press, 1977).

P. Cope and J. I'Anson, 'Forms of exchange: education, economics and the neglect of social contingency', *British Journal of Educational Studies*, 51.3 (2003) 219–32.

R. Dawkins, *A Devil's Chaplain: reflections on hope, lies, science, and love* (London: Weidenfeld & Nicolson, 2003).

G. Deleuze and F. Guattari, *Anti-Oedipus: capitalism and schizophrenia* (R. Hurley, M. Seem and H. Lane, trans.) (Minneapolis: University of Minnesota Press, 1983).

G. Deleuze and F. Guattari, *A Thousand Plateaus: capitalism and schizophrenia* (B. Massumi, trans.) (London: Continuum, 1999).

G. Deleuze, *Difference and Repetition* (P. Patton, trans.) (London and New York: Continuum, 1994).

P. Dennison and G. Dennison, *Brain Gym* (Teacher's Edition, revised) (Ventura, CA: Edu-Kinesthetics Inc., 1994).

N.K. Denzin and Y.S. Lincoln (eds), *Handbook of Qualitative Research* third edition (London: Sage Publications, 2005).

J. Derrida, *Specters of Marx: the state of the debt, the work of mourning, and the new international* (P. Kamuf, trans.) (London: Routledge, 1994).

J. Derrida, 'The future of the profession or the unconditional university (thanks to the 'Humanities', what *could take place* tomorrow)' (P. Kamuf, trans.), *Derrida Downunder Conference*, Sydney, Australia, 2000.

J. Derrida, 'Cogito and the history of madness', in *Writing and Difference* (A. Bass, trans.) (London: Routledge, 2001).

J. Dewey, *Democracy and Education* (London: Macmillan, 1916).

H. Dreyfus, *Being-in-the-World: a commentary on Heidegger's being and time, Division I* (Cambridge, MA: MIT Press, 1991).

H. Dreyfus and C. Spinosa, 'Highway bridges and feasts: Heidegger and Borgmann on how to affirm technology', *Man and World*, 30.2 (1997) 159–78.

H. Dreyfus, 'Responses' in *Heidegger, Authenticity, and Modernity: essays in honor of Hubert L. Dreyfus, Volume I* (eds. M. Wrathall and J. Malpass) (Cambridge, MA and London: MIT Press, 2000, 305–41).

T. Eagleton, *After Theory* (London: Allen Lane, 2003).

R.W. Emerson, *Selected Essays* (ed. L. Ziff) (Harmondsworth: Penguin Books, 1982).

R. W. Emerson, 'Self-reliance', in *Ralph Waldo Emerson* (R. Poirier, ed.) (Oxford: Oxford University Press, 1990).

F. Engels, *The Condition of the Working Class in England* (eds. W.O. Henderson and W.H. Chaloner) (Oxford: Blackwell, 1971).

N. Emler, *Self-esteem: the costs and causes of low self-worth* (York: Joseph Rowntree Foundation, 2001).

G. Fendt and D. Rozema, *Platonic Errors: Plato, a kind of poet* (Westport, CT: Greenwood, 1998).

D. Fincher (Film Director), *Fight Club* (1999).

M. Foucault, *Madness and Civilization: a history of insanity in the age of reason* (trans. R. Howard) (New York, MA: Pantheon, 1965).

M. Frayn, *Construction* (London: Wildwood House, 1974).

S. Freud, *The Standard Edition of the Complete Psychological Works of Sigmund Freud* (ed. J. Strachey, trans.) (London: Hogarth Press, 1981).

S. Fry, *Here's to Plato* (Rectoral Address, University of Dundee, 1995).

F. Furedi, *Therapy Culture* (London: Routledge, 2004).

R. Gaita, *The Philosopher's Dog* (London: Routledge, 2003).

C. Geertz, *The Interpretation of Cultures* (London: Fontana, 1993).

J. Gibson and W. Huemer (eds), *The Literary Wittgenstein* (London: Routledge, 2004).

H. Giroux (2000) *Private satisfactions and public disorders*. Fight Club, *patriarchy, and the politics of masculine violence*. http://www.gseis.ucla.edu/courses/ed253a/FightClub (accessed 10/02/2005).

T. Gisborne, 'Death and bereavement in school: are you prepared?', *Education 3–13* (June 1995) 39–44.

M. Greene and M. Griffiths, 'Feminism and education', in N. Blake *et al.* (eds), *The Blackwell Guide to the Philosophy of Education* (Oxford: Blackwell, 2003).

P. Hadot, *Philosophy as a Way of Life: spiritual exercises from Socrates to Foucault* (ed. M. Chase, trans., with an introduction by A.I. Davidson) (Oxford: Blackwell, 1995).

D. Haraway, 'A manifesto for cyborgs: science, technology, and socialist feminism in the 1980s', in *Feminism/Postmodernism* (L.J. Nicholson, ed.) (London: Routledge, 1990).

M. Heidegger, *Being and Time* (John Macquarrie and Edward Robinson, trans.) (Oxford: Blackwell, 1962).

M. Heidegger, *Poetry, Language, Thought* (A. Hofstadter, trans.) (London and New York: Harper & Row, 1971a).

M. Heidegger, *On the Way to Language* (P. Hertz, trans.) (London and New York: Harper & Row, 1971b).

M. Heidegger, *Building Dwelling Thinking*. In *Poetry, Language, Thought* (A. Hofstadter, trans.) (New York and London: Harper & Row, 1975, 143–63).

M. Heidegger, *The Question Concerning Technology and Other Essays* (W. Lovitt, trans.) (New York: Harper & Row, 1977).

M. Heidegger, *The Principle of Reason* (Reginald Lilly, trans.) (Bloomington and Indianapolis: Indiana University Press, 1991).

M. Heidegger, *History of the Concept of Time* (T. Kisiel, trans.) (Bloomington, IN: Indiana University Press, 1992).

M. Heidegger, *Pathmarks* (W. McNeill, trans.) (Cambridge: Cambridge University Press, 1998).

M. Heidegger, *Elucidations of Hölderlin's Poetry* (K. Hoeller, trans.) (Amherst, NY: Prometheus Books, 2000).

H.L.T. Heikkinen (2002) 'Whatever is narrative research?' in: Huttunen *et al.*, *Narrative Research: voices of teachers and philosophers* (Jyväskylä: SoPhi, 2002).

S. Hetzel, V. Winn and H. Tolstoshev, 'Loss & change: new directions in death education for adolescents', *Journal of Adolescence*, 14 (1991) 323–34.

J. Hillman, *Kinds of Power* (New York: Doubleday, 1995).

J. Hodge, *Heidegger and Ethics* (London: Routledge, 1995).

R. Huttunen, H.L.T Heikkinen and L. Syrjätä (eds) *Narrative Research: voices of teachers and philosophers* (Jyväskylä: SoPhi, 2002).

D. Hume, *Essays: moral, political and literary* (London: Grant Richards, 1903).

R. Jonathan, *Illusory Freedoms: liberalism, education and the market* (Oxford: Blackwell, 1997).

S. Jones, *Almost Like a Whale: the origin of species updated* (London: Doubleday, 1999).

C.G. Jung, *The Collected Works of C.G. Jung*, Vol. 17 (London: Routledge, 1954).

W. Kayzer, *Een schitterend ongeluk: Wim Kayzer ontmoet Oliver Sacks, Stephen Jay Gould, Stephen Toulmin, Daniel C. Dennett, Rupert Sheldrake en Freeman Dyson* [A magnificent accident. Wil Kayzer meets ...] (Amsterdam: Contact, 1993).

R. Keshen, *Reasonable Self-Esteem* (Montreal and Kingston: McGill-Queen's University Press, 1996).

B. Knights, *From Reader to Reader: theory, text and practice in the study group* (New York: Harvester Wheatsheaf, 1992).

D. Kolb, 'Learning places: building dwelling thinking online', *Journal of Philosophy of Education*, 34.1 (2000) 121–34.

P. Larkin, *The Whitsun Weddings* (London: Faber and Faber, 1964).

P. Larkin, *The Whitsun Weddings* (London: Faber, 1971).

C. Lasch, *The Culture of Narcissism: American life in an age of diminishing expectations* (London: Abacus, 1980).

C. Lasch, *The Minimal Self: psychic survival in troubled times* (London: Pan, 1985).

R. Layard, *Happiness: lessons from a new science* (London: Allen Lane, 2005).

J. Lear, *Open Minded: working out the logic of the soul* (Cambridge, MA: Harvard University Press, 1998).

J. Lear, *Happiness, Death and the Remainder of Life* (Cambridge, MA: Harvard University Press, 2000).

J. Lear, *Therapeutic Action* (New York: Other Press, 2003).

E. Levinas, 'The philosopher and death', interview by Christian Chabanis, in E. Levinas, *Is It Righteous To Be?*, 2001 (1982).

E. Levinas, 'Being-toward-death' and 'Thou shalt not kill', interview by Florian Rötzer, in E. Levinas, *Is It Righteous To Be?*, 2001 (1986).

E. Levinas, *Is It Righteous To Be?* (Stanford, CA: Stanford University Press, 2001).

E. Levinas, *Difficile Liberté* (Paris, Albin Michel, 1976).

J-F. Lyotard, *The Postmodern Condition: a report on knowledge* (G. Bennington and B. Massumi, trans.) (Minneapolis: University of Minnesota Press, 1984).

J-F. Lyotard, *The Différend: phrases in dispute* (G. van Abbeele, trans.) (Manchester: Manchester University Press, 1988).

J-F. Lyotard, *Political Writings* (B. Readings, trans.) (London: UCL Press, 1993).

A. MacIntyre, *The Unconscious: a conceptual analysis* (London: Routledge & Kegan Paul, 1958).

A. MacIntyre, *After Virtue* (London: Duckworth, 1982).

T. Madler and G. Connelly, *Why Did Grandma Die?* (New York: Raintree, 1980).

S. Mahieu and R. Vanderlinde, *De professionele ontwikkeling van beginnende leerkrachten vanuit het micropolitiek perspectief* [The professional development of recently graduated teachers from the perspective of micropolitics]. Unpublished master's thesis (Leuven, Belgium: Katholieke Universiteit, 2002).

J. Margolis, 'Unlikely prospects for applying Wittgenstein's "method" to aesthetics and the philosophy of art', in *The Literary Wittgenstein* (Gibson and Huemer, eds) (London: Routledge, 2004, 321–45).

J. McCrone, 'Messing with the mind', *The Guardian*, 12 March 2005.

L. McKinstry, 'Not ill, just naughty', *The Spectator*, 26 Feb 2005.

R. Mestel, 'The arts of seduction', *The Guardian* (23 Jan 1996, Supplement) 12.

A. Miller, *The Drama of Being a Child* (London: Virago, 1987).

G.F. Miller, 'Political peacocks', *Demos Quarterly*, 10 (Special issue on evolutionary psychology) (1996) 9–11.

N. Miller and L. West, 'Connecting the personal and the social: using auto/biography for interdisciplinary research and learning about experience', *SCUTREA Conference Proceedings* (1998), online at: http://www.leeds.ac.uk/educol/documents/000000732.htm (accessed 15 April 2006).

R. Monk, *Ludwig Wittgenstein: the duty of genius* (Harmondsworth, Middlesex: Penguin, 1990).

G.E. Moore, 'Wittgenstein's lectures in 1930–33', *Mind*, 64 (1955) 1–27.

G.S. Morson, 'Contingency and poetics', *Philosophy and Literature*, 22.2 (1998) 286–308.

J. Mosley, *Quality Circle Time in the Primary Classroom* (Wisbech: LDA, 1999).

I. Murdoch, *Metaphysics as a Guide to Morals* (London: Chatto & Windus, 1992).

Personalised Learning website http://www.teachernet.gov.uk/management/newrelationship/personalisedlearning/(accessed 23 May 2006).

Narrative Therapy Centre of Toronto, *About Narrative Therapy*, online at http://www.narrativetherapycentre.com/index_files/Page378.htm (accessed 15 April 2006).

J.H. Newman, *The Idea of a University* (New York: Image Books, 1959).

L.J. Nicholson (ed.), *Feminism/Postmodernism* (London: Routledge, 1990).

C. Norris, *Derrida* (London: Fontana, 1987).

R. Nozick, *Anarchy, State, and Utopia* (Oxford: Blackwell, 1974).

M. Nussbaum, *Cultivating Humanity: a classical defense of reform in liberal education* (Cambridge, MA: Harvard University Press, 1977).

M. Nussbaum, *The Fragility of Goodness* (Cambridge: Cambridge University Press, 1986).

M. Nussbaum, *The Therapy of Desire: theory and practice in Hellenistic ethics* (Princeton, N.J.: Princeton University Press, 1994).

S. Paul (ed.), *Thoreau: a collection of critical essays* (Englewood Cliffs, NJ: Prentice Hall, 1962).

D. Perry, 'Review of the film *Fight Club*', *Xiibaro Productions*, 33.1 (1999), online at www.cinema-scene.com/archive/01/33.html#Fight (Accessed May 16 2006).

R.S. Peters, *Ethics and Education* (London: George Allen and Unwin, 1966).

A. Phillips, *Darwin's Worms* (London: Faber, 1999).

A. Phillips, 'Introduction to Sigmund Freud', *Wild Analysis* (London: Penguin, 2002).

D.E. Polkinghorne, 'Narrative configuration in qualitative analysis', *International Journal of Qualitative Studies in Education*, 8 (1995) 5–23.

M. Power, *The Audit Society: rituals of verification* (Oxford: Clarendon Press, 1997).

J. Rawls, *A Theory of Justice* (Cambridge, Mass.: The Belknap Press of Harvard University Press, 1971).

B. Readings, *The University in Ruins* (Cambridge, MA: Harvard University Press, 1996).

P. Rieff, *The Triumph of the Therapeutic* (London: Chatto & Windus, 1966).

S. Rimer, 'New lesson for college students: lighten up', *New York Times*, 6 April 2004.

R. Rorty, *Contingency, Irony, and Solidarity* (Cambridge: Cambridge University Press, 1989).

R. Rorty, *Philosophy and Social Hope* (London: Penguin, 1999).

S. Rose, The *21st Century Brain: explaining, mending and manipulating the mind* (London: Jonathan Cape, 2005).

D. Rozema, 'Plato's *Theaetetus*: what to do with an Honours student', *Journal of Philosophy of Education* 32.2 (1998) 207–23.

F. Rosenzweig, *The Star of Redemption* (W.W. Hallo, trans.) (Notre Dame: Notre Dame Press, 1985).

F. Rosenzweig, *Understanding the Sick and the Healthy: a view of world, man, and God* (N. Glatzer, trans.) (Cambridge, MA, and London: Harvard University Press, 1999).

A. Ryan, 'Students need help with two things: shedding the burden of unreasonable expectations and getting away from overprotective parents', *The Times Higher Education Supplement* (16 April 2004) 11.

M. Sandel, *Liberalism and the Limits of Justice* (Cambridge: Cambridge University Press, 1982).

E. Santner, *On the Psychotheology of Everyday Life: reflections on Freud and Rosenzweig* (Chicago and London: Chicago University Press, 2001).

D. Schalkwyk, 'Wittgensteins "imperfect garden": the ladders and labyrinths of philosophy as *Dichtung*' in *The Literary Wittgenstein* (Gibson and Huemer, eds) (London: Routledge, 2004, 55–74).

B. Schlink, *The Reader* (C. Brown Janeway, trans.) (London: Quality Paperbacks Direct, 1998).

J. Seery, *Political Theory for Mortals: shades of justice, images of death* (Ithaca: Cornell University Press, 1996).

J. Silin, *Sex, Death, and the Education of Children: our passion for ignorance in the age of AIDS* (New York and London: Teachers College Press, 1995).

D. Smail, *Illusion and Reality: the meaning of anxiety* (London: Dent, 1984).

D. Smail, *Taking Care: an alternative to therapy* (London: Dent, 1987).

D. Smail, *The Origins of Unhappiness* (London: HarperCollins, 1993).

R. Smith, *The Norton History of the Human Sciences* (New York: W.W. Norton, 1997).

R. Smith, 'The demand of language: the justice of the *différend*', *The School Field: international journal of theory and research in education*, 12.1/2 (2001) 61–72.

R. Smith, 'Self-esteem: the kindly apocalypse', *Journal of Philosophy of Education*, 36.1 (2002) 87–100.

S. Smith and J. Watson (eds), *Getting a Life: everyday uses of autobiography* (Minneapolis, The University of Minnesota Press, 1996).

C.H. Sommers and S. Satel, *One Nation Under Therapy: how the helping culture is eroding self-reliance* (New York: St. Martin's Press, 2005).

N. Stadlen, *What Mothers Do: especially when it looks like nothing* (London: Piatkus Books, 2004).

P. Standish, 'Uncommon Schools: Stanley Cavell and the teaching of *Walden*', *Studies in Philosophy and Education* 25.1–2 (2006), 145–57.

P. Standish, 'In her own voice: convention, conversion, criteria', *Educational Philosophy and Theory*, 36.1 (2004) 91–106.

P. Standish, 'Chroniclers and critics', *Pedagogica Historica*, 2007a, forthcoming.

P. Standish, 'Profession and practice: the higher education of nursing', in J. Drummond and P. Standish (eds) *The Philosophy of Nursing Education* (Basingstoke, Hants: Palgrave Macmillan, 2007b, forthcoming).

W. Stevens, *Collected Poems* (New York: Knopf, 1954).

M. Stout, *The Feel-Good Curriculum: the dumbing down of America's kids in the name of self-esteem* (Cambridge, MA: Perseus, 2000).

D. Sudjic, *The Edifice Complex: how the rich and powerful shape the world* (Harmondsworth: Penguin, 2006).

J. Suissa, 'Untangling the Mother Knot: some thoughts on parents, children and philosophers of education', *Ethics and Education* 1.1 (2006) 65–77.

C. Taylor, *Philosophical Papers: vol. 1. human agency and language* (Cambridge: Cambridge University Press, 1985).

C. Taylor, *Philosophical Papers: vol. 2. philosophy and the human sciences* (Cambridge: Cambridge University Press, 1985).

C. Taylor, *Sources of the Self: the making of the modern identity* (Cambridge: Cambridge University Press, 1989).

C. Taylor, *The Ethics of Authenticity* (Cambridge, MA: Harvard University Press, 1991).

H.D. Thoreau, *Walden and Civil Disobedience* (Harmondsworth: Penguin, 1986).

H.D. Thoreau, 'Walking', in L. Hyde (ed.) *The Essays of Henry D. Thoreau* (New York: North Point Press, 2002).

S. Todd, *Learning from the Other: Levinas, psychoanalysis and ethical possibilities in education* (Albany, N.Y.: State University of New York Press, 2003).

R. Usher, I. Bryant and R. Johnston, *Adult Education and the Postmodern Challenge: learning beyond the limits* (London: Routledge, 1997).

G. Vattimo, *The Transparent Society* (Baltimore: Johns Hopkins University Press, 1992).

A. Walker, 'Review of the film *Fight Club*', *Evening Standard*, 11 November 1999, p. 1.

S. Weil (trans. H. Price) *Lectures on Philosophy* (Cambridge: Cambridge University Press, 1978).

R. Wells, *Timothy Goes to School* (London: Kestrel, 1981).

J.P. White, *Education and Personal Well-Being in a Secular Universe* (London: Institute of Education, 1995).

M. White, *Narrative Therapy*, online at http://www.massey.ac.nz/~alock/virtual/white.htm (accessed 15 April 2006).

B. Williams, *Plato: the invention of philosophy* (London: Phoenix, 1998).

P. Winch, *The Idea of a Social Science* (London: Routledge, 1958).

L. Wittgenstein, *Philosophical Investigations/Philosophische Untersuchungen* (G.E.M. Anscombe, trans.) (Oxford: Basil Blackwell, 1953).

L. Wittgenstein, 'A lecture on ethics', *Philosophical Review*, 74 (1965) 3–12.

L. Wittgenstein, *Lectures and Conversations on Aesthetics, Psychology and Religious Belief* (ed. C. Barrett) (Oxford: Basil Blackwell, 1966).

L. Wittgenstein, *Zettel* (eds. G.E.M. Anscombe and G.H. von Wright; G.E.M. Anscombe, trans.) (Oxford: Basil Blackwell, 1967).

L. Wittgenstein, *The Blue and Brown Books* (2nd ed.) (Oxford: Basil Blackwell, 1969).

L. Wittgenstein, *On Certainty/Über Gewissheit* (eds. G.E.M. Anscombe and G.H. von Wright, D. Paul and G.E.M. Anscombe, trans.; reprinted with corrections) (Oxford: Basil Blackwell, 1979).

L. Wittgenstein, 'Remarks on Frazer's Golden Bough' in C. Luckhardt (ed.), *Wittgenstein: Sources and Perspectives* (Hassocks, Sussex: The Harvester Press, 1979, 61–81).

L. Wittgenstein, *Culture and Value/Vermischte Bemerkungen* (ed. G.H. von Wright; P. Winch, trans.) (Oxford: Basil Blackwell, 1980).

L. Wittgenstein, *Tractatus Logico-Philosophicus* (D. Pears and B.F. McGuinness, trans.) (London: Routledge and Kegan Paul, 1992).

M. Wrathall and J. Malpass (eds) *Heidegger, Authenticity, and Modernity: essays in honor of Hubert L. Dreyfus, Volume I* (Cambridge, MA and London: MIT Press, 2000).

P. Wynnejones, 'Beyond this life's outposts: children's books, bereavement and death', *Spectrum* (1994) 15–28.

S. Žižek, *The Fragile Absolute: or, why is the Christian legacy worth fighting for?* (London: Verso, 2000).

# Index